Context and Cognition

Context and Cognition

Ways of Learning and Knowing

Edited by Paul Light
and George Butterworth

 LAWRENCE ERLBAUM ASSOCIATES, PUBLISHERS
1993   Hillsdale, New Jersey   Hove and London

Originally published 1992

Published in the United States and Canada by Lawrence Erlbaum Associates, Inc.

Lawrence Erlbaum Associates
365 Broadway
Hillsdale, New Jersey 07642

Library of Congress Cataloging-in-Publication Data

Context and cognition : ways of learning and knowing / edited by Paul
  Light and George Butterworth
        p.   cm.
    Includes bibliographical references and index.
    ISBN 0-8058-1392-6. -- ISBN 0-8058-1393-4 (pbk.)
      1. Context effects (Psychology) 2. Schemas (Psychology)
    3. Cognitive psychology. 4. Knowledge, Psychology of. I. Light,
    Paul. II. Butterworth, George.
    BF378.C72C65   1993
    153--dc20   92-44674
                                              CIP

Books published by Lawrence Erlbaum Associates are printed on acid-free paper,
and their bindings are chosen for strength and durability.

Printed in the United States of America
10 9 8 7 6 5 4 3 2 1

Contents

Chapter 1

Context and cognition in models of cognitive growth

George Butterworth, *University of Sussex*[1]

Introduction

The study of cognitive development in children has moved through three identifiable phases in the last twenty years. First, there was a shift from a focus on intellectual processes within the individual child, as in the classic research of Piaget, to a concern with social cognition in the 1970s and 1980s very much influenced by the resurgence of interest in Vygotsky. This shift reflects a move away from attempting to explain cognition as a process located solely within the individual, towards an understanding of the interpersonal context of cognitive growth. The shift from 'cold blooded' to 'warm blooded' cognition drew attention to the ways in which thought processes and cognitive growth are socially situated but contextual factors were for the most part seen only as moderators of cognitive growth. Work on cognitive development has recently entered a third phase, in which theorists are beginning to stress an *inextricable* link between contextual constraints and the acquisition of knowledge. Moreover, the physical context is being reunited with the social, within the thought process. The contemporary view tends to be that cognition is *typically* situated in a social and physical context and is rarely, if ever, decontextualized.

How can we explain this movement towards an analysis in terms of situated cognition? Two important trends may be discerned in the recent literature. First, work on the relation between perception and cognition in young children has drawn our attention to the extent to which *perception* enters into the development of thought. Second, work on *language and thought*, especially in relation to the social foundations of knowledge, has drawn our attention to the child's need to understand what adults mean when they pose questions designed to reveal children's reasoning capacities.

1

Our intention in editing this volume was to update our book on social cognition (Butterworth and Light, 1982) with respect to recent trends in the literature on social cognitive development and to show how thinking is situated in the physical, social and cultural context which gives it its form. The aim is to illustrate, through reviews of theory and empirical research, various aspects of this recent trend to *situate* accounts of cognitive development. The chapters in this volume focus on the contextual sensitivity of reasoning in mathematical and other scientific domains, in everyday life and in the school. The chapters examine contextual sensitivity in relation to ecological theories of perception and cognition, and they contrast intuitive reasoning in mathematical and other scientific domains with the child's difficulty with reasoning in formal contexts, such as the school. A central concern is the generalizability of knowledge and its transfer from one context to another.

Perception and situated cognition

Two lines of research in the 1970s and 1980s gave a particularly strong impetus for a focus on the relation between perception and cognition in development. The first of these was the study of reasoning in pre-school children which revealed greater cognitive competence than had previously been acknowledged. Peter Bryant (1974) offered an influential critique of Piaget's theory, based on the argument that reasoning in pre-school children depends on their perception of the relationships among the elements of a task. He showed that for simple Piagetian tasks, such as making inferences, or making judgements about numerosity, and for perceptual problems such as perceiving the orientation of an oblique line, the pre-school child makes judgements relative to the perceived context. Bryant's analysis drew attention to the context or framework on which the young child relies to make relative (rather than absolute) judgements. It was argued that young children depend on deductive inferences in such perceptually based tasks, and of course, this was contrary to the received Piagetian view. A great debate ensued on the nature of the competence revealed by experimental modifications of Piagetian tests, such as in the 'transitive inference' task, in pre-operational children (see for example Chapman, 1988, pp. 348 ff.).

The second contribution to an emphasis on the relation between perception and cognition came from the discovery of the perceptual competence of babies. This work was influenced by the 'direct realist' ecological theory of J.J. Gibson, whose ideas motivated so many of the demonstrations that perception may have an influence in structuring thought (see Butterworth, 1990, for a review). The implication is that if the infant's perception of reality *is* adequate (rather than a buzzing, blooming confusion as had long been assumed) then the Piagetian, constructionist programme needs to explain how babies may perceive objective properties of reality before they have had the opportunity to construct this competence. On the ecological view, perception is *necessarily* situated within the ecology since it consists in obtaining information from the active relation between the organism and a structured environment. Indeed, it is the process of perception that situates the organism in the environment. The evidence from infancy suggests that perception is a 'module' or component of the cognitive system that is antecedent to thought and language and that may contribute to the mastery of reasoning.

These programmes of research served to draw attention to the relationship in development between perceiving and knowing. They did not directly implicate contextual factors in cognitive growth. But as even the slightest acquaintance with Gestalt psychology will reveal, what is perceived as 'figure' in reversible visual illusions depends entirely on what is perceived to be 'ground'. Perception *presupposes* context in deriving meaning from experience. The recent emphasis on the importance of perception in cognitive development draws our attention to the ecological frameworks for experience. When perception is construed as an aspect of cognition, as has recently begun to be the case, this naturally contributes towards a new understanding of thinking as 'situated in the world'. This contrast with the Piagetian account of thinking as gradually approximating formal logical operations, as the child slowly overcomes deficits in basic reasoning abilities.

Language and situated cognition

The recent focus on the social basis of cognition also helps explain how language itself is understood through the social context. Margaret Donaldson (1978) published a series of influential studies that purported to show that versions of Piaget's tasks which were socially intelligible to pre-school children revealed a previously unsuspected competence in perspective-taking, conservation and class inclusion. In Donaldson's terms, her situated tasks make 'human sense' because they draw on everyday social experience, with which the child is very familiar. Both Donaldson and more recently Michael Siegal (1991) take the view that much of the pre-school child's difficulty in reasoning arises because the child cannot comprehend the adult's specialized language. The argument is quite subtle. It is not just that the child lacks knowledge of language, rather the child's errors arise in an *active* attempt to discover what the adult actually *means* by the questions being asked. We shall see this issue arising at a number of points in the present volume. As Donaldson (1978, p. 38) puts it:

It may turn out to be a very long journey from the primary understanding of what people mean by the words they speak and by their concomitant acts to the ultimate and separate understanding of what *words* mean. Perhaps the idea that words mean anything – in isolation – is a highly sophisticated notion, and a Western adult notion at that.

Various examples of the interpenetration of language, context and reasoning, some taken from Piagetian psychology, such as the conservation problem, proportional reasoning, and class inclusion are discussed in different chapters in this volume (Roazzi and Bryant, Chapter 2; Mercer, Chapter 3; Goodnow and Warton, Chapter 9). Just one well-known example will help to make clear the subtle interplay of perception, language and social interaction which is involved.

McGarrigle and Donaldson (1974) reported a beautiful experiment, which has become known as the 'naughty teddy' study, a variant of Piaget's traditional number conservation task. First of all, the child is asked whether two rows of counters arranged in parallel lines contain the same or a different number. The child readily agrees that the number of counters is the same when the length of the rows is identical and each counter is opposite another. Then, under the control of the experimenter, a glove puppet known as 'naughty teddy' rushes in and lengthens one of the rows of counters, just as in the conservation test. The child is then asked whether the longer row contains the same or a different number of counters than the shorter one. Most children between 4 and 6 years now 'conserve', that is, they give the correct answer that the number of counters has not changed, even though they fail to conserve under the standard testing conditions of the conservation task.

Light (1986) has questioned whether the child really demonstrates the logical requirements of conservation when giving the right answer. Just as the child may be (mis)led by the adult's behaviour in the standard test into supposing that length is relevant to number, they may equally be led by the social interaction taking place around the accidental transformation into supposing that the number of counters remains the same. He suggests that children may be giving the right answer for the wrong reasons. What really matters is what cues are available in the interaction as to the relevance or irrelevance of the transformation. What determines the child's apparently correct (or incorrect) response is whether the child's attention is drawn by the adult to transformations that are relevant for understanding conservation of number (or volume or weight) or to irrelevant cues.

On this view, the child's problem in understanding the adult's language becomes one of ascertaining the referent of the adult's utterance. In other words, the problem for the child is one of determining the object of joint attention with the adult. When the adult deliberately rearranges the display and asks questions about number, the child reasonably takes it that perhaps a change in length may have something to do with what the adult means by 'number'. The implicit message given by the adult is, 'Take notice of this transformation, it is relevant to questions about whether the number is the same or different.' When the rearrangement is made to happen accidentally, then the child interprets the adult's question, in relation to the whole context, as merely a check to establish agreement that the number has not changed. Light argues that the child is discovering the meaning of the language through social interaction in the testing situation. This applies both when the wrong answer is given and to the situation where the right answer is volunteered. The child learns about quantity terms by interpreting their meaning in relation to socially intelligible contexts. We might add that the task shows how attention and perception are inextricably linked with the child's judgements about number.

These demonstrations therefore suggest that the child's difficulties with conservation tasks, at least in part, arise in achieving an understanding of what the adult means. The child in discourse with the adult enters into a relationship of unequal power, where the child takes the adult's behaviour in context as a means to understand what is required. As Goodnow and Warton (Chapter 9) point out, the particular class of problems often involved in Piagetian tasks are those amenable to criteria of scientific proof, where a correct answer exists. Different criteria for validation may actually apply to understanding socially relevant events. Typical cognitive developmental testing situations, where experimenters are seeking exact answers, may nevertheless depend on how the child applies judgemental criteria to the *social* interaction.

These new insights into pre-operational reasoning do not rule out entirely Piaget's theory that development also involves a change in the child's underlying logic. By the age of 8 or 9 years, the answer to conservation questions is obvious to the child who has entered the concrete operational stage. It is still possible for Piagetians to argue that the context sensitivity of reasoning, revealed by these recent studies of the pre-school child, gives way to a more generalized understanding, at least with respect to the classic Piagetian tasks. On the other hand, as Girotto and Light point out (Chapter 8), even adults may perform poorly on tasks of hypothetico-deductive reasoning, when the contents of the premises are remote from everyday experience. A completely deductive system of reasoning, context-free and independent of any particular content, seems never to be fully achieved. What may be being highlighted in the current phase of cognitive developmental research is the progressive reintroduction of the *ecology* into Piaget's *evolutionary epistemology* (Piaget, 1971).

In summary, the perceptual, cognitive and social threads in recent explanations of cognitive development have been relatively distinct, but they seem now to be merging. The focus on the Chomskyan distinction between competence and performance, so prevalent in the early attempts to evaluate Piagetian theory in the 1970s and 1980s (when the search was still on for a context-free cognitive substrate), is giving way to the question as to whether cognition is *always* situated? The recent trend is in favour of a situated analysis in which cognitive competence is defined as a function of the context and content of knowledge structures. The question of whether and how reasoning even proceeds in the direction of a fully hypothetico-deductive system is still open, and needs to be assessed in the light of recent evidence for the context dependency of thinking.

Before turning to these issues it will be useful to consider two points in more detail. The first is the definition of 'context' and the second concerns how recent trends in developmental research may relate to the nature of explanation in cognitive developmental theory.

Defining context

It is surprising how often the definition of 'context' is left implicit in developmental theory and indeed some of the contributors to this volume are content to rely on implicit definition. A commonsense approach might focus on the physical, social or cultural setting of a particular intellectual task. Beyond such general statements, what is meant by context often remains unanalysed. It is possible, however, to proceed through a series of definitions, from the most general to the more specific, in an attempt to establish what different theorists may hold in common.

Cole and Cole (1989) elaborate what they call a 'cultural-context' view of development. They point out that the word comes from the Latin *contexere* meaning 'to weave together', 'to join together' or 'to compose'. The context in their definition is the interconnected whole that gives meaning to the parts. Variations in the cultural context may give different meanings to otherwise identical behaviours, through the historical experience of the different cultural groups. Cole and Cole particularly emphasize the manner in which social contexts are differentially 'scripted' in different societies. That is, cultures transmit, through their language and their material structure, generalized guides to action. These are sometimes known as 'pragmatic action schemes' (Cheng and Holyoak, 1985).

Cole and Cole describe several ways in which the culture influences the child's development: they suggest that cultures influence development by arranging the *occurrence* of specific contexts. To give their example, the Bushmen of the Kalahari Desert are unlikely to learn about conservation by taking baths or pouring water from one glass to another; nor are the children growing up in Western cities likely to encounter many contexts which will foster skills in tracking animals. The relative *frequency* with which particular contexts are encountered will foster different skills, such as skiing in snowy countries, or making pottery or weaving in simple subsistence societies

(Childs and Greenfield, 1980). These relatively culturally specific activities may be *associated* with other contexts, and with different *responsibilities*, such as selling products, which will in turn foster further culturally specific types of number skills. Furthermore, as Goodnow and Warton (Chapter 9) argue, contexts can coexist in such a way that individuals may participate simultaneously in several culturally constrained modes of knowing. Children may be adept at mathematics in the streets and they may also need to perform at maths in the schools. Not only mathematics but also botany, biology, physics and medicine are practised in everyday contexts and these forms of traditional knowledge impact on formal methods of tuition (George and Glasgow, 1988). A pluralist perspective on contextual effects enables an understanding of when approximation is a sufficiently accurate method of reasoning, as when cooks solve problems of quantities in baking by using rough approximation, rather than by exact measurement of proportions. The appropriate context may call up the appropriate strategy.

The argument advanced by Cole and Cole is that reasoning typically involves the ability to call up an appropriate scheme, or context-sensitive rule, derived from experience, in regularly occurring settings. These 'pragmatic reasoning schemes' may be abstracted from everyday social experiences in culturally specific contexts. The correspondence between pragmatic action schemas and logical structures is examined by Girotto and Light (Chapter 8) for a number of cases. Examples of a correspondence between the logic of implication and commonly occurring types of social interaction pattern are the 'conditional permission schema' (if one wishes to take a particular course of action then one must satisfy a particular precondition) or the 'obligation schema' (if a particular condition occurs, a particular action must be taken). What is striking about these examples is that the logical structure actually *exists in a social reality*, it is not a mere abstraction, as in more dessicated tests of reasoning. In fact, a recent twist to this argument is that apparently abstract tasks, such as the Raven's progressive matrices test, or the Wason selection problem, may in fact be the most acculturated in the sense that their performance requires extensive experience within a culture which values this type of intellectual perform-ance. Hence such tasks differentiate between members of the population and are the least accessible to the majority because they pose their logical problems in a format that is remote from most of everyday life (Richardson, 1991; Johnson-Laird, 1985). The point is that everyday reasoning is generally based on types of culturally specific knowledge, whose represen-tation is evoked by the appropriate context. On this view the context and content of thought are inseparable from the reasoning process.

While context tends most frequently to be defined in terms of cultural and social location, it is possible further to differentiate the concept. Culture is most readily transmitted through language and as Mercer (Chapter 3) says, the linguistic context refers to the whole set of external features relevant to the analysis of an utterance. The cultural context as *transmitted* through language is nevertheless *expressed* within a particular set of *physical* circumstances, whether in the school or in the streets. What is relevant to discourse in the physical world in turn depends on processes of attention which have both interpersonal and intrapersonal aspects. As Roazzi and Bryant (Chapter 2) point out, the identity of perception of a particular situation by different participants depends upon the identity of their referential framework. So, even when tasks have identical content, differences in processes of referential communication may nevertheless result in different outcomes from otherwise identical processes of reasoning.

The argument we would pursue is that contextual factors operate at different hierarchical levels and have specifically identifiable effects through language, perception and attention which situate the individual in a physical and social reality. On this view, the perceptual field provides the public frame of reference within which socially shared acts of communication occur. Language, developmentally speaking, marks the attainment of another cognitive level, and refers to the objects which exist in the space held in common by speaker and listener. The perceptual field may have priority in development and for referential communication (Butterworth and Jarrett, 1991), and it may be the first contextual determinant on which other contexts are founded. The interpenetration of perception, thought, language and culture, when viewed developmentally and in a pluralist perspective, may provide an explanation for many of the phenomena of situated cognition described in this book.

Deductivism, contextualism and realism

Do these changes in emphasis in the recent history of cognitive developmental psychology constitute a 'paradigm shift' in the nature of explanation? It is probably too early to say; the evidence is not all in and many questions remain to be resolved. It is interesting to note, however, that Bhaskhar (1984) identified three modern theories of explanation that parallel, in some respects, the changes in cognitive developmental theories we have outlined. These he called deductivist, contextualist and realist explanations.

On the deductivist view, to explain an event is to 'be able to deduce a statement of it from a set of initial (and boundary) conditions plus universal laws' (p. 140). For example, that a material conducts electricity is logically entailed by the initial condition that the material is metal and the law that all metals conduct electricity. Specific deductive explanations can be subsumed under more general, abstract, inclusive or basic explanations. That is, deductive explanations are relatively independent of specific content or context. It seems fair to say that deductive explanation is generally characteristic of Piaget's approach to cognitive development, though it should be said that Piaget himself was aware of the limitations of this position.

Bhaskhar says a contextualist explanation consists in a social exchange between an explainer and an explainee that resolves the puzzlement of the explainee. The explanation may depend on the pragmatic or social features of the interaction or it may depend on the heuristic content of the explanation. Contextualist explanations involve syntactic and semantic considerations, familiarity, plausibility and pragmatic considerations such as relevance. This is reminiscent of the emphasis in social cognitive developmental psychology on pragmatic action schemes and pragmatic reasoning schemes operating in culturally specific contexts.

Realism is 'the philosophical position that there are perceivable objects and events whose existence does not depend on being perceived or thought about . . . a real world exists and does not rely for its existence on being experienced . . . and this objective reality is known, at least in part' (abridged from Michaels and Carello, 1981). The Gibsonian theory of direct perception, which has influenced much developmental research, takes a realist stance, in that it is argued that perception is from the outset a means of direct, non-inferential contact with the real world. Bhaskhar (1984, p. 362) goes into detail about varieties of realism but it is sufficient for our purpose to stress, as he does, that realism is given as 'a presupposition of our causal investigations of Nature but our knowledge of it is socially produced and it is the nature of objects which determine their cognitive possibilities for us' (p. 363). According to Bhaskhar, realist explanations attempt to combine the situated insights of both deductivist and contextualist explanations. A realist explanation, however, both suffers from and yet acknowledges the limitations of deductivist and contextualist positions since 'deducibility under covering laws is neither necessary nor sufficient for adequate explanation and consensually negotiated explanatory exchanges may mystify as well as emancipate' (p. 141). In other words, from a realist perspective, no explanation may ever be entirely satisfactory but a situated, realist account is the least unsatisfactory! On this view, scientific explanation differs from everyday explanation not so much in form, as in conceptual content, circumstances of production, and empirical, logical and contextual controls.

The realist formulation may be useful in reuniting aspects of the classical literature on the development of reasoning with the contemporary concern for situated cognition. For example, a realist perspective helps in explaining why making expectations explicit in quantitative reasoning tasks, with a focus on the concrete problem to be solved, assists the child to arrive at the correct answer because reasoning is thereby situated in reality (Roazzi and Bryant, Chapter 2). Furthermore, as Lave (Chapter 5) argues, the central question is not whether problem situations are real dilemmas or hypothetical puzzles; the crucial question is whether they are *authentic* dilemmas, whether imagined or real, which will offer opportunities to improvise new solutions. The realist perspective makes ecological validity, or authenticity, an inherent aspect of the reasoning process.

Situated cognition

A realist formulation, then, helps to situate cognition; it gives reasoning an everyday quality because it draws attention to the different ways in which contexts recruit thinking. It does not require a description of reasoning that begins from the strict rules of formal logic; rather thinking begins in the ecological constraints from which physical problems and social encounters are derived. Hatano (1990) has suggested that situated reasoning includes such 'real world' knowledge as 'intuitive physics', 'intuitive psychology', 'intuitive biology' and 'intuitive mathematics'. These domains help us to understand objects in the physical world and to understand why people behave as they do; they provide a means of understanding the natural and social environment and enable basic rules of inference to be applied. Such knowledge arises through informal, everyday experience but it is analogous to the formal, scientific disciplines taught in schools or universities. Everyday knowledge is based on observation and experiment and it has adaptive, heuristic value. The developmental interface between everyday, situated cognition and more formally acquired knowledge within the same domain is seen as a transition from 'novice' to 'expert'. This may involve apprenticeship, verbal instruction, or schooling before fully conceptual knowledge is acquired. Even then, *transfer* between everyday knowledge and formal knowledge may be incomplete because external constraints continue to exercise an influence on cognitive processes. In some domains, such as intuitive psychology or intuitive biology, the distance between the naive and the expert scientist is arguably less than in other domains, such as physics.

Hatano and Inagaki (Chapter 7) argue that children first of all reason from their own basic experience, by abduction to the specific case in question. Shank (1991), in an electronic mail discussion, has defined the concept of abduction as follows: 'Abduction . . . is the mode of logic first discussed by Peirce, that allows for reasoning from basic experience to the case at hand. An example of an abductive syllogism is: This bean is white; all the beans from this bag are white; it is plausible that this bean is from this bag.'

Shank suggests that the inherent logic is derived from perceptual categorization, an operation that *situates* the mind in the world. This seems to complement the position of Hatano and Inagaki (Chapter 7), who argue that decontextualization, to the extent that it occurs, arises through the construction of mental models. A need for greater understanding is initially aroused by perception of incongruous events, it is developed and supported by dialogue and peer group approval, and it flourishes if mental modelling is unhindered by the immediate need for a definitive solution to the problem. According to Hatano and Inagaki, construction of a mental model (internalization) enables generalization across various contexts through reasoning by analogy with aspects of the situation where the problem was first encountered.

Everyday mathematics is another good example of how a particular knowledge domain may function in a situationally constrained fashion. Several chapters in this volume serve to illustrate this point (Roazzi and Bryant, Chapter 2; Schliemann and Carraher, Chapter 4; Lave, Chapter 5). Children and adults, using situated strategies, can solve everyday mathematical and proportional reasoning problems whereas they fail to solve the same problems couched as more formal word problems typical of the school. Many important questions are raised by these displays of situationally constrained competence. First, is 'street mathematics' making use of the same cognitive operations as school mathematics? There is some evidence that intuitive mathematics proceeds by additive operations, whereas the difficulties encountered with the same problems set in a more formal way at school may arise because they demand application of multiplication procedures. Since the same answer can be obtained through different operations, the difference between street and school success may amount to a difference in the appropriate strategy. If so, competence is neither revealed nor concealed by the context. Rather, as Lave (Chapter 5) argues, school-based learning is as much *situated* (in the school) as is reasoning in any other context. To explain the failure or partial 'transfer' of everyday reasoning to formal situations requires a detailed analysis of the social processes which go on in the supposedly formal context. When such an analysis is carried out, as Lave shows for school learning, it becomes clear that children engage in 'subterranean practices' whereby they engender, through social processes, ways of giving meaning to the mathematical word problems that they are set. The 'subterranean' social processes enable the children to situate word problems and establish a mathematical culture among themselves, in the school. This analysis shifts attention away from the traditional dichotomy between 'concrete' and 'theoretical', 'intuitive' and 'abstract' problem-solving, towards the factors that engage attention and give meaning to activity. The learner is always situated in a particular social context; evidence to support this point of view can be found not only in mathematical reasoning but also in other forms of creativity, such as when children collectively write a play (Baker-Sennett, Matusov and Rogoff, Chapter 6).

An important but neglected factor determining how situated individuals actually *feel* themselves to be within any problem-solving domain is the extent to which tasks appropriately harness their intentions. Lave (Chapter 5) points out that in the days when formal mathematics learning was restricted to a few masters, there was no contradiction between the intention to learn and the expertise towards which the individual was being socialized. Today everyone is taught arithmetic in school but this universal socialization is not necessarily matched by clear practical goals for teaching, since the intentions which guide teaching practice are not continually renewed with respect to changing social demands. Hatano and Inagaki (Chapter 7) make a similar point in contrasting children's learning of biology when caring for animals as part of an imposed school routine, with the much richer learning that ensues when the child's own goals are harnessed in rearing pets. Simply to insist on the contextualization of thought is not enough to explain its nature and development. A proper understanding includes knowledge of what motivates problem solving, expressed not only in terms of the goals of the individual but also in terms of the intentions of society as defined within the various opportunities on offer for the cultural transmission of knowledge.

Conclusion

With hindsight, we can see that earlier accounts of cognitive development were overly 'essentialist' in their emphasis on the logical structure of tasks which children can solve at different ages. Contextual factors and their influence in cognitive development were ignored. Much of the literature in the 1970s and 1980s was devoted to debates about the relation between cognitive competence and performance, where performance was somehow conceived to reflect or to mask an underlying competence. This focus on supposedly underlying cognitive processes began to change when the role of perception in the foundations of thought was more thoroughly explored. This, together with work on the relation between language and thought in pre-school children, led to the realization that the preoccupation with the competence/performance distinction may have been misleading. Perhaps competence is a function of contextual variables and this is why performance varies from context to context. Although these issues are not by any means resolved, researchers from different traditions are now converging on what promises to be a more detailed understanding of thinking and its development. The collection of chapters presented here suggests that the field may be on the verge of a new synthesis. A perspective is emerging that will provide an ecological foundation for the development of thought and action in culturally constrained contexts. 'Cold blooded' cognition was replaced by 'social cognition' and this emphasis, in turn, has given way to 'situated cognition' in the last decade. A realist conceptual framework, as advocated by Bhaskhar, offers the opportunity for a synthesis of the situated social and physical bases for the development of reasoning. It is an inevitable corollary that the type of explanation which emerges will be less precisely circumscribed than, say, the Piagetian view, and it may complement rather than entirely replace it. Hopefully, the juxtaposition of the chapters we present here will bring the elaboration of such a synthesis a little closer.

Note

1. Thanks to Roger Goodwin and Paul Light for their helpful comments on this chapter.

References

Bhaskhar, R. (1984), 'Definitions of "Explanation" and of "Realism"', in W.E. Bynum, E.L. Browne and R. Porter (eds), *Dictionary of the History of Science* (Princeton, NJ: Princeton University Press), pp. 140–2, 362–4.

Bryant, P.E. (1974), *Perception and Understanding in Young Children* (London: Methuen).

Butterworth, G.E. (1990), 'Events and encounters in infant perception', in A. Slater and G. Bremner (eds), *Infant Development* (Hove: Lawrence Erlbaum), pp. 73–84.

Butterworth, G.E. and Jarrett, N.L.M. (1991), 'What minds have in common is space: spatial mechanisms serving joint visual attention in infancy', *British Journal of Developmental Psychology*, pp. 55–72.

Butterworth, G.E. and Light, P.H. (1982), *Social Cognition: Essays on the development of understanding* (Brighton: Harvester Press).

Chapman, M. (1988), *Constructive Evolution: Origins and development of Piaget's thought* (Cambridge: Cambridge University Press).

Cheng, P.W. and Holyoak, K.J. (1985), 'On the natural selection of reasoning theories', *Cognition*, 33, pp. 285–313.

Childs, C.P. and Greenfield, P.M. (1980), 'Informal modes of learning and teaching: the case of Zinacanteco learning', in N. Warren (ed.), *Studies in Cross Cultural Psychology (Vol. 2)* (New York: Academic Press).

Cole, M.M. and Cole, S.R. (1989), *The Development of Children* (San Francisco: Freeman).

Donaldson, M. (1978), *Children's Minds* (Glasgow: Fontana).

George, J. and Glasgow, J. (1988), 'Street science and conventional science in the West Indies', *Studies in Science Education*, 15, pp. 109–18.

Hatano, G. (1990), 'The nature of everyday science: a brief introduction', *British Journal of Developmental Psychology*, 8, pp. 245–50.

Johnson-Laird, P.N. (1985), 'Deductive reasoning ability', in R.J. Sternberg (ed.), *Human Abilities* (New York: Freeman).

Light, P.H. (1986), 'Context, conservation and conversation', in M. Richards and P. Light (eds), *Children of Social Worlds* (Cambridge: Polity Press).

McGarrigle, J. and Donaldson, M. (1974), 'Conservation accidents', *Cognition*, 3, pp. 341–50.

Michaels, C.F. and Carello, C. (1981), *Direct Perception* (New Jersey: Prentice Hall).

Piaget, J. (1971), *Biology and Knowledge* (Edinburgh: Edinburgh University Press).

Richardson, K. (1991), 'Reasoning with Raven – in and out of context', *British Journal of Educational Psychology*, 61, pp. 129–38.

Shank, G. (1991), 'Thoughts on abduction', electronic mail discussion, XLCHC network, University of California, November.

Siegal, M. (1991), *Knowing Children* (Hove: Erlbaum).

Chapter 2

Social class, context and cognitive development

Antonio Roazzi, *Universidade Federal de Pernambuco*
Peter Bryant, *University of Oxford*

Context and social class

The evidence that the context in which children are given cognitive tasks has a huge effect on their performance in those tasks is virtually irrefutable. There are now many completely convincing demonstrations that children perform much better in one condition, or context, than in another, despite the fact that both contexts make exactly the same logical and cognitive demands. Usually the contexts which cause children the most difficulty are the traditional conditions in which some very well-known cognitive tasks, such as the conservation problem and the class inclusion problem, are administered. In other circumstances the same children often manage the same problem with much greater success (Rose and Blank, 1974; McGarrigle and Donaldson, 1974–5; Light, Buckingham and Robbins, 1979; Roazzi, 1986). Such contextual effects have also been found in educational tasks. For example, children who work in street markets in Brazil make arithmetical calculations more effectively at their market stalls than in their classrooms (Carraher, Carraher and Schliemann, 1985).

There is another notable fact about the cognitive and intellectual tasks that have proved so sensitive to variations in context. These are all tasks which have proved a great deal more difficult for working-class than for middle-class children. Many studies have shown that working-class children perform at lower levels than middle-class children in Piagetian tasks (Amann-Gainotti, 1979; Barolo, 1979; Barolo and Albanese, 1981; Carotenuto and Casale, 1981; Carraher and Schliemann, 1982; Perret-Clermont and Leoni

14

[described in Doise and Mugny, 1984]; Roazzi and Dias, 1987). To give one example in more detail, Perret-Clermont and Leoni (1984) compared the performance of Swiss children from different socio-economic backgrounds in a liquid conservation task. Seventy-one per cent of the disadvantaged children failed this task: the figure for children of the same age who suffered no socio-economic disadvantage was only 33.3 per cent. Roazzi and Dias (1987) found much the same pattern with English children in a liquid conservation task and Carraher and Schliemann (1982) report similar results with Brazilian children in a number conservation task.

Our reason for mentioning these two striking sources of differences in children's performance in intellectual tasks – the context in which the task is given and the social background from which the child happens to come – is the possibility that there might be a relationship between the two. In general, the studies which have established the striking superiority of the middle-class children have been given to them and to their working-class peers in the traditional form – in other words in the context that has proved least favourable to children's performance in general. Therefore it is quite possible that the class difference might be one of sensitivity to context: working-class children might be more sensitive to context – hindered more by the traditional versions of the intellectual tasks – than middle-class children are.

There are plausible reasons why this might be so. The traditional versions of cognitive tasks which children find quite difficult are, as Margaret Donaldson (1978) has argued, usually formal and bereft of concrete meaning. In form they resemble the kind of problem that is likely to be posed to children in a school setting. It is quite possible that middle-class children will be better prepared by their parents and their environment for problems in this form than working-class children are. To make this point convincingly, however, we must examine in more detail the nature of the effects of variations in context.

The nature of contextual effects

The contextual manipulations that have had an effect vary greatly from one experiment to another, and so it is hard to propose a simple and precise rule to define what makes some contexts help and others hinder young children's cognitive performance. One can, however, point to several powerful factors. One such factor, on which we shall concentrate in this chapter, is the degree of *explicitness* about the nature of the task. This is particularly clear in work on the conservation problem. The traditional conservation procedure can be criticized for not making it clear to children that the judgement they are being asked to make is a quantitative one. In the traditional form of the task children are simply asked first to look at and to compare two quantities which are identical both quantitatively and perceptually. The fact that the two quantities also look exactly alike may mislead the child into thinking that the initial, pre-transformation, question, and also the question asked after the transformation, are about the perceptual appearance of the two quantities and not about their actual amounts. So, when the experimenter transforms the appearance of one of the two quantities, the child, seeing that they are different and thinking the question to be a perceptual one, answers that they are no longer the same.

Carraher and Schliemann (1985) examined four groups of 4- and 5-year-old children in two versions of the conservation of discrete quantities (number of tokens) task and two of the conservation of continuous quantities (length of pieces of string) task. Two groups were submitted to the traditional Piagetian versions of each task and, accordingly, first established the equality between the quantities through perceptual comparison. The other two groups underwent a modified version of each task where, instead of a perceptual comparison, the child was initially asked to make a quantitative comparison between the two quantities. The 5-year-olds did a great deal better in the modified version (60 per cent and 45 per cent conservation answers for discrete and continuous quantity, respectively, in the modified version as opposed to 27 per cent and 0 per cent in the traditional version).

Gelman (1982) pursued much the same hypothesis and reached much the same conclusion in a training experiment with 3 and 4 year olds. She gave one group of children a version of the conservation task in which they had to count the number of objects in each of two rows in the first part of the task and then compare them on the basis of their number. Then the appearance of one of the rows was altered and the children were asked the usual conservation question. After this experience the children were given several traditional conservation problems. They performed well in these later tasks, and a great deal better than children who had not made the same numerical comparisons in the previous task. Once again, an explicit emphasis on quantity and on counting led to better performance in a conservation of number task.

The argument for the importance of explicitness sits uneasily with another well-known claim about contextual effects in the conservation task. This is the claim for *incidentality*. It has often been suggested that young children do much better in versions of the conservation task in which the perceptual transformation appears not to be a central part of the experimental proceedings. The claim here is that in the traditional version of the conservation experiment young children are misled by the emphasis which the experimenter puts on the transformation. According to this argument, children think that because the experimenter has deliberately changed the quantity, they should now change their previous judgement – the one that they made before the transformation. Since that judgement had been that the two quantities are equal, they now feel it right to judge the two as unequal.

We have mentioned a certain awkwardness between this argument and our plea for the importance of explicitness. This is because some of the evidence for incidentality seems to show that young children can solve the conservation task when nothing is done to make its quantitative nature more explicit.

We shall describe the results of a study by Light, Buckingham and Robbins (1979) of the effects of incidentality in order to illustrate this conflict. We have turned to this study because it seems to be by far the most replicable of this genre of experiments (Bovet, Parrat-Dayan and Deshusses-Addor, 1981; Miller, 1982).

Light *et al.* (1979) gave 6-year-old children one of two different versions of the conservation task. In one, which was called the Incidental condition, pairs of children were told that they were going to play a board game with pasta shells and that they had to start the game with an equal amount of shells. Each child was given a glass, the pasta shells were divided into two equal portions and each portion was put in one of the glasses. However, just before starting the game, the experimenter noticed that one child's glass was chipped and said that it was unsafe and had to be changed; then this child's shells were transferred to another different-shaped glass, and the children were asked whether they still had the same number of shells as each other. In the other condition, the Standard condition, pairs of children were simply given the traditional conservation task.

The results of this study were striking. Twenty-six children out of forty succeeded in the Incidental condition, and only one out of forty in the Standard condition. The authors concluded that children do better 'when the transformation was rendered incidental to the proceedings' (p. 309).

If this very large difference between the two conditions is due entirely to one condition being 'incidental to the proceedings', the study would indeed create considerable difficulty for our hypothesis about explicitness. But there are reasons now for doubting whether this really was what told the two conditions apart. There is another possibility which conforms more closely to our hypothesis, and that is that the game-like Incidental condition helped children not because of the incidentality but because it emphasized the quantitative nature of the problem. In the Standard condition the children could have judged the two quantities as equal because they looked the same. The Incidental condition, on the other hand, could have discouraged the child from making a perceptual comparison and led him or her to make a genuinely quantitative comparison. In the latter condition the children knew that they had to start with the same amount, not just with two sets of shells which looked much the same as each other.

Some recent research (Light, Gorsuch and Newman, 1987) supports this alternative idea. The study which was with 5-year-old children was a complex one, but its strongest result came from a comparison between two kinds of conservation task. One was a Game task which started with pairs of children being told that they were going to play a game with dried peas and that it was essential that they should start the game with the same amount of peas. The peas were divided into two piles, one for each child, which the children judged to be equal, and then the two children's piles were put into different-shaped containers. Notice that this procedure involves no 'incidental' manoeuvres. The other task – the Standard task – took exactly the same form, except that the children were told nothing about a game; so this task was equivalent to the standard conservation procedure.

The Game task turned out to be much the easier of the two. What is the reason for this difference? A rather unattractive possibility, but one which we cannot rule out, is that the children were simply more engaged in and more motivated by the Game task than the Standard task. A second possibility is that the Game task drew the children's attention to the quantitative nature of the questions that they had to answer. The authors themselves prefer this latter possibility and argue for 'the facilitatory effects of placing an emphasis on fairness of distribution' (p. 78).

Their conclusion fits well with our argument about explicitness, although it should be noted that the initial quantitative comparison takes a different form from the equivalent comparisons in the studies by Carraher and Schliemann and by Gelman. In those studies the comparison was one of absolute number: the children counted the two quantities. In the study by Light *et al.* (1987) the children did not count: the initial equality of the two quantities in the Game condition was established by a fairly approximate division – that is, the children made a *relative* not an *absolute* comparison in this case. We make this point now because recent evidence (Desforges and Desforges, 1980; Miller, 1984; Frydman and Bryant, 1988) points to young children's adeptness at making relative comparisons on the basis of sharing, and it is useful to remember that relative judgements of quantity may be as important in children's early mathematical development as absolute judgements based on counting.

We conclude that one major determinant of children's performance in any quantitative task is the extent to which they realize that it is a quantitative task. It also seems that this is a factor which can be quite easily manipulated by varying experimental conditions. Some contexts help children realize the quantitative nature of the task much more than others do.

Turning again to the question of social class, we have asked in a general way whether working-class children are more sensitive to contextual differences than middle-class children. We can now make this question more precise. Do working-class children fail more in the traditional versions of various cognitive tasks because they have particular difficulty in grasping the quantitative nature of these tasks? Do these children need more information, of an explicit kind, than middle-class children in order to understand that the judgements they are being asked to make are quantitative ones?

Class inclusion and the context of the street market

One of the most significant pieces of evidence demonstrating that working-class children are sensitive to the context in which they have to solve intellectual problems is the study by Carraher, Carraher and Schliemann (1985). They looked at the daily use of mathematics by young Brazilians (9 to 15 year olds) working in commercial activities. Their sample was composed of sons and daughters of poor migrant workers who had moved to Recife, a state capital in the north-east of Brazil. These children represent a ready source of income to a nuclear family because they contribute to the family's income by working alone cleaning windshields, shining shoes in the town centre, or gathering paper, plastic containers, metal scraps and other waste products. They also often work with other family members as street vendors, selling coconuts, corn on the cob and other goods. These activities require them to carry out arithmetical operations such as subtraction, addition, multiplication and sometimes division.

Carraher, Carraher and Schliemann (1985) bought items from these children in the market, thus giving them mathematical problems (for example, the cost of the items, the amount of change) in informal conditions. At another time the experimenters gave the same children the same mathematical problems in a more formal way, either as straight sums or as word problems which concerned concrete situations. The children solved the problems in the informal situation more easily than they solved the formal problems.

This striking study raises an obvious question. Will the same effects be found in other, more traditional, cognitive tasks? It is just possible that the dramatic contextual effects, so clearly shown by Carraher *et al.*, are restricted to the computational routines which the street vendors have to learn in order to ply their trade. In that case the study, although important in itself, would have little bearing on children's general cognitive development. On the other hand, the phenomenon demonstrated by Carraher *et al.* might be a general one, and in that case it should be possible to demonstrate similar effects in other logical tasks.

For this reason, one of us, Roazzi, in co-operation with Terezinha Nunes,[1] carried out a further study of sixty Brazilian working-class children (aged 6–9 years) who were also street vendors, and this time we looked at class inclusion. (This study also included a group of sixty middle-class children of the same age who had no experience at all of selling goods in markets, although that fact, as we shall see, prevented a genuine comparison across the two social classes.)

We shall first describe what happened with the street vendors. We designed a class inclusion task which took place as part of a sales transaction:

the children, unknowingly, participated in the research during the normal course of customer–vendor interaction. The interviewer, as a casual purchaser, searched among the goods for two classes of objects or of foods (for example, mint and strawberry chewing gum) of the same price per unit, which were clearly members of the same superordinate class (in our example the class of chewing gum).

Next, the interviewer checked if the child understood that the two subclasses (mint and strawberry chewing gum) were part of the larger class (chewing gum) by asking: 'Which kinds of chewing gum do you have?' If the child knew, without any doubt or perplexity, how to include the two subclasses in the bigger class, the interviewer then picked up four units of one subclass (i.e. mint chewing gum) and two units of the other subclass (i.e. strawberry chewing gum) and showing the child the pieces of chewing gum, the interviewer asked: 'Do I pay more for the mint chewing gums or for the strawberry chewing gums? Why?' 'For you to get more money is it better to sell me the mint chewing gums or is it better to sell me the chewing gums [the class inclusion question]? Why?'

Afterwards, the same children were given a Formal test, which was equivalent to the class inclusion task devised by Piaget and Inhelder (1959) and which had the same logical structure as the Informal test. The children were shown sets of balls of different colours and were asked: 'Are there more yellow balls or are there more balls? Why?'

There was, as we had expected, a large difference between the two tasks. Sixty per cent of the children gave the correct answer in the Informal test and only 23 per cent in the Formal test. Thus the difference between Informal and Formal contexts seems to apply to logical tasks as well as to computational ones. This suggests that the Carraher, Carraher and Schliemann effect is not an isolated or a specific phenomenon.

There are, of course, other possibilities. The order of the two tasks was not, and for practical reasons could not be, counterbalanced. But this almost certainly is not a cause of the difference, because one expects children to do better the second time round, while in fact they did a great deal worse in the second task (the formal one). It is also possible that the difference in the materials in the two tasks (objects to be sold in one and coloured balls in the other) may have had an effect. It seems unlikely to us that this could account for the large difference between the conditions, although this is a factor which certainly should be looked at further.

We conclude that the study shows that these children tended to approach this particular logical problem in a logical way when the problem was part of their everyday activity of selling goods for money.

What about class differences? It is possible, and indeed we think it likely, that working-class children, much more than middle-class children, need the prop of money in order to treat such problems logically. So, it would be interesting to know whether the difference between the two tests is a smaller one in middle-class children. But it was impossible to test this possibility directly in this particular study, for the simple reason that there are no middle-class street vendors. Middle-class children do not work on street stalls in Brazil.[2] For a direct comparison, we turned to the conservation problem.

Conservation, context and class

We had two aims when we set about comparing the effects of context on the way in which 5- to 8-year-old working-class and middle-class Brazilian children manage the conservation problem. We wanted to look at the effects of incidentality, and also at the effects of varying the degree of explicitness in the task.

We will describe our study of incidentality first (Roazzi, Bryant and Schliemann, 1988). We gave thirty-two working-class and thirty-two middle-class children a Standard conservation (of liquid) task and an equal number of children from both social classes an Incidental conservation task. The children who were given the Standard task were shown, in the usual way, an equal amount of lemonade in two identical containers and were asked to compare the two. After the child had judged that the glasses held the same amount, the liquid from one container was poured into a thinner container and we asked the child to compare the two quantities again.

The Incidental task took exactly the same form except that after the child made his or her initial judgement, the experimenter discovered, apparently to his surprise, that one glass was dirty and searched for a cleaner glass (which also happened to be thinner) to put the lemonade in for reasons of hygiene. Thus in the Standard condition we gave the child no particular reason why we transferred the lemonade from one container to another, while in the Incidental condition there was apparently a good reason for doing so, although that reason was incidental to the problem at hand. Notice that this 'incidental' transformation does nothing to make the quantitative nature of the task more explicit, and thus avoids the ambiguity of the original Light *et al.* (1979) Incidental task.

In both tasks we asked the children two questions after the transformation. One was about the amount of lemonade in the two containers, and the other about the relative cost of the two lots of lemonade.

The results were a surprise to us. The middle-class children were better than the working-class children in the Standard condition as we expected, though the difference did not quite reach significance in a chi-squared test. Nine per cent of the working-class children and 25 per cent of the middle-class children answered the question about quantity correctly and were able to justify it properly.

However, we found very little evidence for incidentality. The performance of the children who were given the Incidental task was slightly higher than that of the children who were given the Standard form of the task, but the difference did not reach significance in either social group. Twelve per cent of the working-class children who were given the Incidental problem solved it correctly (as opposed to 9 per cent in the Standard task) and 40 per cent of the middle-class children (as opposed to 25 per cent in the Standard task). Although the difference was greater within the middle-class group it still did not quite reach significance.

These insignificant differences are in strong contrast to the large difference between the Standard and Incidental tasks in the original Light *et al.* (1979) study. This suggests that it was not incidentality *per se* that led to the striking superiority of the Incidental condition in their experiment, but the introduction of a competitive game, as Light, Gorsuch and Newman (1987) have since suggested.

The one significant difference in our study was between the working-class and the middle-class children in the Incidental task. The middle-class scores were significantly higher (12 per cent vs 40 per cent correct) in this task.

Our main question is whether differences between social classes in the conservation task can be explained in terms of differences in the need for explicitness, and so we decided in our next study to look at the effects of explicitness in problems in which the transformation was always an incidental one.

We devised two new tasks for this study, which was also with 5- to 8-year-old working- and middle-class children; again, different children were given the different tasks. In both tasks the instructions were more explicit about the quantitative nature of the task than is usually the case, and both involved measurement in the initial part of the problem. In one task which we call the Quantity task the children had first to share out the lemonade in the two glasses with a ladle. They were asked to put four ladlefuls of lemonade into each glass. One of the two glasses was covered, in order to avoid the possibility of the child making the first comparison on a perceptual basis. The child had to judge the two amounts as equal on the basis of having put the same number of ladlefuls into each glass. Thereafter the procedure was exactly the same as in the Incidental task in the first study.

The other task, called the Money task, was exactly the same except that the child was told that he would have to sell the lemonade and that each ladleful was worth 1 cruzeiro. The child was asked to put 4 cruzeiros' worth of lemonade in each glass. So the emphasis here was as much on the price as on the number of ladles.

Thus we could look at the effects of these two forms of explicitness by comparing the performance of the children given each of these two tasks with the performance of those who were given the Incidental task in the first study where no measurement was involved in the initial part of the task. Since the Incidental task gives us the baseline for children's performance when no particular emphasis is put on quantity, it serves as a control and for this reason we shall now refer to it as the Control task.

The comparison between the Control task and the two tasks (Quantity and Money) in which the quantitative nature of the task was made more explicit, produced some striking results. Figure 2.1 overleaf shows the pattern that we found when we divided children into the usual Piagetian categories (Piaget and Szeminska, 1941): Non-conservers, Intermediate conservers who were inconsistent or who gave the correct answer but could not justify it properly, and Conservers who gave the correct answer and produced the correct explanation for it.

The figure shows that the working-class group clearly benefited from the introduction of more explicitly quantitative instructions. Many more working-class children were classified either as Intermediate conservers or as Conservers among those who were given the Quantity and the Money task than among those given the Control task. The difference between the Quantity and the Control task was mainly in the number of Intermediate conservers. In the Money task, more impressively, the difference was in the number of Conservers.

In the middle-class group the differences were not so impressive. There was no sign that they were any better in the Quantity task than in the Control task: more of them were classified as Intermediate conservers but fewer of them as Conservers in the Quantity than in the Control task. There was some evidence that they benefited from the instructions in the Money task. As many of them were classified as Conservers as in the Control task and more of them as Intermediate conservers in the Money task than in the Control task: but for these middle-class children the difference between the Money task and the Control task was not nearly so great as it was for the working-class children. The upshot was that there were massive class differences, in favour of the middle-class group, in the Control task, but virtually none in the Money task.

Conclusions

The three studies that we have reported certainly confirm the importance of context in experiments on cognitive development, and they provide some evidence about some of the reasons for these contextual effects. As well as this, our data suggest that variations in the context in which cognitive problems are given to young children have different implications for different social groups. This means that some of the differences that have been reported between children from different groups may reflect the different ways in which working- and middle-class children react to particular aspects of the context in which the intellectual tests that produced the differences were administered.

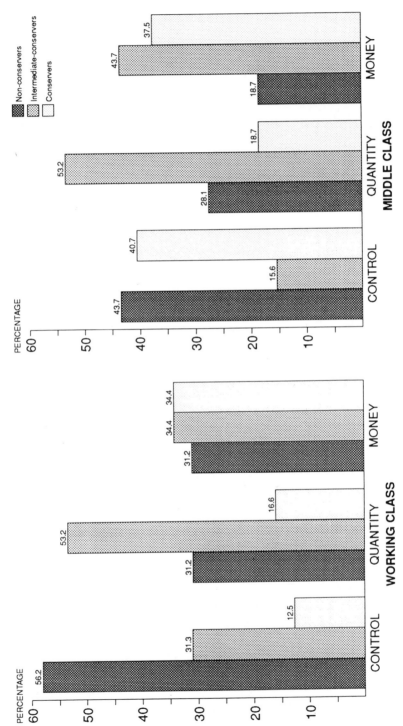

Figure 2.1 Percentage of children falling into the three Piagetian conservation categories in the Control, Quantity and Money tasks.

The most important variable in our studies was the degree of explicitness in the task's procedure. At the very least our results confirm the suspicion voiced by many other people that we cannot take it for granted that children understand the quantitative or logical nature of the quantitative and logical tasks that they are given. The fact that they are so much more likely to answer the post-transformation conservation question correctly when the quantitative nature of the initial pre-transformation comparison has been stressed demonstrates that it helps children to be shown that the questions being asked are about quantity and not about perceptual appearance. The similarity here between our results with liquid and those of Carraher and Schliemann with number is impressive, and suggests that the importance for children of an explicit emphasis on quantity is a general one.

The other main idea about context that we considered was the idea of incidentality. This idea is that the routine of asking children a question about the two quantities, deliberately transforming one quantity and then asking them the same question for a second time, misleads them into thinking that they should change their answer after the transformation, because they believe that the deliberate change that the experimenter has made must be significant in some way. Our own data provided scant evidence for its importance. We were unable to demonstrate that an incidental task is significantly easier than the traditional form of the conservation task. However, our results do not rule out the possibility that incidentality might be important in some circumstances.

Our main aim was to consider the possibility of differences in the effects of context on different social groups. Our idea was that these effects might be more important for working-class than for middle-class children. In effect, we thought that working-class children might be particularly handicapped by the limitations of the traditional context in which cognitive problems are usually given.

Our results give some support to this idea. The striking difference in the way that child street vendors handled the two kinds of class inclusion problems certainly showed that these working-class children are sensitive to contextual changes. But this result does not on its own tell us anything about differences between the two social groups.

The conservation data, on the other hand, do suggest a difference between working-class and middle-class children. Neither group was much affected by our making the task an incidental one, though there were signs that this manoeuvre might have helped the middle-class more than the working-class children. But the introduction of measurement and the consequent increase in the explicit stress on quantity appeared to have an appreciably stronger effect on working-class children than on middle-class children. The working-class children seemed to benefit most from this explicitness, particularly when money is involved.

One can speculate about the reasons for this difference between the social groups (we have already argued that the middle-class children, being better prepared for the school environment, may also be more at home with tasks presented in unfamiliar contexts), but the practical implications of our results are clear. Children in general, and working-class children in particular, are helped when the nature of the task that they are being given is clear and explicit.

Notes

1. Formerly Terezinha Carraher.
2. We did give a version of the informal test to a group of middle-class children in the form of a game. The children were invited to pretend that they were vendors and that the interviewer was a purchaser. The interviewer gave the child a box with several things to sell, such as sweets, chewing gum, etc., and asked the same series of questions as he had asked the street vendors. These children were also given the Formal test later on.
   The pattern of these children's performance was the opposite of the street vendors'. Twenty-seven per cent were correct in the Informal test and 54 per cent in the Formal test. This difference is probably due to an order effect.

References

Amann-Gainotti, M. (1979), 'Conceptions of the world and concrete operations. A comparative study of children from different social classes', *The Italian Journal of Psychology*, 1, pp. 43–52.

Barolo, E. (1979), 'Acquisition of substance conservation in preschool years: the socioeconomic factors', *The Italian Journal of Psychology*, 1, pp. 9–15.

Barolo, E. and Albanese, O. (1981), 'Condizione socio-economiche e acquisizione della conservazione di sostanza', *Ricerche di Psicologia*, 19, pp. 91–103.

Bovet, M., Parrat-Dayan, S. and Deshusses-Addor, D. (1981), 'Peut on parler de precocité et de regression dans la conservation? I Precocité', *Archives de Psychologie*, 49, pp. 289–303.

Carotenuto, V. and Casale, M. (1981), 'Realtá e irrealtá degli stadi di sviluppo mentale', in V. Carotenuto and G. Bellelli (eds), *Sviluppo cognitivo e regolazione della attivitá* (Napoli: Facolta di Lettere e Filosofia).

Carraher, T.N. and Schliemann, A.D. (1982), 'Fracasso escolar: uma queståo social', Mimeo, INEP – Universidade Federal de Pernambuco, Recife.

Carraher, T.N. and Schliemann, A.D. (1985), 'A contagem como mediador da conservaçåo', paper presented at 37th Reuniao Anual da Sociedade Brasileira para o Progresso da Ciência, Belo Horizonte.

Carraher, T.N., Carraher, D.W. and Schliemann, A.D. (1985), 'Mathematics in the streets and in the schools', *British Journal of Developmental Psychology*, 3, pp. 21–9.

Desforges, A. and Desforges, G. (1980), 'Number-based strategies of sharing in young children', *Educational Studies*, 6, pp. 97–109.

Doise, W. and Mugny, G. (1984), *The Social Development of the Intellect* (Oxford: Pergamon Press).

Donaldson, M. (1978), *Children's Minds* (Glasgow: Fontana/Collins).

Frydman, O. and Bryant P.E. (1988), 'Sharing and the understanding of number equivalence by young children', *Cognitive Development*, 3, pp. 323–39.

Gelman, R. (1982), 'Accessing one-to-one correspondence: still another paper about conservation', *British Journal of Psychology*, 73, pp. 209–20.

Light, P.H., Buckingham, N. and Robbins, A.H. (1979), 'The conservation task as an interactional setting', *British Journal of Educational Psychology*, 49, pp. 304–10.

Light, P., Gorsuch, C. and Newman, J. (1987), ' "Why do you ask?" Context and communication in the conservation task', *European Journal of Psychology Education*, 2(1), pp. 73–82.

McGarrigle, J. and Donaldson, M. (1974/1975), 'Conservation accidents', *Cognition*, 3, pp. 341–50.

Miller, K. (1984), 'The child as the measurer of all things: measurement procedures and the development of quantitative concepts', in C. Sophian (ed.), *Origins of Cognitive Skills* (Hillsdale, NJ: Erlbaum).

Miller, S.A. (1982), 'On the generalisability of conservation: a comparison of different kinds of transformation', *British Journal of Psychology*, 73, pp. 221–30.

Piaget, J. and Inhelder, B. (1959), *La genèse des structures logiques elementaires* (Neufchatel: Delachaux et Niestle).

Piaget, J. and Szeminska, A. (1941), *La genèse du nombre chez l'enfant* (Neufchatel: Delachaux et Niestle).

Roazzi, A. (1986), 'Social context in experimental psychology', *Ricerche di Psicologia*, 4, pp. 23–45.

Roazzi, A., Bryant, P.E. and Schliemann, A.D. (1988), 'Context effects on children's performance of conservation task', paper presented at the Annual Conference of the British Psychological Society: Developmental Section, Coleg Harlech, Wales, 16–19 September.

Roazzi, A. and Dias, M.G.B. (1987), 'A influência da experiência socio-cultural em crianças Inglesas. Dados experimentais e exploraç/Ees teoricas na tarefa de conservaçâo', *Arquivos Brasileiros de Psicologia*, 2, pp. 39–56.

Rose, S.A. and Blank, M. (1974), 'The potency of context in children's cognition: an illustration from conservation', *Child Development*, 45, pp. 499–502.

Chapter 3

Culture, context and the construction of knowledge in the classroom

Neil Mercer, *The Open University*[1]

Introduction

References to 'culture' and 'context' have become increasingly common in research into learning and cognitive development, but the concepts are hardly ever explicitly discussed or defined in relation to that field of research. My aim in this chapter is to encourage a more open discussion of their meaning and relevance. The chapter has two main parts. First, I offer some definitions of 'culture' and 'context' and discuss the relevance of these concepts for research into learning (and especially learning in school). I then use some observational data on teaching and learning to illustrate and elaborate that discussion, and in doing so identify what I believe are important features of situated learning.

Culture and context in psychology

The 1980s was an interesting, if unsettled, period for the study of children's cognition and learning. On the theoretical level, there was a growing unease with theoretical perspectives which focused on individual development to the extent that social and interactional factors in learning and development were marginalized or even ignored. Despite widespread dissatisfaction with the theory and methods of earlier research on the educational attainment of children from different cultural groups (e.g. Jensen, 1967; Bernstein, 1971), more recent research on social experience and children's educational progress (e.g. Tizard and Hughes, 1984; Wells, 1985) made it clear that 'culture' could not be ignored. In particular, it seemed that more attention needed to be paid to the relationship between children's experiences within the cultural environments of home and school, and in particular to the form and content of communication between parents and children and between teachers and children. As early as 1971, Bruner (1971, p. 20) had made the point that 'One of the most crucial ways in which a culture provides aid in intellectual growth is through a dialogue between the more experienced and the less experienced', and thirteen years later he was saying 'the process of learning how to negotiate communicatively is the very process by which one enters the culture' (Bruner, 1984, quoted by Edwards and Westgate, 1987, p. 12).

But culture and communication were themes that were not clearly or centrally represented within the Piagetian theory which dominated developmental psychology and which had most influence on educational theory and practice. And so the adequacy of Piagetian theory was questioned (e.g. Walkerdine, 1984; Edwards and Mercer, 1987) and some radical revisions of the Piagetian account of cognitive development were proposed. For example, Light (1986, p. 187) argued that: 'conservation concepts can and should be thought of not as transcendent logical entities but as the historically determined products of specific human purposes and practices ... The child's task, seen in this light, is to gain access to these culturally elaborated abstractions.' The Piagetian perspective has, of course, been staunchly defended, and it is certainly true that critics have focused on the emphases, rather than the scope, of the theory. As Smith (1989) rightly asserts, if you look closely enough, you will find Piaget himself making numerous references to collaboration, culture and communication. But, as Smith also admits, Piaget gave these factors little attention in the practice of his research. It is therefore perhaps not surprising that so many of his followers saw them as having only marginal significance.

Moreover, from the mid-1970s through the 1980s misgivings grew among researchers about how experimental methods had been used to study cognitive development. One important influence was Margaret Donaldson's work (e.g. McGarrigle and Donaldson, 1974; Donaldson, 1978), which showed how strongly experimental results could be influenced by contextual cues carried implicitly within an experimental design or setting. This encouraged the view among researchers that the cultural settings in which learning tasks are attempted are not easily separated from the tasks themselves. It suggested that, to avoid artefacts, learning must be studied 'in context'. Naturalistic, observational methods thus became rather more popular (especially among those researchers with educational interests), and experimental methods were devised which were more sensitive to situational factors. It also seemed that Vygotsky's work (e.g. Vygotsky, 1978), with its recognition of cultural and linguistic factors on cognitive development and learning, might offer a better basis for such observational and experimental research than did Piaget's. Some central features of the 'neo-Vygotskian' perspective on learning and cognitive development which emerged from this period of theoretical reorientation are discussed later in this chapter.

I am suggesting, then, that culture and context became necessary and important concepts for the field of cognitive development and learning – and not just for that part of the field explicitly concerned with cross-cultural differences – once it was accepted that children's performance in problem-solving and other learning activities is inevitably influenced by their response to particular symbolic features of the tasks they face. But this begs the question of what we take culture and context to mean.

Defining culture

Anthropology, of course, is the discipline with first claims on culture. The eminent anthropologist Geertz (1968, p. 641) offered the following definition: 'an historically transmitted pattern of meaning embodied in symbols, a system of inherited conceptions expressed in symbolic form by means of which men communicate, perpetuate and develop their knowledge about and attitudes towards life'. Geertz's definition seems to me to be compatible with the notion of culture employed by Vygotsky (e.g. 1978, 1981). As Scribner (1985, p. 123) points out: 'We find Vygotsky introducing the term "cultural development" in his discussion of the origins of higher psychological functions and in some contexts using it interchangeably with "historical development".' For Vygotsky, the concept of culture offers a way of linking the history of a social group, the communicative activity of its members and the cognitive development of its children.

Having cited Geertz as an authoritative source on culture, I feel bound to admit that his definition may show its age in more ways than simply in his use of 'men' to mean 'people'! Many anthropologists and social theorists have become unhappy with using the term 'culture' because it carries with it so easily an image of a static, enduring body of knowledge, an image which is at odds with the inherent variety of perspective and beliefs to be found even within the most apparently homogeneous social group. Thus Thompson (1984, p. 5) comments: 'There is little evidence to suggest that certain values or beliefs are shared by all (or even most) members of modern industrial societies. On the contrary, it seems more likely that our societies, in so far as they are "stable" social orders, are stabilized by virtue of the diversity of values and beliefs and the proliferation of divisions between individuals and groups.'

Despite these concerns, I have not found any anthropologist objecting to the use of the adjective 'cultural' to describe a particular kind of knowledge (knowledge that is shared and developed between and across generations, that is not derived directly from personal interaction with the physical universe, and which may be expressed in symbolic form) or that all human societies operate a system – a cultural knowledge network – for generating and transmitting knowledge. What is really required, I believe, is not the rejection of the concept of culture but the need for a more robust definition which takes account of notions of power and status, and which reflects cultural pluralism. Thus Maybin in a personal comment has said that her anthropological research on children's 'off-task' talk in school (e.g. Maybin, 1991) involves 'trying to look at children as cultural apprentices, where culture involves various changing and contested meanings, and discourse is an important site for displaying and negotiating those meanings'. From this perspective culture is something which is not just received but which is also revised and re-created by children. It remains a source of meaningful representations of objects and actions, representations which are sociohistorical because they emerge from the historical experience of a social group. Children's interpretations of experience – the meanings they attach to their learning – will, in part, be determined by their involvement with schools and the other institutions of their society. Any educationally orientated study of learning must recognize that schools have their own body of cultural knowledge, and their own ways of communicating and legitimizing knowledge.

Defining context

If anthropology has legitimate claims to the ownership of culture, then linguistics must have similar ones to context. As Crystal's *Dictionary of Linguistics and Phonetics* (1985) explains, in the study of language 'context' is used in four main ways. The narrowest usage, found within formal linguistics, is to refer to 'specific parts of an UTTERANCE (or TEXT) near or adjacent to a UNIT which is the focus of attention ... Words, it is suggested, have meaning only when seen in context' (p. 71). But another, broader definition relates more closely to our present interests:

> Context of situation is a specific term in FIRTHIAN linguistic theory, deriving from the work of the anthropologist Bronislaw Malinowski (1884–1942). In this theory, meaning is seen as a multiple phenomenon, its various facets being relatable on the one hand to features of the external world, and on the other hand to the different LEVELS of linguistic analysis, such as PHONETICS, grammar and semantics. Context of situation refers to the whole set of extgernal features *considered relevant* to the analysis of an utterance at these levels. (Crystal, 1985, p. 72; my italics)

I have included this definition here because it indirectly supports the kind of conception of context which I believe is most useful for the study of teaching and learning. What counts as context for learners, as for analytic linguists, is *whatever they consider relevant*. Pupils accomplish educational activities by using what they know to make sense of what they are asked to do. As best they can, they create a meaningful context for an activity, and the context they create consists of whatever knowledge they invoke to make sense of the task situation.

The success of the process of teaching and learning depends on teachers and learners using talk and other joint activity to build a shared contextual framework which will support future joint educational enterprises. Thus the sociolinguists Edwards and Furlong (1978, p. 57), in their influential study of classroom language in a secondary school, comment:

> It is not a matter of the context determining what is said, because the process is reciprocal. Teachers and pupils create through talk the very context on which they rely to support that talk. They use their knowledge of the context to generate appropriate behaviour, and the appropriateness of that behaviour then serves to define the context in which they interact.

This means that 'context' in this sense is a mental phenomenon, and so not directly available for scrutiny. But the discourse of teaching and learning, wherein context is created and invoked, can be observed and analysed (see for example Edwards and Mercer, 1986, 1987; Mercer, Edwards and Maybin, 1988; Mercer, 1991b and c). For participants in a conversation, useful contextual information may be drawn from shared past experience of doing similar or related tasks together; but it may also draw on a broader cultural base of knowledge, especially that associated with school as a social institution.

Any learning task faced by a child in school is never really decontextualized, because the child will necessarily invoke some prior experience in making sense of the task. And while children may be expected to think and act in school in ways which are not consonant with their out-of-school experience (in many educational tasks they are expected to 'leave their life situations at the door', as Neisser [1976] puts it), the point is that educational advancement depends on the successful accumulation and application of educational experience. This leads me to believe that those who describe the educationally assisted cognitive development of children as a process whereby thought becomes increasingly disembedded from situational contexts (e.g. Donaldson, 1984; Tizard and Hughes, 1984; Wells, 1987; Olson, 1988) seriously misrepresent the nature of that process. I know what they are trying to say, of course: academic problems are often more 'cerebral' than practical, everyday ones, and so seem more 'context free'. But the key to the development of academic competence is not learning to disregard contextual information or solve problems without it, it is learning how selectively to invoke and apply it. As Light (1986, p. 185) puts it, 'Intellectual development, viewed from this viewpoint, is more a matter of recontextualization than of a decontextualization'. Educational success requires the acquisition of a sophisticated contextual frame of reference which allows new problems to be understood in the abstract when they arise. As Street (1984) points out very clearly, Donaldson, Olson and others holding similar views on the development of abstract reasoning fail to see that children's success in tests of logical reasoning depends much more on their awareness of a set of cultural conventions for interpreting a task and communicating the answer than on any ability to handle abstraction. The extent to which children become able – are *enabled* – to bring to a task contextual information which is compatible with those cultural conventions is a measure of the effectiveness of the teaching-and-learning they have experienced.

Tasks and situations

Some psychologists may feel unhappy with a theoretical approach which depends on context being defined as a mental phenomenon. But, for better or worse, such a definition pinpoints the source of some important and enduring problems in psychological research. The experimental artefacts exposed by Donaldson (1978) are the products of problems of shared context, and contextual effects have been revealed which undermine the universality claimed for certain measures of people's general intelligence or educational potential (Labov, 1970; Cole and Scribner, 1974; Neisser, 1976).

Newman, Griffin and Cole (1989, p. 18) describe the emergence of such difficulties within their own research as follows:

> Crudely speaking, the source of the difficulty in making cross-situational cognitive comparisons is that different social constraints operate on people in different contexts, be they in school or out. The psychologist's task (classifying, paired associate learning, logical reasoning) is not a physical object in the world, although it often includes physical objects. A task is, rather, a set of actions, the goal of which is prespecified by the psychologist along with a set of constraints that must be honored in meeting that goal.

All learning is situated, because any task or activity does not exist independently of the ways in which participants (experimenters and subjects, teachers and learners) contextualize it.

This view of learning as situated activity does not necessarily drive us up some non-empirical blind alley. Rather, it suggests that the study of learning, especially in educational settings, must treat context and culture as part of what is being studied, not variables to be partialled out. As Crook (1991, p. 83) puts it: 'Our unit of analysis becomes activity in a *context* and the study of cognitive change, therefore, must dwell on the settings in which understandings are acquired and the circumstances that specify transfers of learning between these settings.' Within an experimental paradigm, it is difficult to get away from the idea that to determine what somebody 'knows' or what they 'can do' a psychologist must isolate them and given them an individualized test. But alternative empirical paradigms exist. For example,

Newman, Griffin and Cole (1989, p. 87) make the following suggestion, which they then put into practice: 'Instead of giving the children a task and measuring how well they do or how badly they fail it, one can give the children the task and observe how much and what kind of help they need in order to complete the task successfully.'

Within both experimental and observational research, an awareness of the significance of culture and context encourages us to study the *process*, not just the outcomes, of learning and to base our generalizations about what is learned in any particular situation on the best available information about how participants contextualize the activity. There is more than one way to go about this. In conversations, talk contextualizes the talk which follows, and so if we have access to the discourse of continuous – or at least consecutive – episodes of teaching-and-learning, we can examine how context is constituted in the talk itself. We can also draw on other sources of information about how people make sense of the activities they do – by talking to them about what they have experienced, or by observing the ways they participate in a range of related events or activities. Once we accept that contextual influences on the process of learning are unavoidable, the choice is whether to leave them there as an implicit 'bug' in the design and procedures of research (as is the case in most psychological research on learning) or to try to take them explicitly into account.

Other disciplines have, in their own way, tried to deal directly with such influences. Consider the following accounts of two learning situations provided by the anthropologist Bloch (in press). He is describing events recently observed in a remote village of the Zafimaniry people of Madagascar. The first event is a lesson in the village school for a group of about nine boys and four girls aged 12 to 14:

> All who are there can read and write to a certain degree. They read other sentences from the board first in unison and then individually. Then they copy them into their book.
>
> They learn a little pointless French vocabulary which was pronounced by both teachers and children in a non-recognizable way. Vocabulary such as the French word for the different fingers of the hand ... *anulaire, auriculaire*, etc. [...]
>
> Also lengthy sums are done such as writing every interval of 50 between 2,500 and 10,000 as well as simple problems. The answers are written in exercise books and corrected individually. On the whole these are much easier than mathematical sums which are being done daily by the same children in dealing with money. [...]
>
> There are also some bizarre grammatical exercises concerning stress in Malagasy. These seem taken from some program ultimately based on the outdated linguistic theories of a famous and delightful Malagasy academic. What was taught however made no sense to the teacher, the pupils or me. [...]
>
> The atmosphere was gloomy, unpleasant ... defeated. The explanation is all too simple ... teaching at this level is meant to be directed to passing the exam which replaces the old BEPC, but all pupils and teachers know that there is no possibility that anybody will get through. (pp. 15–16)

The next event Bloch describes takes place outside school:

> [A]s the result of a cyclone, an unknown bird was blown down near the village. It was brought triumphantly into the village by a group of children who began to examine it. They were particularly amused/interested by its beak which had two strange openings which they decided must be its nose. Then they discussed its peculiar hooded character which they felt meant that it must be a bird of prey, but they worried about what animals it could bite given its small size. Then they noted its wing span and they decided that it must 'fly high'. Finally they noted its webbed feet and decided that it must be a water bird and probably came from the sea and had been blown to the village by the high wind.
>
> It is difficult to imagine a better organized biology lesson but the manner of transmission of this knowledge and the language in which it was put was totally informal, hardly ever consisting of complete sentences. The children interrupted each other, pushed each other. It was clear from their attitude that for them as is true for everybody else, that the knowledge they were demonstrating was not really serious. This attitude is shared by everybody and is linked not simply to the fact that this is stereotypical children's knowledge, but also to the fact that it concerns wild things who are also seen as of no significance to the wise ... fluid and impermanent. (p. 20)

Bloch uses such observations to make the point that to understand the effects of schooling in Zafimaniry society one must first understand how knowledge is organized and evaluated in their culture. *What* is learned is not the only point at issue. In any learning situation, the ways in which knowledge is gained, shared and evaluated are massively influenced by cultural factors.

A neo-Vygotskian perspective

Bloch's examples might encourage us to study how processes of education function as ways of acquiring and sharing cultural knowledge, knowledge which itself serves to contextualize new activities and problems when they are encountered. If we are seriously interested in how children gain educationally relevant knowledge and understanding, the *meaning* of classroom tasks to them cannot be ignored. One of the aims of education is that children's contextual frames of reference should, in certain important ways, progressively approximate those of their teachers; to do science, for example, requires an understanding and acceptance of certain specific, culturally defined methods for pursuing enquiries and a set of conventions for presenting the results, as well as a knowledge of relevant facts. But psychology still offers few insights into how this culturally based, communicative process of cognitive development succeeds or fails. Such insights which have been gained have, I believe, mainly come from research which has its theoretical foundations in Vygotsky: research which has been called 'neo-Vygotskian' or 'cultural' psychology (Crook, 1991; Mercer, 1991c). Neo-Vygotskian theory still requires some considerable development if it is to provide a secure basis for psychological enquiry, but I believe that offers the kinds of concepts which psychology needs if it is to take account of culture and context. One such concept which is particularly relevant to the discussion here is 'appropriation'. (For more general discussions of neo-Vygotskian theory and its educational application, see Mercer, 1990, 1991 a and b.)

Appropriation

The culturally based quality of most learning is represented in the concept of 'appropriation', introduced by Vygotsky's colleague Leont'ev (1981) but recently taken up and developed by Newman, Griffin and Cole (1989). According to Newman *et al.*, it was proposed by Leont'ev as a socio-cultural alternative to Piaget's biological metaphor of 'assimilation'. In saying that children appropriate understanding through cultural contact, the point is being made that 'the objects in a child's world have a social history and functions that are not discovered through the child's unaided explorations' (Newman *et al.*, 1989, p. 62). This is more than a complicated way of saying that children do not need to reinvent the wheel. At the simplest level, it is arguing that because humans are essentially cultural beings, even children's initial encounters with objects may be cultural experiences, and so their initial understandings may be culturally defined. In this sense, appropriation is concerned with what children may take from encounters with objects in cultural context.

Leont'ev uses a child's understanding of what a hammer is to illustrate his point; but here is an example from my own experience. My daughter Anna, when about 9 months old, was offered a toy car to play with by her older brother. Although this was the first time she had seen one at home, she immediately began pushing it along the floor, going 'brrm, brrm' as she did so. The explanation for this surprising but conventional response lay in her regular attendance at a day nursery. Although not given the opportunity there to handle a car, she had been able to observe an older child playing with one. On being given the car to play with, Anna did not need to 'discover' its nature purely through sensori-motor contact to make use of it as a toy. She recognized it as a tool for 'brrm-brrming', because she had *appropriated* from the older child the culturally based conception and function of the toy. Right from the start, it was a culturally defined object, and not simply a bit of material reality which she had to act on to discover its properties and functions.

The concept of appropriation also incorporates the socio-dynamics of the development of understanding in another, more complex, way, because within the educational process appropriation may be *reciprocal*. Thus Newman *et al.* use appropriation to explain the pedagogic function of a particular kind of discourse event whereby one person takes up another person's remark and offers it back, modified, into the discourse. They show how teachers do this with children's utterances and actions, thereby offering children a recontextualized version of their own activities which implicitly carries with it new cultural meanings. Derek Edwards and I (Edwards and Mercer, 1987, Chapter 7) described similar phenomena, using different (but compatible) terminology. We observed that teachers often *paraphrase* what children say, and present it back to them in a form which is considered by the teacher to be more compatible with the current stream of educational discourse. Teachers also *reconstructively recap* what has been done by the children in class, so as to represent events in ways which fit their pedagogic framework. As a feature of classroom education, appropriation is there to be studied. By strategically appropriating children's words and actions, teachers may help children relate children's thoughts and actions in particular situations to the parameters of educational knowledge.

Classroom situations

I will continue by offering an analysis of three rather different sequences of classroom discourse. This analysis is intended to illustrate the relevance of the concepts discussed above, and in particular show how the psychology of teaching and learning might begin to come to terms with context and culture.

Sequence 1 *Key questions*

This sequence comes from the beginning of a lesson in a primary school in East Anglia which was video-recorded for use in an Open University course. The teacher was preparing his whole class of 10 and 11 year olds for a series of computer-based activities on hierarchical classification systems and the use of heuristic 'keys' for creating them and accessing information in them. At this early stage (this is the second lesson of a series), the children were not working at the computers but doing pencil-and-paper activities on 'keys'. (Note: in the transcript, T = the teacher. Punctuation has been added to help comprehension. Emphatic speech is in italics. As the lesson begins, the whole class is seated on the floor in front of the teacher.)

> T: Good morning folks. Now. We're going to um follow up the work we were doing last week on the keys. Can anyone just remind us what do we mean by '*key*'? Colin?
> COLIN: It's a way of finding out what different things are by using some questions.
> T: That's right. Yeh. There was something special about the sort of questions you had to ask, though, wasn't there? What was quite important about the way you asked the questions? Helen?
> HELEN: You had to separate the two . . . You had to separate the things into two groups.

T: Yeh. You had to get them into two groups. So *how* would you, how would you word the question? What type of question would you have to have? Helen?

HELEN: Yes or no.

T: Yes. We had to have a 'yes or no' answer. So you would say something . . . If it was the class, let's say, how might you divide this group into two? Philip?

PHILIP: Girls and boys.

T: Girls and boys. So what would be the question you'd ask?

PHILIP: Er, are you a boy?

T: Are you a boy. Then you'd say 'yes' in your case or 'no' in Heather's case. Right, good. Now that's the basic principle. And how can we go further, say, with the class? Let's say we've already divided into boys and girls. What's another question you can now ask to divide those two groups? [*pause*] Katie?

KATIE: Have they got dark hair?

T: Have they got dark hair? And is that a good question for both groups? Remember, we've got boys and girls. Remember, we've got boys and girls? [*Unintelligible mumble from pupils*]

T: It's a question that applies to both groups that, so it's a good question. That's right. What would be a *bad* question to ask there, which wouldn't fit in with the key? Graham?

GRAHAM: Have you got long hair.

T: Have you got long hair. Why wouldn't that be a good question?

GRAHAM: Because girls might have long hair but boys wouldn't.

T: Right. Certainly now. Nowadays. Might have been a good question 20 years ago.

(Fisher, 1991, pp. 18–19)

In this sequence we can see the teacher first of all attempting to establish some continuity between last week's work and the task in hand. He checks the children's understanding of the central concept of 'key' by eliciting from them what he sees as its crucial features and providing feedback on their answers. He takes up – appropriates – the examples they offer in their responses and uses them to pursue his pedagogic goals. At one level – that of discourse format – the episode is a routine which depends for its realization on a set of cultural conventions about how to do lessons, and so requires an implicit understanding of those conventions on the part of all involved. At another level – that of problem solving – it also is culturally defined as a particular kind of task. The children are asked how they might use questions to divide the class into girls and boys. This requires a 'willing suspension of disbelief', a temporary detachment from the real world on the part of all concerned, for it is obvious that no interrogative procedures would really be required to tell the boys and girls apart. This kind of problem solving is itself a culturally bound activity. Research on 'unschooled' adults in other cultural settings (notably work with the Kpelle of Liberia reported by Cole and Scribner, 1974) shows that such people are often unfamiliar with such procedures and resistant to such deliberate misrepresentations of real-world circumstances.

In one remark – 'that's the basic principle' – the teacher points to what the children are really meant to have learnt the previous week, and what they are concerned with now. They are learning how to construct a classification system through making binary decisions. The procedures they follow are meant to give them practice in doing this; the things they classify (sea-shells, blocks of certain shapes and sizes, etc.) and the particular keys they come up with are, in this situation, of no special educational significance. It is crucial for the learning and the educational progress of these children that they recognize that a principle is being taught and do not focus their attention on more obvious but relatively trivial features of the task. Whether they do so or not will very much depend on how the content and quality of the teacher's talk with them helps them to contextualize the tasks.

Sequence 2 *Maximum box*

In the next sequence we can observe learning taking place, in an event captured by a teacher in a south London school who left a tape recorder running while a group of girls (aged 11 and 12) worked alone together on a maths problem. The problem was this:

> You have a square sheet of card measuring 15 cm by 15 cm and you want to use it to make an open cuboid container by cutting out the corners. What is the maximum capacity the container can have?

For our purposes here, it is useful to focus on one of the four girls, called Emily in the transcript (the other girls are represented as A, B and C). Emily was considered to be quite good at, and confident in, maths by her teacher. At the point the transcript begins, the girls have made a box to the dimensions required, but Emily is unhappy that the box seems to have got 'bigger' despite having lost its corners. This is because she has a fundamental misunderstanding about what they are doing. As you read, try to work out what her difficulty is.

EMILY: This box is bigger than what it should be 'cos if you get 15 by 15 you get 225, but if you times 9 by 9 times 3 you still get 243 and I haven't got that much space in my box.

A: You have.

EMILY: But the 15 by ...

B: It can be, it can work, I ...

EMILY: But surely ...

B: You cut off corners.

EMILY: Yeh but that surely should make it *smaller*.

B: I think that is right.

EMILY [*counting squares marked on the paper*]: Hang on, 1,2,3,4,5 ...

C: You're not going to get 243.

EMILY: I shouldn't get 243 'cos if the piece of paper only had 225 then, um ...

C: Hang on, look ... 9 times 9 times – how many was it up?

A: But don't you remember Emily, it's got all this space in the middle.

EMILY: Yeh, but . . .

A: It's got all that space in the middle.

C: It is right, Emily, it is, it should be that number.

EMILY: But if I have a piece of paper with 225 squares, why should I get more?

A: Because you have all that space in the middle.

EMILY [*sounding exasperated*]: No, it hasn't got anything to do with it. If my piece of paper had only 225 squares on it, I can't get more out of the same piece of paper.

A: You can because you're forgetting, things go *up* as well, not just the flat piece of paper like that.

EMILY: Oh yeh.

A: It's going up.

C: It's going up.

C: It's because, look, down here you've got 3 and it's going up.

A: You're going 3 up, it's getting more on it. Do you see it will be 243?

EMILY: Yeh.

C: It is right, it should be.

> (From the Croydon Oracy Project, reproduced in Open University, 1991,
> pp. A117–18 and audiocassette)

The talk reveals that Emily does not seem to have grasped the distinction between *area* and *volume*. Or, to be more precise, she doesn't seem to understand how a mathematical measure of volume (which she is perfectly capable of calculating) relates to the actual capacity of a three-dimensional object. It is interesting to consider how this kind of misunderstanding could arise for a child who is good at the computational aspects of maths. One possible cause is that doing maths in class is so often a book-bound activity in which few strong connections are made with the world of concrete objects in all their shapes and sizes. It is possible to spend a lot of time calculating areas, volume, angles, gradients and so on, without ever having to consider how these concepts relate to the real world.

Sequence 2 is therefore useful for illustrating how the dynamics of context are an important part of the process of learning, and how educational progress is related to the construction of knowledge as a joint, situated activity. The task creates conditions under which Emily is required to relate her maths to material reality. But by being collaborative, it also offers her the opportunity to participate in discourse which is grounded in the practical task. The learning is in the talk, and the talk is heavily contextualized by the shared experience of Emily and her partners. The talk and the activity force her to revise and extend the contextual framework for her mathematical thinking, and in so doing she achieves a new level of understanding.

Sequence 3 *The Very Hungry Caterpillar*

The final sequence comes from an audio-recording made in a primary school in the West Midlands in 1989. Two children, one 11 and one 5, were working together, pursuing a structured activity but in the absence of their teacher. It is an example of a type of classroom activity common in that school (and increasingly so in other British primary schools) in which an older and younger child work together as 'talk partners' on some specific task (see Madeley and Lautman, 1991 and Meyer, 1991, for fuller accounts of such activities). On this occasion (at which I was present), an 11-year-old girl called Michelle and a 5-year-old boy called Ashley were involved in the retelling of his favourite picture book story, *The Very Hungry Caterpillar* (Carle, 1986). Both Ashley and Michelle have read the book in school, but they do not have it in front of them as they do the activity. (Note: pauses of more than three seconds are indicated by //.)

ASHLEY

MICHELLE

1. Right what's your favourite book Ashley?

2. *The Very Hungry Caterpillar.*

3. Is it a good book?

4. Yea.

5. Can you tell me the story please?

6. Yea//in the light of the moon a egg lay on a leaf//

7. What happened next?

8. Um//

9. Did he wake up?

10. No.

11. He didn't? What happened then? Was it on a Sunday morning?

12. Yea.

13. Right, can you carry on then? On a Sunday morning//did he pop out of the little egg?//

14. Yea.

15. And what happened after that, then?

16. He started to look for food// and on Monday, he ate through one apple, and on Tuesday he ate through two pears, and // on Wednesday he ate through three plums.

17. He was greedy, weren't he? What did he eat on Thursday?

18. Four strawberries.

19. Friday?

20. Four//five oranges.

21. What else did he eat?

22. //Don't know.

23. //On Saturday what did he eat?

24. On Saturday he ate a slice
    of cherry chocolate cake, one
    ice cream, one pickle, one
    Swiss cheese, one//one slice
    of salami.

25. Did he eat anything else?

26. One lollipop//

27. Any pie?

28. Some cherry pie//one cup
    cake//and a sausage.

29. And a sausage. He was greedy
    wasn't he? What else happened?

30. And the next and that night
    he had a belly ache and the
    next day was Monday again and
    he ate through one nice green
    leaf and after that he felt
    much better. Now he wasn't
    small any more he was a big fat
    caterpillar. He built a house
    round himself called a cocoon//
    and he stayed in there for more
    than two weeks and he nibbled
    an 'ole and he pushed his way
    out and he was a beautiful
    butterfly.

31. Lovely.

What happens in this episode can be described as some 'joint remembering'
(Edwards and Middleton, 1986). That is, Michelle and Ashley collaboratively
reconstruct a cultural artefact – the text of a book – from their own partial
contributions to the conversation. We cannot tell from this evidence whether
or not either one of them would have been able to achieve this on their own,
given enough time. The fact is that they do it collaboratively in this situation.
We can draw some obvious conclusions about the learning outcomes of prior
school activities from this episode. One is that, through reading the book,
Ashley has learned not only the plot of the story, but also much of the actual
written language of the book. He has learned the story as a piece of
literature. He also appears to have learned that, in school at least, you retell a
story by keeping as close as possible to the written original. Although he is
not working here with a teacher, he recognizes the key contextual features of
the situation, and so is able to act accordingly. This prior learning on
Ashley's part is not an unproblematic feature of schooling, as Heath (1983),
among others, has shown. Indeed, Heath argues that the disjunction between
the kinds of literacy events, and the modes of storytelling, which

children encounter in school and in their home community is an important and enduring source of educational problems for children of some cultural backgrounds. Ashley has not simply read (or been read) the book and learnt the story, he has *appropriated* the picture book as a cultural artefact, and one which is defined in part by certain social practices in school.

Both children have also clearly learned the discourse requirements for doing this kind of educational activity: there seem to be no problems for them in making the activity happen as a joint enterprise. But in addition, it seems clear that through her school experience Michelle has acquired some pedagogic strategies: she has learned how (in this particular situation) to be a teacher. She sets up the activity through her initial remarks. She asks questions in order to stimulate Ashley's recall (e.g. lines 7, 15, 21) rather than to elicit information of which she is truly ignorant. She gives him a series of 'prompts', switching from general questions to providing more specific clues from the story when she feels he is struggling (lines 7–13, 21–7). She reiterates what he has said (line 29) and provides supportive, evaluative feedback (lines 17, 29, 31). One way in which she perhaps behaves differently from most teachers is that she tolerates very long pauses before offering him further prompts.

In the best Socratic manner, Michelle draws out the whole story from Ashley: she demonstrates that he really knew it all himself. But his realization of his knowledge for the purpose of this activity is achieved by her careful management and support of what could have been for Ashley too difficult and too daunting a task. As Bruner (1985) might put it, she effectively 'scaffolds' Ashley's retelling, helping him achieve something which, although almost entirely dependent on his own prior knowledge, he might not otherwise have done.

Michelle and Ashley's activity can thus be seen to be dependent on a great deal of prior shared knowledge and experience, which serves to contextualize the task in hand (their knowledge of the book, their understanding of the particular task in hand) and which can be easily related to broader areas of cultural knowledge (the language of literature, the format of picture books, the ways teachers talk). Although no teacher is directly involved, Sequence 3 illustrates well how activity, and hence learning, in the classroom is: (a) culturally saturated in both its content and structure; and (b) accomplished through dialogue which is heavily dependent on an implicit context constructed by participants from current and past shared experience. To return to a point made earlier, it surely cannot be appropriate to describe the talk or thinking which goes on here as 'decontextualized' or 'disembedded' (cf. Donaldson, 1984; Tizard and Hughes, 1984; Wells, 1987).

It is interesting to speculate on what might be the educational benefits, for Ashley, of doing this activity. The manner in which Michelle highlights aspects of the structure and content of the story for Ashley may help him learn more about storytelling and books, and so guide his future literary, and literate, experience (Maybin and Mercer, 1990). He will almost certainly come away with his assumptions about educationally appropriate modes of storytelling confirmed. An activity of this kind, successfully completed, could also be expected to increase Ashley's confidence and fluency in demonstrating his knowledge and understanding through talk (a field of competence now formally included in the English National Curriculum). The extent and manner in which he is able to generalize what he has learnt from this particular experience to other related tasks will depend on the symbolic meaning he attaches to particular features of the situation. For better or worse, it is the experience of particular situations like this that shapes children's ability to understand and contribute to that part of our collective understanding that we define as 'educational knowledge'.

Conclusion

I have tried to show some ways in which the concepts of 'culture' and 'context' are vital for the study of learning. I believe that they are required if we are to attend to important aspects of both the *process* and *content* of learning, as it is normally pursued in school and other settings. The acquisition of knowledge should not be theoretically isolated from the processes by which knowledge is offered, shared, reconstructed and evaluated. As Vygotsky suggested, the concept of culture helps us understand learning as a sociohistorical and interpersonal process, not just as a matter of individual change or development. This has particular significance for the study of learning in school, where what counts as knowledge is often quite culturally specific. Culture represents the historical source of important influences on what is learnt, how it is learnt, and the significance that is attached to any learning that takes place. We likewise need a satisfactory definition of context to deal with learning as a communicative, cumulative, constructive process, one which takes place in situations where past learning is embodied in present learning activity, and in which participants draw selectively on any information which is available to make sense of what they are doing. Only by taking account of these situated qualities of learning can we properly begin to describe how people learn.

Note

1. Thanks to Janet Maybin, Brian Street and Barry Stierer for helpful discussion and comments in the preparation of this chapter.

References

Bernstein, B. (1971), *Class, Codes and Control*, Vol. 1 (London: Routledge & Kegan Paul).

Bloch, M. (in press), 'The uses of schooling and literacy in a Zafimaniry village', in B. Street (ed.), *Cross-cultural Approaches to Literacy* (Cambridge: Cambridge University Press).

Bruner, J.S. (1971), *The Relevance of Education* (Harmondsworth: Penguin).

Bruner, J.S. (1984), 'Interaction, communication and self', *Journal of the American Academy of Child Psychiatry*, **23**, 1, pp. 1–7.

Bruner, J. (1985), 'Vygotsky: a historical and conceptual perspective', in J.V. Wertsch (ed.), *Culture, Communication and Cognition: Vygotskian perspectives* (Cambridge: Cambridge University Press).

Carle, E. (1986), *The Very Hungry Caterpillar* (London: Hamish Hamilton).

Cole, M. and Scribner, S. (1974), *Culture and Thought* (New York: Wiley).

Crook, C. (1991), 'Computers in the zone of proximal development: implications for evaluation', *Computers in Education*, **17** (1), pp. 81–91.

Crystal, D. (1985), *A Dictionary of Linguistics and Phonetics*, second edition (Oxford: Basil Blackwell).

Donaldson, M. (1978), *Children's Minds* (London: Fontana).

Donaldson, M. (1984), 'Speech and writing and modes of learning', in H. Goelman, A. Oberg and F. Smith (eds), *Awakening to Literacy* (London: Heinemann).

Edwards, A.D. and Furlong, V. (1978), *The Language of Teaching and Learning* (London: Heinemann).

Edwards, A.D. and Westgate, D.P. (1987), *Investigating Classroom Talk* (Brighton: Falmer Press).

Edwards, D. and Mercer, N. (1986), 'Context and continuity: classroom discourse and the development of shared knowledge', in K. Durkin (ed.), *Language Development in the School Years* (London: Croom Helm).

Edwards, D. and Mercer, N. (1987), *Common Knowledge: The development of understanding in the classroom* (London: Methuen).

Edwards, D. and Middleton, D. (1986), 'Joint remembering: constructing an account of shared experience', *Discourse Processes*, **9**, 423–59.

Fisher, E. (1991), *Project and Video Workbook. EH232 Computers and Learning* (Milton Keynes: Open University).

Geertz, C. (1968), 'Religion as cultural system', in D. Cutler (ed.), *The Religious Situation* (Boston, MA: Beacon Press).

Heath, S.B. (1983), *Ways with Words* (Cambridge: Cambridge University Press).

Jensen, A. (1967), 'The culturally disadvantaged; psychological and educational aspects', *Educational Research*, **10**, pp. 4–20.

Leont'ev, A.N. (1981), *Problems of the Development of Mind* (Moscow: Progress Publishers).

Light, P. (1986), 'Context, conservation and conversation', in M. Richards and P. Light (eds), *Children of Social Worlds* (Cambridge: Polity Press).

McGarrigle, J. and Donaldson, M. (1974), 'Conservation accidents', *Cognition*, **3**, pp. 341–50.

Madeley, B. with Lautman, A. (1991), 'I like the way we learn', in *Talk and Learning 5–16: An in-service pack on oracy for teachers* (Milton Keynes: Open University).

Maybin, J. (1991), 'Children's informal talk and the construction of meaning', *English in Education*, **25** (2), pp. 34–49.

Maybin, J. and Mercer, N. (1990), ' "Scaffolding" literacies: supporting readers in YTS and primary school', in the *Proceedings of the Conference 'Literacy for the 21st Century'*, Brighton Polytechnic, July.

Mercer, N. (1990), 'Context, continuity and communication in learning', in F. Potter (ed.), *Reading, Learning and Media Education* (Oxford: Basil Blackwell).

Mercer, N. (1991a), 'Learning through talk', in *Talk and Learning 5–16: An in-service pack on oracy for teachers* (Milton Keynes: Open University).

Mercer, N. (1991b), 'Computers and communication in the classroom', Unit 7 of *EH232 Computers and Learning* (Milton Keynes: Open University).

Mercer, N. (1991c), 'Accounting for what goes on in classrooms: what have neo-Vygotskians got to offer?', *BPS Education Section Review*, **15**, pp. 61–7.

Mercer, N., Edwards, D. and Maybin, J. (1988), 'Putting context into oracy: the development of shared knowledge through classroom discourse', in M. MacLure, T. Phillips and A. Wilkinson (eds), *Oracy Matters* (Milton Keynes: Open University Press).

Meyer, B. (1991), 'Talk-partners in the infant classroom', in *Talk and Learning 5–16: An in-service pack on oracy for teachers* (Milton Keynes: Open University).

Neisser, U. (1976), 'General, academic and artificial intelligence', in L. B. Resnick (ed.), *The Nature of Intelligence* (London: Chambers/Murray).

Newman, D., Griffin, P. and Cole, M. (1989), *The Construction Zone* (Cambridge: Cambridge University Press).

Olson, D.R. (1988), ' "See! Jumping!" Some oral language antecedents of literacy', in N. Mercer (ed.), *Language and Literacy from an Educational Perspective. Vol. 1: Language Studies* (Milton Keynes: Open University).

Open University (1991), *Talk and Learning 5–16: An in-service pack on oracy for teachers* (Milton Keynes: Open University).

Scribner, S. (1985), 'Vygotsky's uses of history', in J.V. Wertsch (ed.), *Culture, Communication and Cognition: Vygotskian perspectives* (Cambridge: Cambridge University Press).

Smith, L. (1989), 'Changing perspectives in developmental psychology', in C. Desforges (ed.), *Early Childhood Education*, British Journal of Educational Psychology Monograph Series: no. 4 (Edinburgh: Scottish Academic Press).

Street, B. (1984), *Literacy in Theory and Practice* (Cambridge: Cambridge University Press).

Thompson, J. (1984), *Studies in the Theory of Ideology* (Cambridge: Polity Press).

Tizard, B. and Hughes, M. (1984), *Young Children Learning* (London: Fontana).

Vygotsky, L.S. (1978), *Mind in Society* (London: Harvard University Press).

Vygotsky, L.S. (1981), 'The development of higher mental functions', in J. V. Wertsch (ed.), *The Concept of Activity in Soviet Psychology* (Amonk, NY: Sharpe).

Walkerdine, V. (1984), 'Developmental psychology and the child-centred pedagogy: the insertion of Piaget into early education', in J. Henriques, W. Hollway, C. Urwin, C. Venn and V. Walkerdine, *Changing the Subject* (London: Methuen).

Wells, G. (1985), *Language at Home and in School* (Cambridge: Cambridge University Press).

Wells, G. (1987), *The Meaning Makers* (London, Hodder & Stoughton).

Chapter 4

Proportional reasoning in and out of school

Analúcia Dias Schliemann and David William Carraher, *Universidade Federal de Pernambuco*

Schooling and the development of logico-mathematical concepts

For decades studies of the effects of schooling upon the development of logico-mathematical concepts focused on schooled versus non-schooled subjects' performance on logical tasks designed to evaluate cognitive competencies as general and decontextualized abilities. The studies (see, for instance, Greenfield, 1966; Luria, 1976; Stevenson, Parker, Wilkinson, Bonnevaux and Gonzalez, 1978; Sharp, Cole, and Lave, 1979) generally show earlier and greater development in schooled children and adults than in their unschooled counterparts.

A different pattern emerges from studies assessing cognitive competence in familiar contexts. For instance, Gay and Cole (1967) found that unschooled African children performed better than schooled Americans in rice estimation tasks but performed at lower levels on unfamiliar tasks easily solved by schooled Americans. Lave (1977; see also Greenfield and Lave, 1982) found that school experience appeared to contribute favourably to Liberian tailors' performance on school-oriented tasks; however, in work-related tasks, tailoring experience but not schooling was related to performance. Despite their poor performance on school arithmetic tasks, children from low socio-economical levels who work as street vendors in Brazil have been found to solve similar tasks successfully if they are presented in the context of transactions in their workplace (Carraher, Carraher and Schliemann, 1982, 1985). Studies on how workers and students solve experimental problems related to everyday settings (Carraher,

1986, 1988; Schliemann, 1985) show that, unlike students, workers approach these problems as real-life tasks and usually obtain correct or approximate results. As discussed by Carraher, Schliemann and Carraher (1988) and by D. Carraher (1991) the strategies used by subjects with little schooling to solve arithmetical problems are different from those taught in schools but reveal understanding of the same logical principles underlying school algorithms. By contrast, middle-school students have been found to treat the tasks as school assignments and, after a series of written computations, frequently present absurd answers without an awareness of their inadequacy.

Schooling may none the less play an important role. For instance, Schliemann and Acioly (1989), in their analysis of the mathematical abilities developed by lottery bookies in Brazil, found that performance on everyday mathematical tasks was nearly always correct and therefore was not correlated with school experience. However, performance in transfer tasks improved with schooling. Further, response justifications were related to schooling: non-schooled subjects tended to choose empirical or matter-of-fact justifications, while schooled subjects more often verbalized the logico-mathematical relations involved in the procedures they used.

Saxe's (1990) study of Brazilian street vendor youths sheds further light on the issue. He found that the vendors' identification of written numerals and use of written school algorithms to perform computations were strongly related to amount of schooling. Vendors' descriptions of profit, in particular profit per item, appeared to be related to schooling. On the other hand, performance on arithmetic tasks about purchases and change, and ratio comparison tasks, were not related to school experience. Saxe argues that schools not only affect computation routines, but also encourage different ways of thinking about mathematical relations.

Mathematics is an object of study (Douady, 1985) in schools, and mathematical concepts, procedures and representations are formally discussed and studied therein. A great deal of practice occurs in schools through which students are asked to apply what has been taught in order to solve, usually with the aid of written mathematical symbols, problems designed to apply the kind of knowledge supposedly being transmitted. The results of school computations are not actually used, although simulated 'as if' contexts may be provided. Generally, practice tends to be viewed as an end both in and of itself, or as a means of promoting curriculum-related skills and knowledge. By contrast, in 'semi-skilled' activities encountered out of school, mathematics tends to be used as a tool to achieve other aims such as enacting a sale or purchase, or measuring (e.g. determining how much wood to buy for making furniture, or how to build a wall according to a certain scale). Systematic and explicit teaching of mathematical concepts, symbols or procedures appears to be rare in most out-of-school contexts. In schools, numbers devoid of reference to the empirical world (and, later, variables) commonly serve as objects of reflection. By contrast, in work settings, values typically correspond to physical quantities. How knowledge developed in such varied school and out-of-school contexts differs has not been sufficiently explored. We still need further studies that approach schooled and unschooled subjects with tasks that are part of the everyday experience of both groups, allowing evaluation of their real capacities and of the contribution of the different characteristics of their experiences to the construction and consolidation of children's and adults' expertise.

Several issues underlay our decision to focus upon proportional reasoning in order to analyse differences and similarities in knowledge developed in different contexts. First, proportional reasoning has played a prominent role in developmental psychology. In Piagetian theory it is taken as a major landmark in the passage from concrete operational to formal operational thinking (Inhelder and Piaget, 1958). Second, proportional reasoning is a well-studied and particularly thorny area of mathematics education. Not only are proportions explicitly taught in middle-school mathematics, they crop up in a wide range of scientific contexts, including, for example, trajectories, fuel consumption and the expansion of gases. Yet proportional reasoning is notoriously difficult to achieve. Any light that studies of informal mathematics can shed on the issue may be helpful. Third, proportional relations are inherent in some everyday non-academic and non-scientific contexts, particularly in commercial and manufacturing activities. How (and indeed, whether) people tend to develop proportional reasoning in such contexts is an important question in itself. If people with little or no schooling really understand proportional relations in these contexts, or if highly schooled individuals who have difficulty understanding proportionality in school-type settings fail to exhibit such difficulty in informal learning contexts, then there is something important to be understood.

In order to address these issues let us first consider what proportionality is from the point of view of mathematics, then bring the discussion into the field of psychology.

Proportionality

In mathematics, a proportion is an equivalence of ratios expressed as:

$$2:3::4:6 \tag{4.1}$$

or

$$2/3 = 4/6 \tag{4.2}$$

The links between proportions and proportional reasoning can be appreciated when proportions are studied not as isolated objects but rather in the context of reasoning about functions. A variable y is directly proportional to x, or varies directly as x if it can be expressed as:

$$y = f(x) = ax \qquad (4.3)$$

where the real number a is known as the constant of proportionality. The variables are inversely proportional if they can be described according to:

$$y = g(x) = c/x \qquad (4.4)$$

where c is a real number. As (4.3) makes clear, all functions that can be graphed as straight lines passing through the origin of a Cartesian coordinate system reflect direct proportionality,[1] but inverse proportionality will correspond to a parabola.

These statements and observations are applied to the real world by replacing ratios of *numbers* with ratios of *quantities* (Whitney, 1968; Freudenthal, 1983; Vergnaud, 1983; Schwartz, 1988) and mathematical variables with physical variables of magnitudes. Quantities may be expressed through measures of natural units (14 oranges, 7 boys), conventional units of measure ($32.50, 3½ inches) or improvised units of measure (7 giant steps). Our functions will now map (i.e. match) not a set of numbers on to another set of numbers, but rather a set of quantities on to another set of quantities.[2] Our attention in this paper will focus upon simple, direct proportionality (Vergnaud, 1983, 1988); we will thereby leave aside the cases of multiple and inverse proportionality and proportionality associated with Cartesian products.

Simple proportionality corresponds to the case of 'isomorphism of measures', more specifically to cases in which the measures are isomorphic for addition, which means that, given $y = f(x)$, then for all x:

$$f(x' + x'') = f(x') + f(x'') \qquad (4.5)$$

from which it follows that:

$$f(n \times x) = n \times f(x) \qquad (4.6)$$

Diverse situations encountered in daily life can be described according to an isomorphism of measures, perhaps the most ubiquitous being a purchase of goods. If we imagine that y refers to the price (in dollars) and x to the number weight of potatoes (in kg) purchased, then (4.5) corresponds to a statement such as 'The price of 7 kg of potatoes is equal to the price of 3 kg + the price of 4 kg'. To make the relation clearer, we can state:

$$\text{price (7kg)} = \text{price (3kg)} + \text{price (4 kg)} \tag{4.7}$$

Statement (4.6) corresponds to expressions such as 'The price of 30 kg will be 3 times the price of 10 kg of potatoes'. A rational multiplier could also be used but this leaves us with an unwieldy expression in English.[3]

There are many more specific ways of expressing the relationships between the variables price and weight. Here are three examples that refer to the same situation: 'For every additional quarter kg that you buy, you have to pay $.30 more'; 'Each kg will cost $1.20'; 'Each dollar will get you 0.8 kg of potatoes'.

Two fundamental types of problems involving simple proportionality can be discerned and have been studied. *Missing value problems* require one to determine the value of a particular variable given three values: the corresponding value on the other variable as well as an additional pair of values relating the two variables. A typical example is: 'Find the cost of 6 kg of potatoes if 2 kg cost $1.28'. *Ratio comparison problems* provide information from *two* situations and require determining which situation is relatively costlier, heavier, denser, etc. For example, 'One automobile went 75 kilometres in 4 hours whereas a second one went 100 km in 5 hours. Which car went faster (i.e. maintained a greater average speed)?'

When people solve proportionality problems of either type, it is essential to make sense out of their procedures in terms of the mathematical knowledge or understanding their solutions entail. Here is where a function table for simple proportions (Vergnaud, 1983) is useful. We can represent simple proportionality through a two-column table, each of which corresponds to a variable. Each has a pair of values, one from each variable. The first variable refers to the number of candies (*M1*) and the second (*M2*) to price. The problem to be solved is: 'If one candy costs 5, how much do 15 candies cost?'

M1 (number of items)	*M2* (price)	(4.8)
1	5	
15	*x*	

Note that the diagram allows inclusion of the pair or measures where the value of one of the variables is 1. This type of problem is commonly seen as a multiplication problem (5 times 15), not entailing proportions. But, as Vergnaud (1984) pointed out, it is only through understanding of proportionality that multiplication problems of this type can be understood. The value 1 item plays a role in the meaning of the problem even though it is typically ignored in school.

The diagram could also include measures that are all different from 1 as in the following example: 'If 3 candies cost 15, how much do 18 candies cost?':

M1	M2	(4.9)
(number of items)	(price)	
3	15	
18	x	

Vergnaud (1983) showed that missing values problems may be solved through at least three different approaches: the *scalar approach*, the *functional approach*, and the *rule of three* school algorithm.

The *scalar approach* or, as Noelting (1980a, b) prefers, the *within-ratio approach*, focuses upon changes along the same variable or measure space. In such approaches a person compares, for example, how many items were bought in case one (for a given price) with the number of items to be bought in case two. The essential idea is that the relative increase (or decrease) in cost should be directly related to the increase (or decrease) in goods purchased. In this approach each variable remains independent of the other and parallel transformations are carried out on both of them, under the constraint that their proportional relationship is maintained. In the problem depicted in (4.9), the scaler approach would lead to a solution stating that '18 items is 6 times more than 3 items and, therefore, one would need 6 times the money, that is, 6 times 15'.

The *functional* or *between-ratio approach* relies upon relationships between variables or measure spaces. The term 'functional' here is in keeping with our use above, for the emphasis is upon how one variable varies as a *function* of the other variables.[4] This may or may not lead to the explicit use of intensive quantities, that is, measures expressed in 'per' units, such as '0.8 kg per $', but intensive quantities are at least implicit in the approach from the point of view of mathematics. The functional solution consists in computation or the ratio linking the two variables. For the example in (4.9) the functional solution would be: 'Multiplying the number of items by 5: therefore, if one needs 18 items, the amount of money needed is 18 times 5'.

The third approach, the *rule of three* school algorithm, is based in the properties of equivalent ratios and is exclusively applied to missing value problems. Given two equivalent ratios, a/b and c/x, the equalities $a/b = c/d$, $a \times d = c \times x$ must hold and, therefore, $x = (a \times d)/c$.

In Brazilian schools, proportionality problems are introduced to students when they are about 12 years old and the approach relies heavily on the rule of three. Acceptable solutions are only those where the rule of three is correctly applied. Despite intensive training in the rule of three algorithm, school children and adolescents only rarely adopt this kind of solution (see Hart, 1981; Carraher, Carraher and Schliemann, 1984; T. Carraher, 1986; Schliemann and Nunes, 1990).

Let us now redirect discussion toward the psychological concerns motivating our analysis. First, we shall take a selective look at psychological studies of proportional reasoning. Second, we shall focus on the studies of proportional reasoning among subjects with little or no school experience across different contexts. Finally, we shall compare schooled and unschooled youths' solutions to proportionality problems, looking more closely at the similarities and differences in proportional reasoning developed in the context of school and in the context of selling activities.

Proportional reasoning in developmental psychology and mathematics education

Whereas proportions tend to be viewed in schools as a content or subject matter to be covered in mathematics and science curricula, the understanding of proportions assumes an important significance in developmental psychology as a reflection of the general cognitive development and reasoning abilities of children and adolescents. The most influential and theoretically complex position comes from the Piagetian line of research (Inhelder and Piaget, 1958). We will briefly characterize the Piagetian arguments and findings in that area and contrast them with general findings from the area of mathematics education, particularly those of Karplus (1981).

Inhelder and Piaget (1958) undertook an important series of investigations regarding diverse scientific concepts in the hopes of characterizing the changes in thinking associated with the transition from concrete to formal operational thinking. In the course of their collaboration they produced analyses of children's and adolescents' reasoning about density, experimental control, chemical reactions, oscillations of pendula, falling bodies on inclined planes, balance scales, projection of shadows, and several others. Most of these studies, as well as others on probability (Piaget and Inhelder, 1975, first published in 1951), speed (Piaget and Inhelder, 1970, first published in 1946), and enlargement of geometrical figures (Piaget and Inhelder, 1967, first published in 1948) entail proportions and proportional reasoning.

In all these studies, the Piagetian position is singularly clear in rejecting the possibility of children's understanding of proportions before formal operations, and a clear finding from Piagetian studies during the 1940s and 1950s is that before the age associated with formal operations children do not treat equivalent ratios as equal, nor do they compare ratios in a way that reflects an understanding of the property of order. Rather they characteristically display additive reasoning which relies upon additive rather than multiplicative differences between terms of ratios (or they only compare two of the four terms). For example, when a child is asked to enlarge a rectangle while maintaining its form (and hence the ratio of the width to the height), he 'measures the difference [of the length and height] and transfers it to the sides of the rectangle he is constructing; for instance, Mar, who adds 2 cm to a rectangle 4×6 cm because 6−4 = 2, and Ger who ends up with 7×5 cm, starting from 5×3 and transferring 5−3 = 2 cm' (Piaget and Inhelder, 1967, p. 367).

A correct answer in the case of Ger would, of course, maintain the ratio of 5:3 in the second rectangle. One way to do so would be to double each side − a multiplicative comparison rather than an additive one. It is also possible to conceive of the transformation as a matter of preserving the ratio of sides in the ratio of increments to the sides: 'For every 5 units increase in length, there must be a corresponding increase of 3 units in the width.'

Piaget's view was not that the concrete operational children do not happen to get the right answer. Rather, it is *inconceivable* that they could get the right answer through their own reasoning, which is not equipped with the logical structures required for handling proportions.

Piaget's argument is based upon the idea of 'logical proportion' − the equivalence of the relations connecting two terms A and B to the relations connecting two other terms C and D (Inhelder and Piaget, 1958, pp. 314−15). Strange as it may seem, Piaget and Inhelder argued that children must be able to use propositions as the terms of a ratio before understanding ratios of numbers. For instance, they assert (p. 315, adapted symbols) that given statements p and q the following logical proportion holds true:

'p implies q'/'q implies p' = ([not p] and q)/(p and [not q])

It is one thing to assert that proportions, in the normal mathematical sense (as an equivalence of ratios of numbers or quantities), bear a resemblance to logical proportions. However, the assertion that an understanding of numerical proportions *derives* from an understanding of logical proportions is one that demands evidence.

Later, rather less well-known, evidence (Piaget, Grize, Szeminska and Bang, 1977, first published in 1968) was not consistent with the earlier view. Children at the age that should correspond to the concrete operations stage were found to be able to solve correctly proportional problems about the amount of food to be given to eels of different lengths. Piaget's reaction was to alter the analysis of proportional reasoning while maintaining the general position regarding stages of intellectual development. In short, he argued that true proportional reasoning concerns *inverse* proportions. Children at the level of concrete operations could perhaps understand simpler, direct proportions, but this was no longer regarded as authentic proportional reasoning.

Researchers of reasoning regarding *simple or direct* proportionality none the less acquired lots of evidence for the late acquisition of proportional reasoning (see Lovell and Butterworth, 1966, and Lunzer and Pumphrey, 1966, for British subjects and Carraher, Schliemann and Carraher, 1986, for Brazilian subjects). Some researchers (Noelting, 1980a, b; Karplus and associates, see Karplus and Peterson, 1970) were sceptical of early Piagetian findings and argued that simpler tasks, designed to focus explicitly on proportional relations, should be used. The orange juice mixture tasks ('Which mixture will taste more "orangy", 1 cup concentrate in 3 cups water, or 2 cups concentrate in 7 cups water?') and the paper clips task ('How many big clips will Mr Tall's height measure if Mr Short's height measures 3, and if their respective heights are 8 and 6 when measured with smaller clips?') were thought to get around these problems. But even so, diverse studies using these measures (Karplus and Peterson 1970; Karplus, Karplus, Formisano and Paulsen, 1979) conducted in the United States and Europe concluded that proportional reasoning only becomes predominant by the 11th and 12th grades. The overall conclusion from developmental studies of proportional reasoning is that it is only at the beginning of adolescence that simple proportional relations are understood and that many adolescents still have problems in solving the tasks when complicated ratios or inverse proportions are used.

Karplus's tasks were probably easier than Piaget's tasks. They seem however to be quite unusual types of tasks even for school children. It is possible that low performance levels only reflect the novelty of the task and that the same children could solve other proportionality problems if the contents of the problems and the kind of questions asked were somehow related to their previous experience. The fact that children can solve one type of proportionality problem without being able to solve other types is stressed by Karplus (1981) who had found in his previous studies different results for the same children for two different versions of the Paper Clips Task. It is therefore possible that children who fail the easier version of the Paper Clips Task would display understanding of proportionality for problems that are part of their everyday experience.

A study that focused on proportional relations from a point of view that is closer to both e veryday and school approaches to proportions was done by Ricco (1982), who documented children's difficulties and strategies in solving isomorphism of measures problems. Her subjects, although chosen from among those who had not yet received school instruction on proportionality, were regularly schooled children who had intensive school training in the solution of multiplication and division problems. Subjects were told a story about a group of children who went to buy pencils in a shop. Information about the price of a certain number of pencils bought by one child and another number bought by another child was given and, from that, the subject's task was to find out the prices paid by each of the other children, knowing how many pencils each had bought. She found that most eight-year-old subjects use procedures taking into account the proportional relations between the two variables.

It is possible that the tasks traditionally used to assess proportional reasoning in children and adolescents underestimate children's reasoning abilities, since they adopt an approach that markedly differs from proportions as they appear in everyday life. Also, since studies on proportional reasoning involved only schooled subjects, the developmental trends that were found could in fact, at least partially, be explained by the contribution of school attendance. What would happen, however, with subjects who did not attend school regularly, but who deal with proportionality problems in their jobs? What procedures do they use to solve proportional problems and what kind of understanding about proportions do they develop in this context? Are their procedures specific to the kind of problems they usually solve, or are they general procedures that could be applied to any context?

Studies of proportional reasoning out of school

In a series of studies developed among schooled and unschooled children, adolescents and adults in Brazil, we tried to address these questions. We chose to concentrate on simple direct proportionality problems of the missing value type for one main reason: this is the kind of problem that belongs to the experience of both schooled and unschooled children. For the same reason, we chose the relationship between the number of items to be sold and the price as the main context to which the proportional relations properties are to be applied. This particular context is known by both schooled and unschooled children and differences that may be found between them should not be attributed to lack of knowledge about the variables in the problem.

Carraher, Carraher and Schliemann (1982, 1985) found solution of proportional problems among children who work as street vendors and had very low levels of school attendance. The problems these children solve generally consist in knowing the price of one item and computing the price of many. The following transcription of the mental computations performed by a coconut vendor to find the price of 10 coconuts at the unit price of 35 cruzeiros (the Brazilian currency) provides an example of such solution: 'Three are one hundred and five, with three more, two hundred and ten (pause). There are still four. It is (pause) three hundred and fifteen (pause), it seems it is three hundred and fifty' (Carraher, Carraher and Schliemann, 1985, p. 23). Underlying the child's successive steps lies an understanding of the relationship between the two variables, number of coconuts and price to be paid, as proportionally related.

This understanding, however, may be specific to the natural situation it is applied to, as well as to the quantities the subject is dealing with. Despite its limits the scalar approach has the advantage of preserving the meaning of the relations involved in the problem. This led Kaput, West, Luke and Pattison-Gordon (1988) to design instructional materials to improve children's understanding of functions through use of the scalar approach. They found significant progress on proportional problem solving once the children understand the relationship between the two variables in the problems in terms of an isomorphism of measures table.

T. Carraher (1986) documented the understanding of proportional relations among construction foremen. In their work they have to deal with scales of measure indicating what should be the relation between the measures in centimetres shown in the blueprints and the real size of walls to be built. Blueprints usually indicate what scale was used and the real size of each wall. If information about the sizes of some walls is missing, it can be exactly computed from the other information. Carraher showed her subjects blueprints (with no information about the scale used) where real size was shown for some walls but not for others. The preferred strategy among foremen consisted in first finding a relation between the first pair of numbers and then transferring their relation to the second pair. In the following transcript, a foreman was given a blueprint where one of the walls, measuring 9 centimetres in the drawing, was identified as corresponding to a real wall 3 metres in width. The task was to find the real size of another wall measuring 15 centimetres on the blueprint:

> Nine centimetres, 3 metres. Right. This is easy. (E.: Why?) Because it just is. You just take 3 centimetres for each metre. (E.: How did you come up with this so quickly?) Isn't 9 equal to 3 times 3? Then, if [the wall] is 3 metres, 3 times 3, 9. The other one here [on paper] is 15, the wall will be 5 metres. Because 3 times 5, 15. This is an easy one. (Carraher, 1986, p. 535)

Schliemann and Nunes (1990) found that fishermen with little or no schooling gave 95 per cent of correct answers when asked to solve proportional problems where, given the price of one item to be sold, they had to compute the price to be paid for more than one of those items. These problems replicate the problems they found and solved in their everyday activities selling dried fish. Despite everyday experience, where computations always go from the price of one to the price of more than one item, the authors found that most fishermen could also solve verbal proportionality problems designed to test the flexibility and generality of their procedures. Instead of starting with the price of one item, they were given the price of more than one item and asked to compute the price of one. On such items 74 per cent of the responses were correct. They also achieved 79 per cent of correct answers when this type of inverted problem was formulated relating quantity of processed to unprocessed seafood, a relationship they used to refer to in their activities but where no computing problems ever occurred. When the problems asked for the relation between a pair of variables where none of the values had value one, from another pair where values were also different from one, performance was only slightly lower with 60 per cent of correct answers.

The difficulties shown by schooled children and adolescents when they try to solve the proportionality tasks set up by developmental psychologists contrasts sharply with the data on use of proportionality to solve problems that appear in everyday contexts when people compute prices to be paid for items they sell or buy. It is not clear, however, whether the knowledge about proportions displayed in specific everyday contexts is a general knowledge that could be applied to any other contexts, involving different variables. In the next section we will analyse how adults with little or no school experience deal with proportional relations across different contexts, and whether strategies to solve proportionality problems in one context transfer to other contexts.

The identification of a problem as a proportionality problem in different contexts

In order to solve a proportionality problem it must be identified as such. How is this done? And, this achieved, what determines what procedure will be adopted? In school contexts, students do not have to decide about what procedure should be used since all the problems they receive while the topic is taught involve proportionality. Also, the rule of three or some other formal algorithm is the accepted method for solution. In everyday activities, however, not every relation is a proportional relation. Consider for example the relationship between ages in a problem like the following: 'When Mary was 3 years old, John was 10; what is Mary's age now if John is 30?' The format of this problem is very similar to missing values proportionality problems. The relationship involved, however, is not a proportional relation but an additive one. It seems therefore that one must be familiar with the contents of the problem in order to decide whether or not it should be solved via procedures that are adequate for proportional relations.

According to the classical Piagetian position adolescents who have reached the stage of formal operations are supposed to deal with problems involving proportional relations applied to any content (Inhelder and Piaget, 1958). Piaget did later admit (Piaget, 1972) that adults might show formal reasoning applied to contents or areas in which they are more experienced but not to those in which they have no experience. For instance, a carpenter could show formal reasoning when dealing with problems related to the carpentry profession, without being able to apply the same sort of reasoning to other contents. Experience with specific contents would then be a crucial factor in determining use and transfer of a certain kind of reasoning across different situations.

Everyday experience in a certain context, however, might work in two different directions. It might allow for the use of more complex mathematical procedures, but it might also encourage development of strategies that simplify the problem. Consider, for instance, the problem: 'To make a cake with 3 cups of flour, you need 5 large spoonfuls of water; how many spoonfuls do you need if you put in 9 cups of flour?' In everyday school activities the socially accepted solution for this problem is to perform a series of written computations till an exact correct answer is found. In the kitchen, however, this problem can be satisfactorily solved by increasing the amount of water until the dough reaches the right consistency. Social convention regards monetary transactions, on the other hand, as requiring precision. Provided that the unit price does not vary, precision can be achieved only if the ratio of price to quantity is treated as constant; this requires methods consistent with proportional reasoning.

A study of proportional reasoning among cooks in Brazil (Magalhães, 1990; Schliemann and Magalhães, 1990) allows us to look more closely at the role of context and social convention. The study analysed how subjects with little or no schooling solve proportional problems in different known and unknown contexts and whether strategies used in one context would be transferred for the others. Sixty female cooks between 16 and 40 years of age, with three months to one year of schooling and no instruction on proportions, took part in the study.

Missing value proportionality problems were devised in: (a) a sales transaction context; (b) a cooking context; and (c) the context of a pharmaceutical mixture of ingredients. In sales transactions, the isomorphism of measures must be maintained. Cooking allows for approximations. We thought cooks might be uncertain as to how medicinal mixtures should be regarded. Subjects were equally divided into three group. The cooks of one group were first individually given eight recipe problems, followed by four problems about prices, then by a repetition of the recipe problems not solved in the first presentation, and finally eight medicine problems. A second group of cooks encountered the following order of problems: prices, recipes, medicine and recipes (those not solved earlier). A third group did the medicine problems, followed by the four price problems, then the medicine problems not solved in the first trial, and finally the ten recipe problems. The variation in order allows us to make inferences about problem solving before and after solving price problems. The transfer of price problem strategies to other contexts can then be analysed.

Answers were classified into three categories: correct or numerically exact answers; approximate answers that seemed to take into account the proportional relation between the variables; and wrong or absurd answers. As Table 4.1 shows performance *on the first problem context encountered* varied

Table 4.1 Performance by first problem context encountered

First context encountered		Percentage of responses	
	Correct	Approximate	Wrong
Group I: Prices	91.3	0.0	8.8
Group II: Recipes	17.5	50.0	32.5
Group III: Medicine Formulas	10.0	41.3	48.8

Table 4.2 Strategy by first context encountered

First context encountered			Percentage of responses		
	Scalar	Unit price	Estimation	Additive	Other wrong procedures
Prices	17.5	73.8	0.0	3.8	5.0
Recipes	8.8	8.8	50.0	15.0	17.5
Medicine	8.8	1.3	41.3	23.8	25.0

considerably across contexts, despite the fact that the same numbers were used in all settings. While price problems were nearly always solved correctly and never solved approximately, only occasionally were precisely correct answers given to recipe problems and medicine problems and in about half of the instances approximate answers were given.

Strategies also varied across contexts in the first presentation (see Table 4.2). In more than 70 per cent of the price problems the cooks worked out the unit price and used it to determine the total price. For instance, for the problem 'If 2 kg of rice cost 5 cruzeiros, how much do you have to pay for 3 kilos?', one subject answered: 'Each kilo costs 2 cruzeiros and 50 cents; then 3 kg cost 7 cruzeiros and 50 cents'. In 17.5 per cent of the problems subjects first found the relationship between the given and desired number of items and then applied this scale factor to determine the unknown price from the known price.

When recipe problems came first the cooks seemed to be operating according to different principles: in 50 per cent of the answers, estimates were given and justifications tended to be rather informally expressed, as in 'I think that's enough' or 'That's how I do it'. Medicine problems were also frequently solved through estimation (41.3 per cent). Remarkably, roughly one-half (48.8 per cent) of the medicine answers were either additive or outright wrong answers. Wrong answers were not simply wrong; they often

Table 4.3 Performance by order of presentation (% responses)

Group 1	Recipes 18.1	Prices 93.7	Recipes 61.2	Medicine 55.6
Group 2	–	Prices 91.2	Recipes 60.6	Medicine 62.5
Group 3	Medicine 8.12	Prices 90.0	Medicine 27.5	Recipes 54.37

appeared to be obtained by guessing or by performing a meaningless operation upon the given quantities.

Results in the second presentation context were strikingly different from the first. Table 4.3 shows that there was a clear increase in correct answers for both recipe and medicine problems when they followed the money problems. This increase, however, was not so pronounced for medicine problems when they were presented after money problems but before recipe problems. The predominant approaches after price problems were scalar or functional.

These results are relevant to the issue of determining the conditions under which proportional reasoning arises. If the cooks were to be judged on the basis of their results on the recipe and medicine problems considered in isolation, we might be inclined to suppose that they did not possess proportional reasoning skills. However, these same subjects showed that they were perfectly able to solve problems involving the same arithmetical structure when associated with a context (buying and selling) socially defined as requiring its use. All subjects apparently recognized that the same model would apply to the other problems and their subsequent answers tended to be precise and correct.

Transfer was not so easy to unfamiliar problems (medicine) given immediately after price problems. However, when recipe problems were encountered between the price and the medicine problems, performance was much better. The recipe problems appear to have mediated transfer from the price context to the unfamiliar context.

These findings underline the importance of the specific context in the use of proportional reasoning. They suggest that proportionality reasoning may well develop first in a limited range of contexts and about particular contents. Given the proper conditions, similarities of relations can be detected and transfer and generalization become possible. This recognition may then act as a bridge for transfer of procedures to the unknown contexts.

It seems to us that there is no doubt that, even without any specific help from school instruction, the development of proportional reasoning is possible. This does not mean of course that schools cannot influence the development of proportional reasoning. In order to address this second issue we will compare solutions and strategies used by minimally schooled subjects, who deal with proportions in out-of-school contexts, to those used by schooled subjects.

How street vendors and school children solve proportionality problems

Vergnaud, Rouchier, Ricco, Marthe, Metregiste and Giacobbe (1979, see Vergnaud, 1983) analysed, among school children, how the way numbers are located in the isomorphism of measures diagram may facilitate or hinder the solution of missing values problems. They presented 11 to 15 year olds the problem 'In a hours the central heating consumption is b litres of oil; what is the consumption in c hours' in sixteen different versions, each with a different arrangement of numbers so that, for part of them, it was easier to find the solution through a scalar approach, since the numbers describing one variable were multiples of one another. For the other problems the functional approach was easier since the numbers describing one variable were multiples of the corresponding numbers for the other variable. If, as supposed by Vergnaud, the scalar approach is more natural, problems where scalar solutions were facilitated should be more easily solved by the subjects than problems where the functional relations are facilitated. Contrary to their expectations, performance was not affected by whether scalar or functional solutions were more easily available.

The results of Vergnaud *et al.* (1979) for regularly schooled children may not be replicated for children who learn about proportions in an everyday working context. The latter group should also encounter difficulties in solving problems where the direction of computation goes from the price of many items to the price of a smaller quantity of items and problems where the price of one item is smaller than one.

Unlike the young street vendors, primary and middle-school students regularly receive intensive training in multiplication and division, as well as on algorithms entailing multiplicative relationships. This training is often decontextualized, with emphasis on numerical computation rather than on quantities. Despite the well-documented lack of sense of many procedures learned by students in schools, this type of training may help school children to deal with a broader range of number relations than street vendors with low levels of schooling are accustomed to.

The diversity of problems may favour schooled children. As Vergnaud *et al.* (1979) found, children who learn about proportions in schools should be able to deal with a problem regardless of whether a functional or a scalar solution was easier to find. Children who deal with proportions as street vendors, always working from the price of one to the price of many items, should solve problems more easily if the scalar solution entails multiples, but ought to have relative difficulty in working out solutions for problems in which only the functional approach is facilitated by multiples.

Finally, in an inflationary economy like present-day Brazil, the ratio of price to number of items also has a determined direction since the number representing the price of one item is usually an integer greater than one. Therefore, when given the price of more than one item, if the subject chooses to compute the unit price as a step to solving the problem, the usual computation is to divide the price by the number of items, and not the other way around. Computation should be much more difficult if the number indicating the price is smaller than the number of items.

Schliemann and Nunes (1990) compared fisherman's strategies used on proportionality problems with those of students who had everyday experience with price computation, but who also received school instruction on the school algorithm (the rule of three) to solve proportional problems. They found that both fishermen and students prefer to use a scalar approach, not taught in schools. This preference was found even for those problems where functional solutions were (in principle) easier than were scalar solutions. When the functional multiplier was an integer (but the scalar multiplier was not) performance was poorer than when a scalar multiplier was an integer (but the functional multiplier was not).

To analyse the issue further we designed the study reported below (a part of which is reported in Nunes, Schliemann and Carraher, 1990) aimed at comparing school children to street vendor youths' performance and strategies for solving proportionality problems.

Three groups of thirty children each participated in the study. The first group was composed of 11 to 14 year olds, with from two to six years of school attendance, who had not received school instruction on proportionality. These street vendor children came from very poor families in Recife, Brazil. The second and third groups came from upper- and middle-class schools in the same city. Their ages also ranged from 11 to 14 years. The 6th graders had not received instruction on proportions; the 7th graders had.

The ninety subjects were individually interviewed and asked to solve, using whatever means and strategies they wanted, the eight problems shown in Table 4.4. Problems were orally presented but pencil, paper and a pocket calculator were available for use by children. Time was unlimited. They were asked to solve problems aloud. The interviewer probed for clarification when the spontaneous comments of the subjects were not sufficient to determine the problem-solving approach used.

The eight problems were designed so that for four of them it was easier to find a solution through a scalar approach: the scalar multiplier was an integer while the functional multiplier was not. These four problems will be called 'scalar problems'. In the other four problems, the 'functional problems', the functional approach was favoured.

Table 4.4 Problems presented to children

A. Problems with scalar ratio easier to be computed:
   (a) From a smaller to a larger pair:
      Price is larger than number of items:
         3 little cars cost 10 cruzeiros.
         How many cruzeiros do I need to buy 9 cars?
      Price is smaller than number of items:
         10 chewing gums cost 3 cruzeiros.
         How many chewing gums do I buy with 9 cruzeiros?
   (b) From a larger to a smaller pair:
      Price is larger than number of items:
         9 balls cost 21 cruzeiros.
         How many cruzeiros do I need to buy 3 balls?
      Price is smaller than number of items:
         21 chocolates cost 9 cruzeiros.
         How many chocolates do I buy with 3 cruzeiros?
B. Problems with functional ratio easier to be computed:
   (a) From a smaller to a larger pair:
      Price is larger than number of items:
         3 pens cost 9 cruzeiros.
         How many pens do I buy with 21 cruzeiros?
      Price is smaller than number of items:
         9 rubbers cost 3 cruzeiros.
         How many cruzeiros do I need to buy 21 rubbers?
   (b) From a larger to a smaller pair:
      Price is larger than number of items:
         10 comics cost 30 cruzeiros.
         How many cruzeiros do I need to buy 3 comics?
      Price is smaller than number of items:
         30 lollipops cost 10 cruzeiros.
         How many lollipops do I buy with 3 cruzeiros?

In each set of four problems, the first two problems required subjects to determine a missing larger value from a ratio of smaller values. In the other two problems they had to determine a missing smaller value from a ratio of larger values. In half of the problems the number associated with price was larger than the number associated with items; in the other half the relation was reversed. All answers were recorded, transcribed and classified in terms of correctness and strategies used.

As in the cooks study, three types of answers were found: precisely correct, approximate and incorrect. Approximate answers were nearly non-existent for scalar problems (three cases) and rare for functional problems (twenty cases in 480 answers). With the exception of the last problem, the frequency of approximate answers did not differ between groups. In the ensuing analysis correct and approximate answers are collapsed. The proportions of correct and approximate answers for each of the problems in each group are shown in Table 4.5.

A multivariate analysis of variance (MANOVA) with groups (vendors, 6th graders and 7th graders) as a between-subjects factor, and type of problem

Table 4.5 Performance by group (prices in cruzeiros)

Problems with scalar solutions easier

Direction	From small to large		From large to small	
Large number:	Price	Items	Price	Items
Question:	3 cost 10	10 cost 3	9 cost 21	21 cost 9
	9 cost ?	? cost 9	3 cost ?	? cost 3
Vendors	0.93	0.93	0.67	0.73
6th graders	1.00	0.93	0.87	0.77
7th graders	0.90	0.90	0.86	0.80

Problems with functional solution easier

Direction	From small to large		From large to small	
Large number:	Price	Items	Price	Items
Question:	3 cost 9	9 cost 3	10 cost 30	30 cost 10
	? cost 21	21 cost ?	3 cost ?	? cost 3
Vendors	0.60	0.65	0.50	0.33
6th graders	0.87	0.76	0.79	0.38
7th graders	0.87	0.76	0.90	0.56

(scalar-oriented versus functional-oriented), direction of computation (from small to large versus from large to small), and size of numbers (price larger than number of items versus number of items larger than prices) as within-subjects factors was performed in order to evaluate the effects of the different types of problems on subjects' number of correct answers. MANOVA results showed significant main effects for type of problem ($F_{1,75} = 31.77$, p. ‹ 0.001), direction of computation ($F_{1,75} = 28.95$, p ‹ 0.001), and size of numbers ($F_{1,75} = 22.19$, p ‹ 0.001). Scalar-oriented problems were easier for all three groups of subjects, as were problems where direction of computation went from a smaller to a larger pair of the function, and also problems with price stated as a number larger than the number describing number of items.

Overall differences between groups were not significant, but significant interactions were found between groups by direction of computation ($F_{2,75} = 3.09$, $p = 0.05$) and between groups by size of numbers ($F_{2,75} = 6.23$, p ‹ 0.005). Other significant first-order interactions were found for type of problem by relative size of numbers ($F_{1,75} = 7.86$, p ‹ 0.01) and for direction of computation by relative size of numbers ($F_{1,75} = 5.87$, p ‹ 0.02).

The significant interaction between group and direction of computation was mainly due to the sharper decrease in performance among street vendors when the direction of computation went from a larger to a smaller pair. This decrease was attentuated among 6th graders and was very small for 7th graders. The difficulties shown by street vendors in problems where direction of computation was opposed to that usually found when they compute prices in everyday activities seem to be a result of the unidirectionality of their preferred strategies for solving the problems.

The significant interaction between group and relative size of numbers was due to a decrease in performance among both groups of school children when number of items was larger than the number denoting price, while street vendors' performance was not affected by this manipulation in the way numbers appeared in the problems.

Scalar problems with the direction of computation going from a smaller to a larger pair (the first two problems) were solved via mental computation by nearly all subjects and, in most cases (at least 63 per cent of the subjects in each group in the first problem and 80 per cent in the second), via computational strategies focusing on the scalar relation. Street vendors' use of the scalar approach, however, was clearly different from that by 6th and 7th graders. The regularly schooled subjects by far preferred to find the scalar operator for one variable and then multiply the known term by the multiplier to obtain the missing value. Street vendors instead used a building up approach: step-by-step transformations in both variables till the answer was reached. The following protocols illustrate the differences between schooled subjects' and street vendors' strategies when they were solving the second problem:

Subject: André, a 12-year-old street vendor who has been selling popcorn since he was 6.

> E [*examiner*]: 10 chewing gums cost 3 cruzeiros. With 9 cruzeiros, how many chewing gums can you get?
> A [*subject*]: 30. 10 chewing gums cost 3, 20 makes 6, 30 makes 9. With 9 you can buy 30 chewing gums.

Subject: Viviana, a 12-year-old 6th grader.

> E: 10 chewing gums cost 3 cruzeiros. With 9 cruzeiros, how many chewing gums do I buy?
> V: 3.
> E: Why?
> V: Oh, no, wait a minute, 10 chewing gums cost 3 cruzeiros (pause), 30.
> E: Why 30?
> V: 3 times 10 equals 30.
> E: Right, but why did you choose 3 times 10?
> V: Because 9 is equal to 3 times 3 cruzeiros.

Street vendors sometimes mentioned multiplication facts but generally did not give a clear explanation about why they used multiplication to compute the answer.

For scalar problems going from a larger to a smaller pair, scalar solutions were again very popular for all groups, with multiplication used more often by school subjects and successive additions by street vendors. But for these two problems there was also a high frequency, in all groups, of correct answers that were found very rapidly and for which subjects did not reveal their computational strategy. These immediate answers were probably a result of the prompt identification of the scalar relation since computation via the functional relation would require longer processing time, because numbers were not multiples. Another interesting difference between schooled and unschooled children emerged in the third problem in Table 4.4. Here 40 per cent of 6th graders and 43 per cent of 7th graders used a calculator or written computation to work out their answers, and 23 per cent of 6th graders and 47 per cent of 7th graders computed the price of one item. In the same problem, computation of the price of one item was chosen by only three street vendors. No street vendor youths used a calculator nor a written computation routine, even though the necessary instruments were present. Rather, they continued to approach the problems through the same informal strategies used successfully in the former problems. In this situation the fact that they were not versed in the use of calculators and written computations seems to have placed them at a disadvantage. Street vendors who solved the third and fourth problems made use of the fact that 3×7 equals 21 but tended to explain their approach by appealing to the building-up scalar solution, as in the following case:

Subject: Cristiano, a 13-year-old popcorn vendor for one year.

> E: 9 balls cost 21 cruzeiros. I want to buy 3 balls. How many cruzeiros do I need?
> C: 15 cruzeiros, wait, it is wrong, it is 7 cruzeiros. Before you ask me I'm going to explain: 3 times 7 is 21. The 3 belongs to the ball. 6 balls makes 14 and 9 balls make 21.

Street vendors who did not solve the scalar problem where direction of computation went from a larger to a smaller quantity presented confusing answers with descriptions of senseless strategies, as if the problems were not related to the other problems they did solve. This was the case for Carlos solving the fourth problem:

Subject: Carlos, a 13-year-old chocolate vendor.

> E: 21 chocolates cost 9 cruzeiros. How many chocolates can I buy with 3 cruzeiros?
> S: [*after a pause and after counting his fingers*] 9 chocolates.
> E: While you were solving it, you were thinking. Tell me now what were you thinking about.
> C: 9 plus 3 makes 12, 21 minus 12 makes 9.

For functional problems there was an overall drop in performance, especially in the last problem where the direction of computation was different from that used in everyday transactions and the number of items was stated as a number larger than the number stated for price. In this case street vendors' performance fell to 33 per cent and 6th graders' to 38 per cent. While street vendors continued to use mental computation and the scalar approach, with approximate answers appearing more frequently, school subjects more often used calculators, written algorithms and approaches that were more suitable for this type of problem. These approaches were the functional approach, the computation of the price of one item or the computation of how many items could be bought with one cruzeiro as a starting point. These approaches were prevalent among 7th graders. Some of the 6th graders also adopted these two strategies although use of the scalar approach still persisted in an approximately equal number of subjects in this group. Despite their preference for scalar strategies, eleven street vendors worked through computation of the price of one item in the seventh problem. The functional approach, however, was used only once by one street vendor in the last problem.

Use of the scalar approach in functional problems, with direction of computation going from a smaller to a larger pair, required, in most cases, computation of the price of one item as a step towards solution. The example below of a child solving the fifth problem illustrates this combination of procedures:

Subject: Flávio, a 13-year-old ice-cream vendor for two-and-a-half years.

 E: 3 pens cost 9 cruzeiros. With 21 cruzeiros, how many pens can you buy?
 F: 3 pens is 9 cruzeiros, 6 is 18. 1 pen is 3 cruzeiros. 18 to 21 is 3. 6 plus 1 is 7. 7 pens cost 21 cruzeiros.

School children's use of functional solutions was always done through use of the multiplication and/or division operation:

Subject: Edson, 6th grader(s).

 E: 9 rubbers cost 3 cruzeiros. You want to buy 21 rubbers. How many cruzeiros will you need?
 S: This one is really meant to get me. If 9 rubbers cost 3 cruzeiros, then 21 rubbers cost [*pause*]. This one looks like the other one. It is 7.
 E: How did you find out?
 S: Because the triple of 3 is 9, and the triple of 7 is 21. 3 times 3, 9, 3 times 7, 21.

The present study seems to indicate that procedures developed in contexts outside of school have a limited power when proportionality problems appear differently from how they usually occur in everyday settings. The difficulty found by street vendors seems to be in part due to the unidirectionality of the relations and procedures they are used to. But the lack of training in multiplication and division, and in the use of written algorithms and calculators, also plays an important role in limiting their efficiency. Despite these problems, experience in computing prices in everyday contexts seems to be one of the activities that allows the development of understanding about proportionality.

Concluding remarks

While there is a wide consensus among psychologists, educators and mathematicians about what are proportions, there is considerable difference of opinion regarding the nature and development of proportional reasoning. Early, classic psychological studies in the area lent support to the idea that proportional reasoning is manifested only during adolescence and is intimately related to the postulated transition from concrete operational to formal operational thinking. Studies in mathematics education and more recent psychological studies of thinking in familiar contexts have raised findings that disagree in a substantial way with this characterization of proportional reasoning.

Criticisms of Piagetian tasks, as being confounded and overly imbued with scientific concepts, recommended that purer, more mathematical tasks be used.[5] But *purer* tasks are not easier for children and did not bring down the age at which proportionality is fully understood. None the less, careful protocol analyses made it clear that there were conditions – particularly when small integer multiples are used – in which younger children are able to solve proportionality problems. What therefore seemed to be a great divide (concrete to formal) was found to be more continuous than at first thought. The Piagetian analysis of the emergence of proportional reasoning holds that numerical proportions derive from 'logical proportions' involving ratios of statements. So far as we can tell, this claim has not been substantiated.

Recent studies of proportional reasoning leave little doubt that people acquire an understanding of proportionality in the context of purchase of items. Frequently, missing values problems are solved through the derivation of a unit ratio, $n:1$, corresponding to the cost of one unit. This ratio appears to be understood as equivalent to the ratio from which it is derived. Building up strategies based on successive additions that preserve the relationship between the variables in the problem are commonly employed by people with little or no schooling. This strategy is indeed correct but the scalar multiplier is implicit rather than explicit.

Schooling may contribute to the development of proportional reasoning and more powerful strategies for solution of proportional problems in at least three ways. First, by requiring students to learn multiplication and division, scalar and functional multipliers can be explicitly represented. This will be particularly important in dealing with algebraic representations of functions: for example, in understanding the role of the constant a in the linear equation $y = ax + b$. Second, schools explicitly introduce students to rational numbers. One of the difficulties in working with multiplicative structures is that they inevitably require that we encounter means of representing and handling rational numbers. Unschooled individuals commonly have considerable difficulty in handling problems in which the values do not share common factors. Third, schools can establish explicit links between situations otherwise thought to be unrelated. The use of common symbolic representations (written symbols, diagrams, graphs and explanations) can facilitate such linkages. But for transfer to occur successfully, it may be necessary for educators to re-evaluate how they classify and conceptualize mathematics problems. What frequently appear on the surface to be mere problems of multiplication and division of quantities are most certainly problems entailing proportionality.

Psychologists can continue to contribute to the area by clarifying the nature of proportional reasoning and the conditions under which it occurs. There are still important developmental questions to be dealt with and these issues may well yield important implications for mathematics education. Our misgivings with regard to a classic Piagetian approach in no way suggest that proportional thinking is unrelated to development. Certainly, proportional reasoning could not occur at all if there were not cognitive structures available for sustaining the representation and comparison of ratios. But we are equally convinced that proportional reasoning to a large extent involves learning: learning to analyse situations, to express relations, and to derive values. There remains considerable work to be done in showing how learning in out-of-school contexts is, and can be, related to learning in school.

Notes

1. When the y-intercept is not zero, the function does not pass through the origin. In such cases, x and y values are not proportional but *increments* along x are proportional to *increments* along y.
2. We can also map a set of numbers on to a set of (previously unmeasured) quantities through measurement, but this possibility does not concern us here.
3. Rational numbers include integers and fractions, whether expressed as common fractions (1/3, 7/5) or decimal values (1.53).
4. A unit ratio approach (price for one unit, km in one hour, etc.) appears to be a special approach that frequently cannot be classified as either scalar or functional. When a multiplier is clearly expressed as an intensive quantity, we are dealing with a functional approach. But when a person multiplies two values (e.g. 5×15 in the above diagram) it is impossible to identify which is the (scalar or functional) operator. To Vergnaud (1983), however, the computation of the unit ratio in terms of, for instance, the price of one is in fact still part of a scalar approach. Ricco

(1982) found that children prefer to work through the computation of the unit ratio.
5. These criticisms do not apply to the probabilities task.

References

Carraher, D.W. (1991), 'Mathematics in and out of school: a selective review of studies from Brazil', in M. Harris (ed.), *Schools, Mathematics and Work* (London: Falmer Press), pp. 169–201.

Carraher, T.N. (1986), 'From drawings to buildings: working with mathematical scales', *International Journal of Behavioural Development*, **9**, pp. 527–44.

Carraher, T.N. (1988), 'Street mathematics and school mathematics', in A. Borbás (ed.), *Proceedings of the Twelfth International Conference for the Psychology of Mathematics Education* (Veszprém, Hung.: OOK Printing House).

Carraher, T.N., Carraher, D.W. and Schliemann, A.D. (1982), 'Na vida, dez; na escola, zero: os contextos culturais da educação matemática', *Cadernos de Pesquisa*, **42**, pp. 79–86.

Carraher, T.N., Carraher, D.W. and Schliemann, A.D. (1984), 'Can mathematics teachers teach proportions?', in P. Damerow, M. Dunkley, B. Nebres and B. Werry (eds), *Mathematics for All*, Science and Technology Education Document Series, no. 20 (Paris: UNESCO).

Carraher, T.N., Carraher, D.W. and Schliemann, A.D. (1985), 'Mathematics in the streets and in schools', *British Journal of Developmental Psychology*, **3**, pp. 21–9.

Carraher, T.N., Schliemann, A.D. and Carraher, D.W. (1986), 'Proporcionalidade na educação científica e matematica: uma análise de tarefas piagetianas', *Revista Brasileira de Estudos Pedagógicos*, **67** (**156**), pp. 367–79.

Carraher, T.N., Schliemann, A.D. and Carraher, D.W. (1988), 'Mathematical concepts in everyday life', in G. Saxe and M. Gearhart (eds), *Children Mathematics: New directions in child development* (San Francisco: Jossey & Bass).

Douady, R. (1985), 'The interplay between different settings: tool object dialectic in the extension of mathematical ability', in L. Streefland (ed.), *Proceedings of the Ninth International Conference for the Psychology of Mathematics Education*, Noordwijkerhout, Neth., July, pp. 33–52.

Freudenthal, H. (1983), *Didactical Phenomenology of Mathematical Structures* (Dordrecht, Neth.: D. Reidel).

Gay, J. and Cole, M. (1967), *The New Mathematics and an Old Culture* (New York: Holt, Rinehart & Winston).

Greenfield, P. (1966), 'On culture and conservation', in J. Bruner, R. Olver and P. Greenfield (eds), *Studies in Cognitive Development* (New York: Wiley), pp. 225–56.)

Greenfield, P. and Lave, J. (1982), 'Cognitive aspects of informal education', in D. Wagner and H. Stevenson (eds), *Cultural Perspectives on Child Development* (San Francisco: Freeman), pp. 181–207.

Hart, K. (1981), *Ratio: Children's strategies and errors* (Windsor, Berks.: NFER–NELSON Publishing Co.).

Inhelder, B. and Piaget, J. (1958), *The Growth of Logical Thinking from Childhood to Adolescence* (New York: Basic Books).

Kaput, J., West, M., Luke, C. and Pattison-Gordon, L. (1988), 'Concrete representations and ratio reasoning', in *Proceedings of the Tenth Annual Meeting of the International Group for the Psychology of Mathematics Education, North American Chapter* (DeKalb, IL.: Northern Illinois University).

Karplus, R. (1981), 'Education and formal thought: a modest proposal', in I.E. Siegel, D.M. Brodzinsky and R.M. Golinkoff (eds), *New Directions in Piagetian Theory and Practice* (Hillsdale, NJ: Erlbaum).

Karplus, R., Karplus, E.F., Formisano, M. and Paulsen, A.C. (1979), 'Proportional reasoning and control of variables in seven countries', in J. Lochhead and J. Clements (eds), *Cognitive Process Instruction* (Philadelphia PH: Franklin Institute Press).

Karplus, R. and Peterson, R. (1970), 'Intellectual development beyond elementary school. II: Ratio, a survey', *School Science and Mathematics*, **70** (9), pp. 813–20.

Laboratory of Comparative Human Cognition (1983), 'Culture and cognitive development', in P.H. Mussen (ed.), *Handbook of Child Psychology* (New York: Wiley), vol. 1, pp. 295–356.

Lave, J. (1977), 'Cognitive consequences of traditional apprenticeship training in Africa', *Anthropology and Educational Quarterly*, **7**, pp. 177–80.

Lovell, K. and Butterworth, I.B. (1966), 'Abilities underlying the understanding of proportionality', *Mathematics Teaching*, **37**.

Lunzer, A.E. and Pumphrey, P.D. (1966), 'Understanding proportionality', *Mathematics Teaching*, **34**,pp. 7–12.

Luria, A.R. (1976), *Cognitive Development: Its cultural and social foundations* (Cambridge, MA.: Harvard University Press).

Magalhães, V. P. (1990), 'A resolucão de problemas de proporcão e sua transferência entre diferentes conteudos', unpublished Masters thesis, Department of Psychology, Universidade Federal de Pernambuco, Recife.

Noelting, G. (1980a), 'The development of proportional reasoning and the ratio concept: Part I – Differentiation of stages', *Educational Studies in Mathematics*, **II**, pp. 217–53.

Noelting, G. (1980b), 'The development of proportional reasoning and the ratio concept: Part II – Problem structure at successive stages; problem solving strategies and the mechanism of adaptative restructuring', *Educational Studies in Mathematics*, **11**, pp. 331–63.

Nunes, T., Schliemann, A.D. and Carraher, D.W. (1990), 'Proporcionalidade: esquemas intuitivos versus procedimentas escolares', unpublished manuscript, Department of Psychology, Universidade Federal de Pernambuco, Recife.

Piaget, J. (1972), 'Intellectual evolution from adolescence to adulthood', *Human Development*, **15**, pp. 1–12.

Piaget, J. and Inhelder, B. (1967), *The Child's Conception of Space* (New York: Norton).

Piaget, J. and Inhelder, B. (1970), *The Child's Conception of Movement and Speed* (London: Routledge & Kegan Paul).

Piaget, J. and Inhelder, B. (1975), *The Origin of the Idea of Chance in Children* (New York: Norton).

Piaget, J., Grize, J., Szeminska, A. and Bang, V. (1977), *Epistemology and Psychology of Functions* (Dordrecht, Neth.: D. Reidel).

Ricco, G. (1982), 'Les premières acquisitions de la notion de fonction linéaire chez l'enfant de 7 à 11 ans', *Educational Studies in Mathematics*, **13**, pp. 289–327.

Saxe, G. (1990), *Culture and Cognitive Development: Studies in Mathematical under-standing* (Hillsdale, NJ: Erlbaum).

Schliemann, A.D. (1985), 'Mathematics among carpenters and carpenters' apprentices: implications for school teaching', in P. Damerow, M. Dunkley, B. Nebres and B. Werry (eds), *Mathematics for All*, Science and Technology Education Document Series, no. 2562 (Paris: UNESCO).

Schliemann, A.D. and Acioly, N.M. (1989), 'Mathematical knowledge developed at work: the contribution of practice versus the contribution of schooling', *Cognition and Instruction*, 6 (3), pp. 185–221.

Schliemann, A.D. and Magalhães, V.P. (1990), 'Proportional reasoning: from shops, to kitchens, laboratories, and, hopefully, schools', *Proceedings of the Fourteenth International Conference for the Psychology of Mathematics Education*, Oaxtepec, Mexico.

Schliemann, A.D. and Nunes, T. (1990), 'A situated schema of proportionality', *British Journal of Developmental Psychology*, 8, pp. 259–68.

Schwartz, J. (1988), 'Intensive quantity and referent transforming arithmetic operations', in J. Hiebert and M. Behr (eds), *Number Concepts and Operations in the Middle Grades* (Reston, VA: Erlbaum/National Council of Teachers of Mathematics), pp. 41–52.

Sharp, D., Cole, M. and Lave, C. (1979), 'Education and cognitive development: the evidence from experimental research', *Monographs of the Society for the Study of Behavioural Development*, 44 (1–2), serial no. 179.

Stevenson, H., Parker, T., Wilkinson, A., Bonnevaux, B. and Gonzalez, M. (1978), 'Schooling, environment and cognitive development: a cross-cultural study', *Monographs of the Society for the Study of Behavioural Development*, 43 (3), serial no. 175.

Vergnaud, G. (1983), 'Multiplicative Structures', in R. Lesh and M. Landau (eds), *Acquisition of Mathematics: Concepts and process* (New York: Academic Press).

Vergnaud, G. (1984), 'Understanding proportion, fraction and ratio at the primary level', paper presented at the Fifth International Congress on Mathematical Education, Adelaide, Australia.

Vergnaud, G. (1988), 'Multiplicative Structures', in J. Hiebert and M. Behr (eds), *Number Concepts and Operations in the Middle Grades* (Reston, VA: Erlbaum/National Council of Teachers of Mathematics), pp. 141–61.

Vergnaud, G., Rouchier, A., Ricco, G., Marthe, P., Metregiste, R. and Giacobbe, J. (1979), 'Acquisition des structures multiplicatives dans le premier cycle du second degré', RO no. 2, IREM d'Orleans, Centre d'Étude des Processus Cognitifs et du Langage.

Whitney, H. (1968), 'The mathematics of physical quantities: Part I: Mathematical models for measurement', *American Mathematical Monthly*, 75, pp. 115–38.

Chapter 5

Word problems: a microcosm of theories of learning

Jean Lave, *University of California*

Introduction

This paper charts some of the converging lines of thought, research and argumentation that point to a theory of situated learning as a possible next step in understanding the learning and teaching of mathematics. The story might begin almost anywhere in Western history. I have arbitrarily picked the date 1478. In that year, when the *Treviso Arithmetic* was printed (Swetz, 1987), the relation of math learning and everyday experience may have been less of a conundrum than it is today. There existed no contradiction between specialized mathematical education and universal socialization for everyday living, as there is today. At that time there were only a few master computers. They accepted future merchants as short-term apprentices. In this socially organized math practice the apprentices learned from the master computers the math they needed to carry out typical business transactions.

The word problems in the *Treviso Arithmetic* are remarkably modern-sounding, or at least the mathematical intentions displayed in the problems:

> A merchant has 10 marks and 6½ ounces of silver of a fineness of 5½ ounces per mark. He has 12 marks of another kind which contains 6½ ounces per mark. He has 15 marks of another kind which has a fineness of 7¼ ounces per mark. And from all this silver he wishes to coin money which shall contain 4¾ ounces of fineness per mark. Required is to know the amount in the mixture, and how much brass must be added. (Swetz, 1987, p. 156)

But the similarity ends with the problems as read. Today everyone is supposed to learn math in school. Most children going through public school math curricula will not be merchants or mathematicians. Instead of helping a specialized clientele, teachers are engaged in a far more diffuse practice. They are charged with two tasks: creating or replacing existing everyday math procedures while at the same time helping to determine the relative mathematical preparedness of children who will grow up to take different economic and social positions.

These general goals for teaching children in society today shape curricula, the organization of classroom lessons, policies about universal school attendance, testing, grading, tracking, and much else about schools. But this misses the point I wish to make: these goals are not some short list of high-priority, compatible values – they are *contradictory*. The basic sociocultural structuring forces they represent shape not only the organization of schools, classrooms and lessons, but math learning as well.[1] Furthermore, what I have referred to as the goals of universal socialization on the one hand and the production of socially unequal distributions of knowledge and power on the other are not goals at all. For they configure our choices without either of them being acceptable as an adequate solution to the mathematical needs of the society. Their articulation sets the basic conditions within which practical goals are forged in particular instances for particular schools, classrooms and subject matters. Since any given set of practical goals is a resolution to these contradictory principles, they are (a) never wholly satisfying nor satisfied, and (b) they are therefore stable only in the short run.

Even this is too simple a view. For it is so difficult to acknowledge the conflicting conditions that govern the development of specific educational goals, that there is enormous pressure on schools as systems to avoid clarifying practical goals for math learning in school altogether. It strikes me that we become paralysed whenever a question is raised concerning what relations should hold between math instruction forms and people's lives (as opposed to next year's school lessons). It seems illustrative of this point that researchers have only recently begun to explore the uses of math in everyday life. For the most part, the community of researchers has accepted uncritically platitudes about 'replacing weak everyday practice' and 'preparation for this high-technology world' without giving high priority to finding out just what these might mean.[2] I want to consider what might constitute goals for math learning, then, in the light of research on everyday mathematical practice and without losing sight of the social forces that create the conditions for generating such goals. Meanwhile, I have ventured some way from the subject of word problems. The discussion to follow will focus on relations between the social structuring of education in Western culture and that peculiar cultural device.

Differences in the social organization of knowledge and learning affect the meaning of word problems. How can that be? For one thing, a word problem is one way to express beliefs about how everyday experience and mathematics should be related in order for math learning to take place effectively; a word problem may be viewed as a microcosmic cultural–symbolic instrument. Word problems in today's sociocultural order are intended to ground abstract math in familiar terms for beginners who are assumed to have (only) a concrete grasp of math in their daily experience. Word problems also reflect a theory of learning, an epistemological, cognitive and social account deeply embedded in Western thought of how knowing and understanding change and grow. The theory is about cognition and the institution of schooling as well (Lave, 1988). It involves the belief that to know something requires that the learner be separated, or distanced, from the situated experience to be known; that the learner must abstract features of the experience, generalize about them and then transport them into a variety of novel situations in which they can be recognized to apply. Schools are often referred to as places where people learn 'out of context', learn general concepts, or are to be prepared for the world outside school.

Why would school math include word problems, given this theory of learning? Well it is not clear that there *are* continually renewed intentions which guide this practice in our society – perhaps school math includes word problems 'because they are there' (and have been for several hundred years). It may be that there is some felt sense that word problems offer practice in miniature, or even exact practice, for the situations of everyday life in which math learners will need to apply what they have learned in school. This in turn implies that such connections to life experience *motivate* learners. Word problems are used with the intention of illustrating mathematical principles. This cultural device may also be a means of transmitting the message to children that they really *will* need the math they are learning when they grow up and move into the world. The very process of solving word problems takes its form directly from the theory of learning: abstracting out the numbers and operations from a situation, operating on them in abstracted form, drawing a conclusion or generalization about the results, then reinserting the results into the situation. And finally, learning what arithmetic word problems are about, when those everyday scenarios are in fact greatly stylized and distanced in other ways from the scenes and experiences they depict, is a sustained process during which children absorb a genre of puzzle-solving activity. Their experience with this genre teaches them to give different meaning and value to certain experiences in school and to other aspects of their lives, including what they come to call 'real' math and the 'other' math of everyday activity.

The chasm between school and everyday life

All is not well with math learning in our system of school education. Cognitive psychologists have carried out research over the last fifteen years that makes plain the limited nature of many children's grasp of school mathematics, and have arrived at conclusions about the causes of their difficulties. This work highlights as one significant culprit the gulf between math learning in school and the everyday experience of children trying to bring their intuitions to bear while learning math in school. For example:

> It may be possible to help the weaker learners become stronger by giving them explicit help in drawing the connections between the formal rules they are taught and their more intuitive and informal knowledge of certain mathematical principles. Although there is regularly some effort to teach the principles and justifications underlying school arithmetic procedures this effort is not usually very sustained. More important, it does not aim to explicitly link school math with children's intuitive knowledge about mathematics. (Resnick, 1986, p. 33)

In fact, this diagnosis reveals the double character – the weakness as well as the presumed strength – of the theory of learning that insists upon the separation of the learner's experience from the learning process.[3] Unfortunately, such separation leads to new genres of activity rather than to enrichment of ongoing activity, and for learners, it leads to the compartmentalization and trivialization of school and/or other kinds of life experience as they are separated from each other.

Word problems are not simply a value-free educational or mathematical technology. They provide occasions for talk and activity. There is a discourse of word problems – a set of things everyone knows how to say about word problems or that can be expressed in 'word-problemese', issues and questions that come up when people begin to talk about them; and things that are not or cannot be said within this framework (cf. Geras, 1972; Cohn, 1987). These are stylized narratives about assumed general cultural knowledge that (even) children can be expected to have. They are not about particular children's experiences with the world. The problems themselves are stylized representations of hypothetical experiences – not slices of everyday existence. If you ask children to make up problems about everyday math they will not make up problems about their experienced lives, they will invent examples of the genre; they too know what a word problem is. Saljo and Wyndhamn's research (1992) shows how children situate their math practice differently in different settings. They presented school children with a postage table and asked them to figure out how much postage to put on a letter of a certain weight. The exercise took place in several settings, and children responded accordingly. In the post office 8th graders handed the letter to the person behind the counter with the scale and asked, 'How much?' In social studies class they read the table and picked the next highest postage. Given the identical problem in the context of a math class they figured out the postage due to three decimal places. A first step in the argument follows: word problems are clearly part of 'real' school math, and are thereby implicated in the maintenance of the division between 'real' and 'other' math.[4]

Children's intuitions about the everyday world are in fact constantly violated in situations in which they are asked to solve word problems. This discontinuity by itself may help create the division between 'real' and 'other' math by conveying the message that what children know about the real world is not valid, in two ways: by the fact that word problems are about aspects of only hypothetical experience and essentially never about real situations. And further, in real situations that might plausibly be claimed to be comparable to the hypothetical ones (e.g. grocery shopping), quantitative relations are assembled and transformed by methods quite different from those used in school, and in many cases these methods draw on the world and others in it to generate calculational activity and results in ways that would be classed as cheating or failing in school. The upshot, where school lessons make implicit claims that word problems model the everyday world, is a challenge to children's grasp of their own experience. Brenner has made close observations of Hawaiian pre-school children's experience with money before and after they enter the Kamehameha school. She reports that pre-school children typically go to the store carrying quarters or a one dollar bill – more than they need – and bring back change. She goes on to say that:

> Naming of money precedes more quantitative concepts. Children tend to talk about the name of a coin rather than its numerical value. Thus they learn money as an ordinal system in which coins are organized by their relative value rather than their absolute relationship to each other . . . Buying is nearly errorless . . . and gets lots of social support. (Brenner, n.d.)

By contrast, in school the approach is additive: kids are taught to group pennies, then pennies and nickels then pennies, nickels and dimes. The school curriculum does not capitalize upon children's understanding of money (e.g. relating coins to the dollar bill). Nor do the prices and quantities in textbook problems bear any realistic relation to children's experience. The result is a division for the children between their ideas of money in and out of school. Brenner demonstrated this by interviewing individual children at intervals across the school year. A young child who answered questions about quarters and dollars early in the school year, at the end says, 'I don't know them any more. I only know pennies and nickels now because we don't do dollars in school' (Brenner, n.d.). The implication to children is that everyday experience is to be valued negatively. And, as our research on adult math practice confirms, adults, like children, believe that math is important but that they cannot do it, or, for the most successful, that they cannot do it as well as they should (Lave, 1988).

Word problems are at one and the same time both math problems and claims about math in everyday life (including how it should be done). In order not to reflect or help to perpetuate that debilitating division between everyday experience and (math) learning in school, it seems important to analyse two aspects of this genre more carefully: on the one hand, the contrast between everyday experience as portrayed in word problems and in its experienced forms, and on the other hand, what it means to 'have a problem' in school and in other circumstances. Questions like these have been central to research on everyday math practice, and will be discussed in the following section. This leads to a more general discussion of learning in everyday practice. Then I will go back to word problems in school, exploring math practice in the classroom from the perspective of learning-in-practice.

Everyday math research

One of the first questions that comes to mind when the researcher proposes to venture past the schoolyard fence is whether school math does 'travel' serviceably across the school–life bridge, into the everyday world. All of the research on everyday math shows that it is effective and accurate (Carraher *et al.*, 1982, 1983; Carraher and Schliemann, 1982; Scribner and Fahrmeier, 1982; Scribner, 1984). At the same time, there is very little evidence from these studies that school-taught math procedures are used in any clearly identifiable manner in settings that are not school-like. Quantitative problems in everyday life tend to be dilemmas for which resolutions are invented on the spot – in fact, everyday math is characteristically an improvised rather than an algorithmic, or mechanically reproduced, or 'routine' practice. In everyday situations numbers are hard to find, but once determined are often preserved for future use; quantitative relations are related to other relations rather more often than they are to each other; problems and solutions define each other; problems can be abandoned, resolved, or reformulated as well as solved. Thus, people seem to 'own' their own math problems outside schools in ways they usually do not in school. And problem resolutions often generate further conflict. Adult Math Project research has led us to realize that *what* activity people are engaged in shapes what they will see as problematic. For instance, grocery shoppers do not initiate individual purchases with unit price comparisons. They do not consider price comparison calculations until their choices are reduced to a single pair of grocery items so similar that a decision is impossible on the basis of their qualitative characteristics. When calculation becomes the decision-method of choice, they establish the ratio of the two prices or quantities, whichever is easier, and then check to see which ratio is the larger. Other results of the everyday math research are described here in telegraphic form, in a list of some of the salient characteristics of everyday math practice (Murtaugh, 1985; de la Rocha, 1986; Lave, 1988).

1. The problem solver, activity, other people, and the world help solve problems, often so integrally that it is not possible to assign one location to the problem, the problem-solving activity, or the resolution. Research on

a helicopter transport ship navigation team plotting the ship's position offers an excellent example (Hutchins, 1992).

2. The formation, resolution and consequences of math problems are dilemma-driven; what will be seen as problematic in ongoing activity will emerge in and from that activity. In the supermarket one is doing grocery shopping (which might involve the occasional calculation) – not 'doing mathematics in a supermarket setting'. This distinction will appear again in discussing the 'everydaying' of math in word problems versus the possibility of 'mathematizing' experience (see Lave, 1988, Chapter 5, for a general discussion of the articulation of structuring resources in the production of activity of which 'everydaying' math and 'mathematizing' everyday experience are examples).

   In ongoing activity, actors' intentions are engaged in what they are doing. When that activity poses conflicts, difficulties, in short *dilemmas*, they *engage* in resolving them. The notion of 'dilemma' here is to be distinguished from that of 'problem' as in 'arithmetic word problem'. Word problems are a genre of puzzle. This does not guarantee that they will never be experienced as intention-engaging dilemmas. But whether they are (or not) depends on the nature of ongoing activity and where people's intentions are engaged.

3. Where the world is a good model of itself, whole-person enactment of quantitative relations in activity makes better sense than 'doing math'. (If I had six oranges and you wanted two of them, I would offer you a couple or you would reach over and take them. In the act of stirring the pancake batter I feel the proportions of milk and flour.) These whole-person engagements in assembling relations of quantity might be called 'problems of sense'.[5]

4. Math activity decreases over time within a given social practice. People move routine calculations into the social organization of artifacts and actions, as dieting cooks do in the kitchen (e.g. 4 swallows = 4 ounces), to minimize mathematical activity which gets in the way or makes life more difficult (de la Rocha, 1986). In the *Guardian* recently, an interviewer asked a British engineer why he designed a bridge the way he did – the question was occasioned by the collapse of the bridge. He said he chose the design because it was easy to make calculations for.

5. Most activity systems within which people organize their daily experience have these characteristics and do not offer resources for learning mathematics as a discipline.

   In sum, math learning in everyday practice is situated, dilemma-driven, and the processes for 'mucking about' with quantitative dilemmas are improvised in the process. Ongoing activity shapes what learners will perceive to be dilemmas for them. Problem solving involves the total resources of activity, persons, and the setting of the problem solver.[6] Such learning engagement does not seem to constrain learners, nor for that matter does it guarantee them either concrete or abstract understanding of their activity, its meaning, its relations with other aspects of their lives or its implications for themselves as knowing beings. Old dichotomies like the abstract/concrete, general/particular ones do not, therefore, supply restrictions on the concept of everyday activity. 'The everyday' is a broad category that may be usefully characterized as any activity that reoccurs frequently as part of common social practice. The notion from conventional views of learning that knowledge is to be transferred to *novel*, unrelated situations also seems inappropriate in this frame of reference, made irrelevant by the exceptional rarity of new situations and novel activities in everyday life. Even when they do occur it is unlikely, to say the least, that an individual encounters such an event alone (D'Andrade, 1981; Lave, 1988, Chapter 2). There do appear to be restrictions on what math is learnable when 'doing mathematics' is not the central, ongoing activity. We shall return to this point. But first, given that children attend school five days a week, forty weeks per year for twelve years, it seems reasonable to reconsider school math learning as a kind of everyday practice.

School math as situated activity

The first step in applying a situated theory of learning to the school math classroom is to recognize that this theory does not make the conventional distinction inscribed in the putative gulf between school and the everyday world. From this perspective math in school *is* situated practice: school is the site of children's everyday activity. If school activities differ from the activities children and adults engage in elsewhere, the view of schooling must be revised accordingly; it is a site of specialized everyday activity – not a privileged site where universal knowledge is transmitted. What kinds of specialized activity take place in schools? To answer the question requires an investigation of the everyday practice of children in classrooms. We can bring to the task ideas about learning derived from everyday math research, analysing math learning in a 3rd grade classroom in a bilingual school in Santa Ana, California, as situated learning in practice.

My collaborator, Michael Hass, and I looked closely at the process of development of the math practice of eleven bilingual Hispanic children in this class, following them through a three-week unit on multiplication and division facts. This group, the most accomplished of the three groups into which the room was divided, brought to these lessons almost as much knowledge as they finished with. They could solve, on average, half of the problems on a forty-problem test given before and after the unit (Hass, n.d.). There were differences in pre-test scores between children in the group. But the performances of the less successful converged over time with those of the more adept, so that all finished with roughly the same level of performance on the final test. In contrast with explanations which typically focus on the teacher's skill at transmitting knowledge, and individual children's motivation, we sought an explanation for these results in the everyday practice of the children (which included the teacher's participation in, and her effects on, learning activity as well). Hass discovered, by following the children's activities closely, that in the three-week period, the children were deeply engaged in math work during individual work time (about 75 per cent of class time) while they invested minimal attention and involvement in ongoing activity during the teacher's instruction sessions (about 25 per cent of the time). In these three weeks the children gave no evidence of having adopted *any* of the specific strategies demonstrated by the teacher during instruction periods.

The children sat around a table for workbook sessions. There was a great deal of interaction among the children at the table. The children began their group work sessions by making sure they agreed on what they were supposed to do. They co-ordinated the timing of their activity so as to work on approximately the same problems at the same time. They asked each other for help and helped each other without being asked. They collaborated and invented procedures. They discovered that the multiplication table printed in their book could be used to solve division problems, an opportunity for mathematical discussion of which the teacher was unaware. Each of the eleven turned in nearly errorless daily practice assignments. On the rare occasions when one of the students consulted the teacher for individual help, the information gleaned in the interaction quickly spread around the table. Essentially all problems were solved using counting and regrouping strategies. These were not presented in lessons and were not supposed to be used.

The children had unintended opportunities to invent problem-solving methods, combining shared strategies in the classroom with those they brought with them to the classroom (see Brenner, 1985, for evidence of syncretic math practice in Vai classrooms in Liberia). But they employed them so as to produce the appearance of having used the teacher's procedures, for which she took a correct answer as evidence. Interviews with the teacher suggested that she was unaware of the interactive math activity of the children; the children when interviewed individually reported that they consulted the teacher when they had difficulty solving problems.

In sum, the teacher, text and workbooks prescribed in detail how the children should act – what their everyday practice of math should be – while the children produced a different practice. When the teacher prescribed specific new procedures for carrying out multiplication and division operations, the children did not adopt the prescribed practice, nor did they take the risk of failing to get the correct answer. They engaged in familiar, improvised, co-operative processes of arithmetic problem solving instead. They developed their practice of learning math in the classroom cautiously, out of known quantities. They drew on a wide range of resources afforded them by the math workbook activity, other children and the setting (including, occasionally, the teacher). Their practice was aimed at success or at least survival in the classroom – a specialized ongoing activity – rather than being focused on deep understanding of mathematics. It is now possible to see how the distinction between 'real' math and 'other' math is generated in the classroom. By working out answers using their own techniques and then translating them into acceptable classroom form in their workbooks, the children generated this powerful categorical distinction for themselves. It is not necessary to search beyond the classroom for the generation of this distinction. The dilemmas which seemed to motivate this practice were ones about performance and blame avoidance. In this setting, where salient classroom activities were about control, order and performance, and where major dilemmas for children were ones of managing to succeed or survive, teacher-mandated math problem solving was not the dilemma that engaged their intentions.

Earlier I stated that I proposed to look carefully at what it means to have a math problem in school and in other settings. The 3rd grade math class study provides an opportunity to do so. Two cross-cutting dimensions of differentiation among problems may be distinguished. First, while math puzzles are sometimes truly engaging dilemmas, quite often the ones presented to children in school are only hypothetical problems. They are not dilemma-motivated and do not engage the intentions of problem solvers. Children engaged in mathematical dilemmas are engaged with opportunities to improvise new mathematical practices, that is to learn math. We may ask whether the school math class offered a rich set of math learning opportunities. If the Santa Ana 3rd grade is typical, the answer would be a pessimistic one. For it appears that the performance-oriented aspect of schooling (driven primarily by the elite preparation side of the schooling contradiction) so engages children's intentions that even legitimate problems are experienced in hypothetical terms.

The second dimension encountered in the everyday math research cross-cuts the first. It applies to both dilemma-motivated and hypothetical problems. There are problems of sense – ones that can be addressed by whole persons in activity. These often are not formed as canonical math problems, and are resolved through the transformation of quantitative relations in ongoing activity and with the setting. Problems of sense contrast with problems of scale. The latter occur in circumstances in which learners have no access to the object or activity they would like to understand except through some form of special representation, for which math is an important instrument in many cultures including our own (astronomical calculations would be a good example). Word problems more often than not turn problems of sense into problems of scale, thereby destroying any claim that they reflect everyday experience. This situation does not offer rich opportunities for learning mathematics.

Relations sketched in the preceding pages among broad cultural beliefs, institutions, practices and academic theories call into question the assumptions underlying the theory of learning at a distance from experience. These relations are complex and occur at several levels. In Western cultural practice schooling *is* separated from other activity systems. Alumni of schooling further distinguish in culturally appropriate ways between, on the one hand, what they have learned in school and how it should be valued and applied in their lives, and, on the other hand, the content, value and application of what they have learned elsewhere in their lives. These cultural assumptions and practices are compatible with the dichotomous theory of learning which permeates both the school as social institution and the everyday school experience of its alumni. But this compatibility is not to be taken as evidence supporting the theory of learning-at-a-distance. Rather, in taking a close look at learning-in-practice in schools and in other settings, empirical evidence contravenes the belief that people learn at a distance from daily practice in the school, while learning in practice elsewhere.

A theory of situated learning, by contrast, starts with the view that everyday activity is just that: that people learn in practice wherever that practice takes shape within activity systems; that classroom practice provides opportunities to learn whether intended or not; and that the improvised math practice that results may bear little relationship and certainly unintended relationships with the teaching curriculum. Math might be thought of as a kind of action whose meaning is not determined by the fact that it is *math*, but by its place in a sociocultural system of activity – be it schooling, the household, or an occupation. The social organization and interrelations of different forms of math practice have both intended and unintended consequences for what people learn about math and what they learn about the meaning of math, about themselves as math learners, and about themselves as powerful people – or not. In different historical settings math, like love or music, has different meanings, in different situated activities, with different co-participants. 'Situated', as the term is used here, does not imply that something is concrete and particular, or that it is not generalizable, or not imaginary. It implies that a given social practice is multiply interconnected with other aspects of ongoing social processes in activity systems at many levels of particularity and generality.

Implications of a situated theory of learning

If we adopt this changing view of relations between math in practice in classrooms and kitchens and street corners, what kinds of practical goals can be imagined for children who are still learning math in school?[7] Especially since there is now evidence that 'preparing children for everyday life' is not particularly compelling as a goal – nor is preparing them for a high-technology world (but that is another story). I want to transform the question a little, into the familiar terms posed for us by the dilemmas surrounding word problems as educational devices, as these in turn reflect the conventional theory of learning. Let us begin with the troublesome gulf between school and everyday experience which appears more as a barrier to learning than as a defence of especially powerful forms of learning. There are at least two ways in which some researchers have tried to build better bridges between schooling and the rest of the world. And there is a move afoot to concentrate on a different kind of bridge (one to the profession of mathematics). For my own part, I would like to suggest careful consideration of the kind of traffic to be encouraged back and forth. Each of these alternatives may be elaborated further.

First, it could be argued, given the efficacy of everyday math practice, that such practice provides the resources with which to replace or at least enhance school math. This in effect gives primary responsibility for the math curriculum to everyday life outside school. But it should be plain from the analysis of math learning as situated practice that we cannot simply send children out into the everyday world to learn math, no matter how effective and benign the processes of quantity transformation are in such settings. The learning opportunities provided by other ongoing activities do not create strong possibilities for increasing deep understanding of math.

Second, there has been recent work aimed at importing better versions of real-life scenarios into word problems (e.g. Schoenfeld, 1987, p. 37). Other notable attempts include the work of Bransford *et al.* (1988); they have devised messy problems that invite children to invent mathematical dilemmas within constraints given by the scenario. I have argued that there is a paradox involved in this strategy for bridging the experience gap (though this does not keep it from supporting creative learning opportunities – for example, Lampert's 1985 lessons around 'The voyage of the Mimi'). In the real world, serious problem solvers are intent upon inventing ways to reduce or eliminate the need for calculation and quantitative problem solving (see the Weight Watchers research, de la Rocha, 1986). This is likely to conflict with the expectations embedded in elaborated word-problem scenarios. There is another paradox as well: math class *is* real, everyday practice, and so (to take an example offered by Lesh, personal communication) is lawn-mowing, but organizing a lawn-mowing business in math class is neither real lawn-mowing practice nor real school practice. However, realism may not be the key to bridge building. Thus, an imaginary lawn-mowing business may work well as an instrument for engaging children in math problem solving if it offers occasions for them to engage their intentions in mathematical dilemmas. The crucial question is whether the problem-solving situations are real dilemmas or hypothetical puzzles. Authentic dilemmas that furnish opportunities to improvise new practice may be either imaginary or real.

Third, let us shift the focus from the relevance of particular *problems* to learner's everyday lives, to the relevance and form of *mathematical activity* claimed to be appropriate in situations in which word-problem-like problems might arise. It is possible to distinguish between two ways of conceiving of relations between math and daily life, whether in the construction of word problems in math lessons or in quantitative relations in the supermarket. The word-problem writer might well think to herself: 'What are the ways that shopping in the supermarket affords us opportunities for raising issues about various topics in mathematics?' With the answer in hand, she could begin to do something that might be called 'everydaying math' (e.g. if the shopper plans to buy five pounds of potatoes for five dinner guests, and then meets a friend and invites that friend to dinner, how many . . .) The alternative is to mathematize everyday experience – here is an example from a colleague who lay awake one night listening to rain drip down the drain pipe running from the roof to the driveway outside her bedroom, attention riveted by the periodic sound, unable to sleep. She began to count the number of raindrops in ten-second periods of time, watching the clock by her bed. Then, still unable to sleep – but hopeful – began to try to figure out by what percentage the drip rate was slowing down over time. 'I figure I understand what a second derivative of the rise in water level is now,' she said, 'after my husband told me that was what I was doing.' Big messy word problems, in which the learner has a good deal of leeway to decide just what the problem is, give learners opportunities for 'mathematizing' experience in ways that 'everydaying' math lessons cannot.

This suggests that perhaps learning practices that are effective in various settings (including even subterranean practices in school) might usefully be allowed to surface in legitimate classroom practice. Reciprocal teaching and other forms of co-operative learning may well have this effect, given their improvisational and dilemma-driven character. These do seem to be characteristics of successful math practice everywhere – outside school and in the 3rd grade classroom whose practice we observed closely. Co-operative learning also reduces performance dilemmas and enhances ongoing engagement of attention and intentions in math argumentation and math dilemma resolution.

Fourth, it is possible to take the math practice of professional mathematicians as a model for children's math practice in school. The argument has appeared in recent math learning literature: mathematicians' practice is an everyday practice. A mathematician works for days or months or years to develop a proof, trying out a variety of arguments and strategies and searching for patterns of findings that lead to deeper understanding of mathematical structure. This differs from math teachers' practice, for mathematicians are not primarily engaged in retrieving or passing on received wisdom. This suggests a possible long-term goal for math education: engaging children in early phases of an apprenticeship to mathematical masters, so that they learn how to *do* what mathematicians do, or at least, experience a way in to how they do it – that is, the cognitive apprenticeship research, and especially Schoenfeld's concept of mathematical culture in the classroom (Lampert, 1985; Schoenfeld, 1987; Collins, Brown and Newman, 1990). This approach changes the content and raises the level of expectations about what math all children should learn. But it has its problems. Raising expectations about what all children should learn does not resolve the tension between the goals of general socialization and elite selection (see note 7 below). What is missing is other, rather than professional, goals – and they are needed for both children and teachers.

Situated-learning theory speaks on this issue. It recommends a reconception of the process by which experiences in and out of school are brought into relation with each other. This generates a different model of appropriate 'traffic' across the bridges between school and the other sides of life. It conceives the process of learning as one in which math culture is collectively generated in the classroom in such a way that it changes relations for school alumni between everyday experience and their mathematical practice. Perhaps school alumni are the right bridge builders to construct relations (for themselves) between school math culture and the rest of their lives. It is not clear just how much immersion in a mathematical culture is required, but at the end of this mathematical experience, its graduates should be able to infuse mathematical meaning into their everyday experience when they own the problem, and engage their intentions in mathematizing it. Here is an example of what that might look like, from another colleague, who likes to think about math:[8] 'I see a California lilac bush, and wonder if the flowers are arranged in a Fibonacci sequence around the perimeter ... I wonder what the power spectrum of a blackbird song is like? Does it have two big formants? It certainly sounds that way to my ear!'

Math practice in the classroom could be seen as a special cultural activity of its own (rather than as a resource for replacing some other inferior practice), and becoming a participant in that culture as a possible goal for classroom math practice (Schoenfeld, 1987). If successfully drawn by math learners, connections with everyday life would be a result of becoming part of that mathematical culture, as children find themselves with a 'mathematizing' way of looking at their experience with space, time, quantity, pattern, process, and probable and improbable events. The kinds of connections between math and life that math-learning researchers desire might better be thought of as the end product of effective math learning rather than as initial conditions for learning math.

I have suggested two new relationships implied by a theory of situated learning: the first involves rethinking the mathematization of experience – something that might also be termed the situating of math in ongoing activity – as a valuable end product of math education. This stands in contrast with the view that math must be 'everydayed' as an initial condition for math learning. A second shift, given new theoretical glasses for looking at classroom math practice, is a move away from the relation that looms so important because of its theoretical and institutional history – that between the 'everyday', or 'concrete', and the 'theoretical', scholastic abstraction of school math – towards a different distinction: that between things (real and imaginary) that do and do not engage learners' intentions and attention, and give meaning to the activity they are engaged in and definition to 'what's going on here, what am I doing now?' The real trick may not be one of finding a correspondence between everyday problems and school problems, but making word problems truly problematic for children in school – that is, part of a practice for which the children are practitioners. Given lively imaginations, it does not matter whether the problems conform to life experience, but it is important that they engage the imagination, that they become really problematic.

Social forces at several levels converge to make children's performance in the classroom problematic, while at the same time working against the likelihood that mathematics will engage the children's intentions with a similar consistent intensity (Lave, 1990a; Lave, 1990b; Lave *et al.*, 1988). Suppose that through the development of a mathematical culture in the classroom, the use of reciprocal teaching and apprenticeship learning, it would be possible to make math learning available as the everyday, ongoing activity in math classrooms. This would not put an end to the contradictions that shape school culture. Instead we should expect the contradiction between learning and evaluation now located in the learner as performer in the classroom to shift to the teacher's position in the system of schooling. Issues of authority and improvisation in the classroom, contradictions of control (e.g. Apple, 1979; McNeil, 1986) make it unlikely that teachers can sustain for long the kind of improvised practice that makes it possible for math problems to be the dilemmas that motivate children to work and play with math.

All of this suggests two points for further discussion. One is research on how math teachers might more easily employ co-operative learning strategies in such a way that their teaching links strong goals for learners with an improvisational approach for reaching them. In the course of exploring this approach new makes and styles of math problems are emerging. They may continue to look like word problems, but they are likely to mean something as different from current word problems as current word problems are different from the merchants' problems of the 1500s. The other point is to take as central to research on math learning the dilemmas of teachers within those activity systems known as schools, as they attempt to sustain (for themselves and their students) everyday life in school as a curriculum for learning mathematics as a practice.

Conclusions

A word problem is not just a word problem: it is a form of action whose significance is fashioned by word-problem solvers. It enters into their everyday activity in school in ways that lead them to draw on their everyday math experience, to treat word-problem solving activity as 'real math', to see themselves as inadequate partly because they believe that they should apply it in a particular form and they know they do not use it that way in other everyday circumstances. Mathematics becomes tied up in meanings associated with received wisdom and it has no intuitive connections with everyday experience. The supposedly everyday experiences of this genre are far from mundane, and problems are designed to provide occasions for practice at *separating* math from experience, rather than mathematizing it. That is, the activity of solving word problems and the contents of word problems in school are not the same as 'the same' activity or contents embedded in other systems of activity in other parts of life; they are integrally generative of the practice and the meaning of word-problem solving.

A claim was made at the beginning of the paper that word problems mean something different now than in 1478, and I have attempted to explain the grounds and reasons for this claim. The meaning of activity, its actions (dilemma-engagements) and operations (of which math word problems are an example), and its instruments, objects of consumption, subjects, products and productive processes, are produced and reproduced (and they change) within the activity system of which they are a part. Thus, the meaning of word problems does not lie in their mathematical properties but in their role in the activity system of schooling, or dieting, or becoming a merchant in Venice in the 1500s. Different intentions, differently engaged, will impel action and give meaning to it in varied ways. This is a major principle of a theory of situated activity (including situated learning).

Notes

1. To understand the structuring of knowledge, activity and meaning in the classroom requires a sociological analysis of school and of knowledge. In the present context I can only illustrate this view in the most minimal of forms.
2. When educators talk about the general goals of schooling it is unusual to hear a plea for everyday expertise that is not coupled with references to the need to prepare children for technical occupations as well. This is just another version of the contradiction inherent in schooling between socialization and unequal preparation. Pronouncements which juxtapose the two sides of the contradiction without acknowledging the conflict between them can only be platitudes, for they fail to address the fact that some particular *resolution* to the conflicts thus engendered must emerge in every concrete instance.

3. But the double character of the theory that values learning at a distance while devaluing learning in experience should serve as a warning that any theory that simply reverses the values associated with schooling and so-called embedded learning situations (e.g. Dreyfus and Dreyfus, 1986) should also have a double character and attendant drawbacks.

4. There is other evidence about word problems as a genre: Liberian tailors can do 'pure numerical' problems and 'concrete' button array problems, but if they have not been to school, they have difficulty with word problems. Further, tailors who *have* been to school can do word problems better than either numerical or button problems. Were there any developmental progression from 'concrete' to 'abstract' problem-solving, the unschooled tailors should be better at word problems than at numerical problems, and schooled tailors better at button problems than word problems. (See Lave, in preparation.)

5. There are also problems of scale, ones the problem solver cannot engage with in embodied activity (of which a bit more later). This distinction between problems of sense and scale is Olivia de la Rocha's (1986).

6. School as a specialized system of activity is organized to *prevent* broadly inclusive aids to problem solving. Teachers and texts own problems, there are rules to prevent interaction among problem solvers, and so on. Indeed, the methods of everyday quantitative transformations are officially *inappropriate* in classrooms. Even so, children in school use their knowledge of the stylized characteristics of the genre itself, and whatever other resources are available (e.g. patterns of problems or answers, patterned formulae by which the teacher generated the problems, their knowledge of what a correct answer ought to look like).

7. There are correspondences between strategies for developing math curricula and different resolutions to the basic contradiction that shapes schooling as a social institution. Goals emerge from a variety of weighted articulations between principles of universal socialization and elite preparation. Where socialization is ranked highly among educational goals, it is possible to imagine schools sending children out to learn math in the everyday world, or taking the view that since everyday math is effective and versatile, schools might become institutions that offer supplementary means for augmenting or enhancing everyday practice. Alternatively, there is the standard view, which gives greater weight to elite preparation than socialization. In this case street math may be presumed not to exist, or not to be worthwhile, and emphasis would be on replacing it with 'real' math. This position has been under critical examination throughout the paper. Third, it could be argued that schools should concentrate on producing a small number of highly trained professional mathematicians. This is presumably further in the direction of elite preparation than current thinking about public schooling. (But if we look at what schools actually *do*, this is what they are most effective at, as purveyors of math.) Fourth, it could be argued that everyone should be socialized into high levels of mathematical competence, but here it must be said that this begs the contradiction: schools are organized to take in *everyone* but to put out *ranked and graded alumni*, no matter what the general level of competence. How elite or egalitarian the result is is not determined by this general level. Further, the forms of learning that seem most effective at present in distributing knowledge widely among children are ones that mitigate against individualistic testing and ranking policies. The goal of socializing children to a high level of math knowledge

is dubious because it fails to specify *what* high levels of mathematical competence are for (everyday living? High-technology occupations?).

8. But the process of arriving at this cultural viewpoint for relating math and life is full of ironies in the current world. It appears that word problems are the ultimate test of understanding when the learner cannot do much math, and this genre becomes utterly irrelevant for learners in advanced math courses. Here is a description of the process by a computer scientist with a college degree in math: 'Through grade school, then algebra and geometry – so long as you keep having word problems – word problems are the hardest thing to do. You don't really understand math until you can do them. You know that if you have really appropriated the math, word problems (the real test of your understanding) should be doable. If you can't do them, it proves that you've just been doing math by "plug and chug". And of course, no one can do the word problems. In college math you never see a word problem again. Word problems look like a real joke. Either there, or maybe when you begin to tutor and teach math, is when you realize this. So while you *cannot* do the math, the [word problems] look crucially important, and when you get past them they seem pointless. The only way to succeed at word problems is to see through them. A corollary is that people drop out of math *because* they buy in.'

References

Apple, M. (1979), *Ideology and Curriculum* (London: Routledge & Kegan Paul).

Bransford, J., Hasselbring, T., Barron B., Kulewicz, S., Littlefield, J. and Goin, L. (1988), 'Uses of macro-contexts to facilitate mathematical thinking', in R.I. Charles and E.A. Silver (eds), *Research Agenda for Mathematics Education: Teaching and assessment of mathematical problem solving* (Hillsdale, NJ: Erlbaum).

Brenner, M. (n.d.), 'Numeracy and the child's world', unpublished manuscript, Kamehameha Center for Development of Early Education, Honolulu, Hawaii.

Brenner, M. (1985), 'Arithmetic and classroom interaction as cultural practices among the Vai of Liberia', unpublished doctoral dissertation. University of California, Irvine.

Carraher, T., Carraher, D. and Schliemann, A. (1982), 'Mathematics in the streets and schools', unpublished manuscript, Universidade Federal de Pernambuco, Recife.

Carraher, T., Carraher, D. and Schliemann, A. (1983), 'Na vida, dez na escola, zero: os contextos culturais da educacão, matematica', *Cadernos de Pesquisa*, **42**, pp. 79–86.

Carraher, T. and Schliemann, A. (1982), 'Computation routines prescribed by schools: help or hindrance', paper presented at NATO conference on the acquisition of symbolic skills, Keele, England.

Cohn, C. (1987), 'Sex and death in the rational world of defense intellectuals', *Signs: Journal of Women in Culture and Society*, **12** (4), pp. 687–718.

Collins, A., Brown, J.S. and Newman, S. (1990), 'Cognitive apprenticeship: teaching students the crafts of reading, writing, and mathematics', in L.B. Resnick (ed.), *Knowing, Learning and Instruction: Essays in honour of Robert Glazer* (Hillsdale, NJ: Erlbaum).

D'Andrade, R.G. (1981), 'The cultural part of cognition', *Cognitive Science*, **5**, pp. 179–95.

de la Rocha, O. (1986), 'Problems of sense and problems of scale: an ethnographic study of arithmetic in everyday life', unpublished doctoral dissertation, University of California, Irvine.

Dreyfus, H. and Dreyfus, S. (1986), *Mind over Machine: The power of human intuition and expertise in the era of the computer* (New York: The Free Press).

Geras, N. (1972), 'Althusser's Marxism: an account and assessment', *New Left Review*, **71**, pp. 57–86.

Hass, M. (n.d.), 'Cognition-in-context: the social nature of the transformation of mathematical knowledge in a third grade classroom', Social Relations Graduate Program, University of California, Irvine.

Hutchins, E. (1992), 'Learning to navigate', in S. Chaiklin and J. Lave (eds), *Understanding Practice* (New York: Cambridge University Press).

Lampert, M. (1985), 'Mathematics learning in context: the voyage of the Mimi', *The Journal of Mathematical Behavior*, **4**, pp. 157–67.

Lave, J. (1988), *Cognition in Practice: Mind, mathematics, and culture in everyday life* (Cambridge: Cambridge University Press).

Lave, J. (1990a), 'The culture of acquisition and the practice of understanding', in J. Stigler, G. Herdt and R. Shweder (eds), *Cultural Psychology: The Chicago symposia* (Cambridge: Cambridge University Press).

Lave, J. (1990b), 'Views of the classroom: implications for math and science learning research', in M. Gardner, J. Greeno, F. Reif and A. Schoenfeld (eds), *Toward a Scientific Practice of Science Education* (Hillsdale, NJ: Erlbaum).

Lave, J. (in preparation), *Tailored Learning: Apprenticeship and everyday practice among crafsmen in West Africa*.

Lave, J., Smith, S. and Butler, M. (1988), 'Problem solving as an everyday practice', in R.I. Charles and E.A. Silver (eds), *Research Agenda for Mathematics Education: Teaching and assessment of mathematical problem solving* (Hillsdale, NJ: Erlbaum), NCTM paper.

McNeil, L. (1986), *Contradictions of Control: School structure and school knowledge* (New York: Routledge & Kegan Paul).

Murtaugh, M. (1985), 'A hierarchical decision process model of American grocery shopping', unpublished doctoral dissertation, University of California, Irvine.

Resnick, L. (1986), 'Constructing knowledge in school', in L.S. Liben and D.H. Feldman (eds), *Development and Learning: Conflict or congruence* (Hillsdale, NJ: Erlbaum).

Saljo, R. and Wyndhamn, J. (1992), 'Solving everyday problems in the formal setting: an empirical study of the school as context for thought', in S. Chaiklin and J. Lave (eds), *Understanding Practice* (New York: Cambridge University Press).

Schoenfeld, A. (1987), 'When good teaching leads to bad results: the disasters of "well taught" mathematics courses' *Educational Psychologist*.

Scribner, S. (ed.) (1984), *Cognitive Studies of Work*, special issue of the quarterly newsletter of the Laboratory of Comparative Human Cognition, **6** (1 & 2).

Scribner, S. and Fahrmeier, E. (1982), 'Practical and theoretical arithmetic: some preliminary findings', Industrial Literacy Project, Working Paper no. 3, Graduate Center, CUNY.

Swetz, F. (1987), *Capitalism and Arithmetic: The new math of the 15th century* (La Salle, IL.: Open Court Press).

Chapter 6

Sociocultural processes of creative planning in children's playcrafting

Jacquelyn Baker-Sennett, Eugene Matusov, Barbara Rogoff, *University of Utah*[1]

LESLIE: [*complaining about making too many changes in the play*] If we make up the whole thing over again it will be too hard.

CAROL: No it won't.

ROBIN: No it won't.

LESLIE: We can't do it all right now.

ROBIN: Yes we can. We almost already have. When we think of the parts, we think of the play!

KIM: Yeah!

CAROL: Yeah!

KIM: We just think of who the people are and . . .

ROBIN: . . . and what they're going to do . . . And then we can organize it.

(Snow White, Session 3)

This chapter explores the sociocultural processes of creative planning through an examination of the process of children's collaborative creation of a play. We argue that creative planning processes are grounded in practical considerations of sociocultural activity, in a wedding of imagination and pragmatics. Original, workable ideas evolve from a process that is the synthesis of spontaneous improvisation and organized, directed activity, as individuals participate with others in sociocultural activities. We examine how a collaborative interactional system develops in the process of planning, and how this social organization is essential to the planning process, as a group of young children plan a play. We follow the germs of the children's ideas as they are offered, critiqued and elaborated by each other, and consider the

93

role of classroom structure, teacher support, and fairy-tale scripts as cultural aspects of the event.

Our purpose is to develop the argument that creative planning involves flexible use of circumstances in the pursuit of goals. We work from a contextual perspective in which individual cognitive and social activity is seen as constituting and constituted by sociocultural processes. That is, the development of original and workable ideas can better be understood when we consider the social, cultural and institutional contexts in which creative planning takes place. We make the case that creative planning involves an active, dynamic social process that involves both advance planning and on-line improvisation. In order to follow the creative planning process we must trace the development of the social and cultural conditions in which creative planning occurs.

Creating as a social cognitive activity

Traditionally, researchers have considered both planning and creating as *individual* endeavours. This assumption can be attributed, in part, to the methodologies that have been employed. Researchers have typically examined children's ability to arrive at problem solutions under contrived circumstances, working on a task alone, under the direction of an adult experimenter in controlled conditions. But firm experimental control and focus on solitary thinking is ill-suited for an investigation of children's flexible and spontaneous problem solving. In everyday activities taking place outside of the laboratory context, creative planning is often a flexible, collaborative venture (Vygotsky, 1978; John-Steiner, 1985; Csikszentmihalyi, 1988; Rogoff, 1990).

Planning typically occurs in elaborate sociocultural systems that may be invisible under isolated laboratory conditions. Although recent research suggests that collaborative processes may facilitate planning and creating (Bouchard, 1971; Weisberg, 1986; Azmitia, 1988; Radziszewska and Rogoff, 1988, 1991), there is limited information on how children plan under their own direction, outside the laboratory context (although Tudge and Rogoff [in preparation] are studying collaborative spatial planning in video games). Likewise, there is little work that focuses on how personal, interpersonal and cultural processes together contribute to the development of creative plans (but see John-Steiner, 1985, for a sociocultural account of creativity in renowned thinkers and artists; and Rogoff, Lacasa, Baker-Sennett and Goldsmith [in preparation] for a study of how the planning of Girl Scout cookie sales and delivery involves sociocultural, interpersonal and individual processes). The present study focuses on how the interpersonal and cultural processes of an activity constitute and are constituted by planning processes when children engage in a collaborative long-term project with a fluid product.

Our use of the word 'social' relates to the sociocultural contexts in which cognitive processes such as creative planning are embedded and to the process of the emergence of relations between children that are essential to group creative planning. When planning a play, children need to develop the play itself and to develop a means of co-ordinating with each other to design the play. Their planning of the play is inherently embedded in their planning of how they as a group are going to plan the play; their interpersonal processes are organized towards the goal (among other goals) of producing an entertaining play. This is consistent with Gearhart's findings (1979) that 3 year olds planning pretend shopping trips learned to adjust their planning process to take each other's plans into account, rather than simply expecting other children to serve as pliable tools for the execution of their own plans.

A sociocultural approach focuses us on the *process* (rather than the products) of creative planning and brings to attention the importance of flexibility in creative planning. Planning is inherently a creative process that involves foresight as well as improvisation in the face of changing circumstances and anticipation to be able to take advantage of unpredictable events. Although research on skilled planning emphasizes the development of planning in advance (Brown and DeLoache, 1978; Wellman, Fabricius and Sophian, 1985), successful planning involves flexibly and opportunistically altering plans in process (Pea and Hawkins, 1987; Gardner and Rogoff, 1990). Since we cannot anticipate all aspects of our planning endeavours, it is often both advantageous and efficient to plan opportunistically, developing and adjusting plans during the course of action (Hayes-Roth, 1985; Rogoff, Gauvain and Gardner, 1987). The necessity of flexibility in planning is made much more apparent when research examines the sociocultural context of planning, in which co-ordination with others, cultural tools, institutional constraints and opportunities, and unforeseen events are the objects of study rather than being seen as 'noise' to be controlled, as has been the case in most research on planning to date.

An investigation of children's playcrafting

Our discussion is based on videotaped observations of children's collaboration in developing a play. The group involves six 7- to 9-year-old girls who planned and performed their own take-off on a fairy-tale in their 2nd/3rd grade classroom during ten planning sessions extending over one month.

This study departs from most previous studies in following the creative planning process from start to finish, in studying group collaborative processes rather than individual or dyadic problem solving, and in examining problem solving in an open-ended project rather than a problem that involves a pre-existing script or algorithm for solution. Our goal was to examine the playcrafting process in as natural a situation as possible, to tape the playcrafting process as it unfolds in a setting that was not of our design.

Playcrafting sessions, rather than individual subjects, are our unit of analysis. We followed the group's ideas as they developed across time, with individual contributions woven together. We are not attempting to separate out individual contributions to examine the characteristics of individuals as independent units, although we do, of course, attend to how each child's contributions are woven together in the whole effort. Our focus on the development of the event is consistent with a contextual event approach (Rogoff, 1982; Rogoff and Gauvain, 1986) and with the method of activity theory (Leont'ev, 1981).

Our analysis concentrates on one play, *Snow White*, that was produced as part of the writing curriculum in a 2nd/3rd grade classroom in an 'open' non-traditional school where creative activities such as playcrafting are common and children are routinely expected to collaborate on classroom projects and to organize their own activities. Interpersonal problem solving and management of one's own learning activities are an explicit part of the curriculum. The classroom teacher serves as a resource and guide in a 'community of learners'. Thus, the cultural context of the children in this classroom is one that includes sustained attention and creativity in child-managed collaborative projects, with comfortable use of adult assistance and guidance but not dependence on adult management.

Children were assigned by their teacher to plan and perform their own versions of a fairy-tale. (The class chose four tales to make into plays; *Snow White* was one of two in which the group attempted to create a new version of the play rather than just to enact a traditional version.) Over the course of one month each group planned and practised its play with intermittent assistance from the classroom teacher and a student teacher, and then performed its play for classmates and adult visitors.

The teacher's role in structuring the task

Preparing the planning and writing task

Before initiating the project the teacher conducted library research on fairy-tales, set up a fairy-tale reading centre in a corner of the classroom, showed students a video presentation of *Rumplestiltskin*, and 'piggy-backed' this group project with an individual fairy-tale writing assignment. The teacher explained: 'I see this as a learning experience that you will learn all sorts of skills from. You will be doing some reading and some writing. You will do planning and organizing. These are all skills that we are trying to learn.'

The teacher, in conjunction with the students, structured the task by listing common elements of fairy-tales (e.g. begins 'Once upon a time', has a happy ending). This list was later copied from the blackboard to a posterboard and remained visible to the students throughout the month. The teacher also provided the groups with an important organizational tool for their planning of the plays: a coloured sheet of paper on which each group was to list the participants, the play's title, the characters, the setting and main events (including problem and solution).

Structuring the collaborative process

The teacher viewed this project not only as a cognitive task (it was clearly part of the reading and writing curriculum for teacher, students and parents alike), but also as a challenging social task. She attempted to maximize student success on the interpersonal problem-solving processes as well as the planning of the plays themselves.

Groups were formed with attention to the academic and interpersonal strengths of the individual children. After the teacher helped the students generate a list of fairy-tales and select four to produce, she asked students to select their first and second choices. During recess the teacher (assisted by a parent volunteer) grouped students according to their preferences and according to her perception of individual cognitive and social strengths and weaknesses:

> PARENT: I think that would balance the group.
> TEACHER: Uh huh. We haven't put anybody in here with real strong writing skills.
> PARENT: Sarah's pretty good, isn't she?
> TEACHER: Mmmm, she's OK, but she won't take a leadership role. Um, who . . . I'm kind of wondering is if we got Jason in there, he could be a leader.

When the students returned from recess the teacher told them which group they were in, and emphasized that their task would be socially as well as cognitively challenging. She offered suggestions for successfully working as a group and for managing inevitable social struggles:

> TEACHER: You'll vote as a group and you'll say, 'OK, do we want to do it the old way or the modern way?' and everybody will have to discuss it and say the pros and the cons. When having a little group there are certain things that make it positive and certain things that make it hard. One guy has an idea and says, 'MODERN! MODERN! I want it modern.' Does that help the group?
> KIDS [*in unison*]: No!
> TEACHER: Or if some kids just sit there and don't say anything, does that help the group?
> KIDS [*in unison*]: No!
> TEACHER: OK, so you have to figure out a way to make the group work. What if I

said, 'I have seen groups that have too many chiefs and no indians?' What do I
mean? Leslie . . .

LESLIE: That means that too many people are taking over the group.
TEACHER: Everybody want to be the boss and nobody listens. So that might be a
problem that you might have to solve with your group. Because you always need
some workers and some listeners. Part of this will be figuring out how to make
your group work . . . There will be some adults in the room to help but a lot of
the time it will just be up to you to say 'wait a minute, we need to compromise'
or 'we need to vote on it', rather than just one guy taking over.

Thus, by establishing groups that she believed would be cognitively and
socially balanced and by providing students with a number of organizational
strategies for planning and managing social relations, the teacher prepared
the groups to embark on their project.

Once the groups began their projects, the teacher occasionally served as
mediator of disputes, stepping in to ask the children how they could decide
issues and encouraging their reflection on the *process* of solving interpersonal
problems. At a key point in the first session of *Snow White*, she suggested that
departing from the traditional tale (an idea she had earlier suggested in
encouraging creative adaptations of the tales) might help the girls escape
from their difficulties, which had to do with differences in recall of the
traditional tale. The idea of creating an adaptation brought the girls together
and formed the basis of the rest of their sessions.

From across the room the teacher observed the group to make sure that all
was going well, and during some later sessions she observed and made
practical suggestions. She was occasionally asked for information (on spelling
and on whether minor changes are allowed in the assignment). Her role was
to monitor and support the girls' efforts; the decisions on how to plan and
develop the play belonged to the group. During a number of later sessions
the student teacher attempted to organize the group, but his efforts were
generally rejected, as the group was already organized in a way that he did
not seem to detect, and his style was one of intervention rather than of
observation and support. (The classroom teacher informed us that the
student teacher's overzealous attempts to manage are a typical strategy used
by student teachers, who feel responsible to do something, but are not yet
skilled in observing and subtly assisting a group in solving its own problems.)

Method for examining the course of events

To examine how the girls' organization and ideas evolved over the course of
the project, we first described the girls' discourse and actions throughout
each of the sessions (ten records of twenty to eighty single-spaced pages
each). Each of the authors checked and corrected the transcripts against
video and audiotaped records of the sessions, usually clarifying some points

but seldom disagreeing on overall interpretation of the events. Then with the use of the transcripts and videotapes, we abstracted a summary of the creative planning activities (a forty-five-page document). This summary version of the ten sessions was further abstracted to produce a chart of the events as they occurred over the ten sessions. Figure 6.1 overleaf presents the chart of the creative planning activities of the group during ten planning sessions, concentrating on transitions in the group's focus of planning. The classification system of Figure 6.1 emerged from our successive abstractions of the planning process over the ten sessions, as well as from concepts of planning derived from the literature and previous research on planning. It represents the transitions of the group from abstract levels of planning, to determining the events of the play, to detailed decisions regarding specifics of the production and practice of the actions that have been decided:

Level 1. **How to plan planning** the play and establish rules for handling disputes,

Level 2. **How to plan** the play, co-ordinate pieces, resolve competing ideas, and keep on track in planning,

Level 3. **Deciding on the main themes and events** and ensuring coherence of the events and their motivation,

Level 4. **Deciding on specifics** such as props, costumes, dialogue and action, as well as who will play what character,

Level 5. **Acting on** what has already been decided, with only local improvisation and adjustment.

The events abstracted by these five levels account for almost 100 per cent of the ten sessions in which the children prepared their play, with the exception of one brief segment noted below. In the following sections, we describe the group's use of these levels of planning as they develop the play.

The course of planning

During the ten planning sessions, activities proceeded for the most part from the general to the specific (Levels 1 and 2 to Level 5, in Figure 6.1). On the first day the group spent most of their time developing a general story framework (Levels 2 and 3), trying to arrive at consensus based on individual memories of the traditional version of *Snow White*. However, each girl had seen either one or two different versions of the tale (one produced by Disney and the other by Fairy Tale Theater). Thus, they could not arrive at a consensus by referring to *the* traditional version of the fairy-tale. Since the two versions are quite different, the task was complicated and the girls could not decide which production to adopt. With assistance from the teacher in

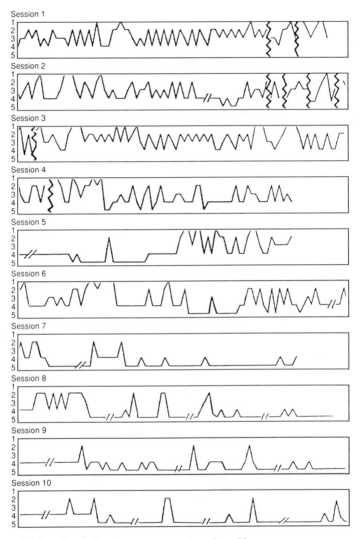

Figure 6.1 Levels of planning across sessions 1 to 10.

Key

Level 1. How to plan planning the play/establish rules for handling disputes
Level 2. How to plan the play/co-ordinate pieces/resolve different ideas/keep on track
Level 3. Deciding main themes and events/coherence and motivation of the events
Level 4. Deciding props, costumes, dialogue and action/who plays what
Level 5. Acting what has already been decided, with local improvisation and adjustment

Each point indicates a topic change, either within a level or across levels.

 indicates a breakdown in group planning; a dead end with high feelings

indicates that the level continued longer than shown

attempting to resolve disputes regarding the 'real' story, at the end of the first session the girls decided to modify the traditional story model and collaboratively to develop 'twists' on the traditional story (Levels 1, 2 and 3).

During the second and third sessions, there was still a great deal of planning how to plan (Levels 1 and 2), with greater emphasis on deciding the main theme and events of the play (Level 3). In the second planning session the girls moved from the creation of a general story model to the development of a script of lines and actions (Levels 3 and 4). In the third session there was still great attention to how the play should be planned, deciding how to divide and distribute roles, and attempting to make these decisions (Levels 1 and 2).

A shift in activities took place about the fourth session, as can be seen in Figure 6.1. During the first three sessions the groups planned in advance, 'out of action', sitting around a table and discussing many ideas that would later be incorporated into their play. During the fourth session, the girls began to practise what they had planned. While practising, they improvised, planned 'in character', and practised planned events. The shift was entirely managed by the children, as were almost all the moves between levels of planning in the first sessions (the major exception being the teachers' intervention in suggesting a modification of the tale at the end of the first session).

Essential to the first four sessions was building a *social foundation* to allow the girls both to complete the cognitive aspects of their task and to work effectively as a group. Once this foundation was built, the group was able to communicate and plan 'in action' during the course of the remaining sessions, which they treated as practice sessions. From the fourth session, the girls spent a great deal of time practising – a phase that they marked by labelling it as such, as well as by changing the physical setting from working around a table to rehearsing in the hallway outside the classroom. From sessions four through ten the group spent incrementally more time rehearsing, planning in character and improvising, and less time planning out of action (see Figure 6.1).

Advance planning and planning during action

The girls engaged in flexible, opportunistic planning (Hayes-Roth and Hayes-Roth, 1979; Rogoff, Gauvain and Gardner, 1987), beginning with a greater balance of advance planning (especially Levels 1, 2 and 3) during the first four playcrafting sessions and then focusing to a greater extent on planning during action (especially Levels 3, 4 and 5). During the course of action old plans were modified, new plans developed and improvisations emerged. Planning during action is not an appendage or consequence of advance planning, but rather an integral aspect of opportunistic planning.

Advance planning involved the organization of future activity through building action sequences, co-ordinating participants, and considering material resources either before the activity started or during a pause. During the first four playcrafting sessions when the *Snow White* team planned the story theme and main events, and checked the coherence of the events and their motivation, they worked out of character and usually without action. This advance planning was necessary for the group to establish a consensus regarding the theme and events of the play as well as to develop a group working relationship that was necessary for the planning process. Although the girls often plunged into planning at a detailed level during the first four days, one or another of them soon brought the group back to the more abstract levels of planning the theme, events and motivation of the play as a whole, without which the concrete levels of planning could not be co-ordinated.

The girls each took leadership roles in managing the return of the group to advance planning at different times. On the first day, one girl repeatedly moved the group back to planning main events when the group spent too long planning props or other specifics; however, when she mentioned that she forgot to list the dwarves under 'characters', another girl took the responsibility for maintaining the more abstract planning level, as she suggested staying at a general level: 'Just say dwarves; don't give the names.' On the second day, a third girl showed a consistent pattern as peacemaker and organizer, by turning the conversation away from disputed topics to fun or simple topics, and then reorganizing at a higher level of planning soon after. Each of the other girls also provided leadership to the group in moving the work along at a general planning level, with comments on not bothering with costumes or props *yet* and on not taking too long improvising a particular scene (e.g. 'We can figure that out later'; 'This is good enough for now'; 'Pretend the scene's over, and then . . .').

Much of what occurred during the ten playcrafting sessions involved planning during action. Some of this improvisational planning was of necessity, when the group needed to cope with their plans being detailed by absences of group members, with later lack of agreement or of understanding by group members who had been absent, and with running out of time at the end of a session before a process came to conclusion. While these 'inconveniences' are carefully controlled in most laboratory planning sessions, during everyday endeavours they are the occurrences that make the creative planning process a challenge and provide opportunities for breaking to new patterns. The skill, for many, is being able to turn unplanned events into opportunities. Take, for example, Kurt Vonnegut's description of his reliance on improvisation during the writing process:

> [Writing is] like make a movie: All sorts of accidental things will happen after you've set up the cameras. So you get lucky. Something will happen at the edge of the set and perhaps you start to go with that; you get some footage of that. You come into it accidentally. You set the story in motion, and as you're watching this

thing begin all these opportunities will show up. (Vonnegut in Winokur, 1990, p. 252)

Creativity in planning
The 'trick' for both experienced writers and novice playcrafters is to be able flexibly to anticipate change and adapt to unexpected occurrences throughout the course of the planning process. Plans often do not go as anticipated, and it is virtually impossible to anticipate all of the obstacles and opportunities that will arise during the course of events. Thus planning during action, involving flexibility and alertness to new opportunities and problems, provides fertile ground for creative solutions. Perkins (1981) discusses how Picasso's creation of Guernica involved 'accident and intention, the balance of luck and foresight in creative process' (p. 21). Perkins quotes Arnheim's description of the work:

> An interplay of interferences, modifications, restrictions, and compensations leads gradually to the unity and complexity of the total composition. Therefore the work of art cannot unfold straightforwardly from its seed, like an organism, but must grow in what looks like erratic leaps, forward and backward, from the whole to the part and vice versa. (p. 19)

Most of the planning during action that we observed was not in response to intruding events, but was instead the means by which the girls managed the complexities of creating a complex play and of co-ordinating their often discrepant ideas. On many occasions, the girls elaborated on the idea mentioned by another person, with the collaborative product reflecting a creative advance that is more than the sum of the individual contributions.

For example, the development of the idea of having the evil stepmother give Snow White a poisoned banana instead of a poisoned apple can be followed across a number of events and ideas from different individuals across the ten sessions. At the end of the first session, when the teacher suggested making an adaptation of the play to resolve their dispute, one girl's immediate response was to suggest using a poisoned lemon to change the original version. The girls together brainstormed other poisoned foods that could be used, among which was the poisoned banana; this was what got written on their planning sheet. In the second session, the girls discussed the adaptation written at home by one of the girls, which involved the prince punching the princess in the stomach and her throwing up all over him. Another girl suggested using chewed-up banana to create the effect, and the girls all wrote down 'banana' on their papers. When they practised the play in the later sessions, the evil queen gave the princess a poisoned banana and the princess pretended to vomit when the prince kissed (not punched) her. However, the pretend vomiting deterred all of the girls from playing the prince, a role they otherwise wanted. In the final performance, the poisoned banana remained but the vomiting had disappeared. Thus the development of several events involving the banana reflected the girls' adjustment to practical constraints, their creative use of each other's ideas to advance the group product, and the process of adjustment of the plan over time.

Another example involved the use of a fortuitous circumstance in creating a scene. During the first session, the girls considered how they could have a talking mirror, and a number of possibilities were discussed, one of which was to have a hole in a mirror with an actor speaking in the hole. All six girls participated in this discussion, which ended without resolution as one girl brought them back to the need to focus on main events. Nothing more was done with the mirror issue until the ninth session, when the evil queen went to look in a pretend mirror but was inconvenienced by the student teacher who was right where she wanted the mirror to be. She told him to move. But his being there seemed to have prompted the idea of having a person play the mirror, and she asked a classmate to come over to be the mirror and told her the mirror's line. This feature was replayed in the tenth session, and appeared in the final performance as well. In this example, the creative planning built on an intrusion to develop a creative germ that had been mentioned long before. Related processes have been observed in children's pretend play in early childhood (Göncü and Kessel, 1988).

Planning during action: in character or improvisation
We observed two types of planning during action: planning 'in character' and improvisation. Planning in character took place during activity, within the context of rehearsals or planning of script lines. It typically involved filling in gaps in dialogue or action or communicating the need for a character to appear on stage without breaking the momentum of the rehearsal. In the following example from the seventh session, the group had not yet discussed an ending for the play. Since it was inefficient to stop the rehearsal in order explicitly to plan an ending, Robin (as the wicked stepmother) took the initiative and summarized the finale, in character and without interrupting the course of action: 'Then the prince gets his wizard to turn all my mirrors black every time I look in them. So that I die if I look in them. OK?' Once this plan had been devised, during subsequent rehearsals the group was able to remember the course of events and add dialogue and action through improvisational techniques.

When improvising, the girls planned and carried out actions and events simultaneously, performing 'according to the inventive whim of the moment' (McCrohan, 1987; Dean, 1989). Improvisation differs from planning in character in terms of communicative focus. In the previous example, Robin explicitly communicated the plan to the group. However, in the following improvisational example the action and the plan were synonymous. In earlier sessions the group had decided on using a poisoned banana and that the dwarves would carry the princess over to a glass coffin. During the seventh session, the group improvised the dialogue:

CAROL: It's a banana! She's not breathing.
STACY: It looks a bit peculiar.
CAROL: She's not breathing! Come on let's carry her.
STACY: Try CPR!
CAROL: Let's carry her off.

Improvisation allows for spontaneous modifications and elaborations without the need to reflect verbally on the plan and often without the need to establish verbally mediated consensus. If an improvised line or move seemed jarring, this led to discussion either in character or out of character.

Since the group had established consensus early on about the play's overall structure and had developed shared modes of communication, during the later playcrafting sessions they could short-cut many of the formal negotiations and plan during the course of action.

Choosing advance planning and planning during action

The group evidenced struggles in managing a flexible adjustment of planning to blend the advantages of both advance planning and planning during action. On a number of occasions, the group evidenced tension between proceeding through advance planning or through planning during action. They had numerous discussions about writing the script all out versus putting the play together through acting, as in this example from the fifth session:

> Leslie asks: 'Do you want to write scripts or do you want to take the play part by part?'
>
> Heather suggests writing part of the script, then doing that part, then writing more script.
>
> Leslie urges writing a script to avoid forgetting their lines, and suggests getting out of costume to write scripts. Eventually the girls write scripts.
>
> Robin suggests: 'Why don't we all work together on one big script and then we can get it copied? So we can all work together on one script.' [*a solution to the problem of co-ordination*]
>
> The girls write, agreeing to focus on the first part of the play and just listing the names in abbreviated fashion.
>
> Leslie remains concerned with co-ordination: 'What if one person wants to say something and the other . . .?'
>
> Robin reassures: 'It will probably be all right.'
>
> They write some more, and again Leslie worries about advance planning: 'I just figured out our problem. We don't know how the story *goes*.'
>
> Robin reassures that planning in action will work: 'We are just kinda making the story up as we go – as we act.'
>
> Leslie is content: 'Oh. OK.'

At times, the student teacher intervened to encourage more advance planning, urging the group to resolve each conflict before going on. However, the girls largely ignored him. His suggestions would have been likely to lead to stalemates, with the group stuck on disputes, rather than to creative solutions.

Contrast with children's individual planning during writing

The *Snow White* group's skilled movement between advance planning and planning during action, adjusting planning across levels of detail, contrasts with the literature on children's planning of written compositions (Flower and Hayes, 1980; Hayes and Flower, 1980; Bereiter and Scardamalia, 1987). Seminal work by Bereiter and Scardamalia (1987) found that elementary school children write by simply putting down the next thing they think of, without thinking about the composition at a meta-level, planning or creating an abbreviated plan in the form of notes that differ significantly from later completed text.

The *Snow White* group used more sophisticated planning than that found by Bereiter and Scardamalia. During the first four playcrafting sessions children planned at a global rather than sequential level of detail by creating a story theme and events, examining the coherence and flow of the story. During the final seven playcrafting sessions the group modified, improvised and rehearsed their plan. At times, when hindered in making progress on the overall plan, the group would dip into planning at some level of detail, shortly to return to the more general level with greater consensus or renewed ideas.

The girls wrote abbreviated plans on paper on a number of occasions (listing the characters, sometimes with abbreviations of actors' names). For example, when one girl suggested that everyone write down their parts and what they want to say and then discuss it all together, she added, 'You don't need to really write every word.' These abbreviated plans and management of levels of planning by 2nd and 3rd graders were qualitatively more sophisticated than those produced by Bereiter and Scardamalia's sample of 6th graders who planned details in sequential order.

What might account for the discrepancies between Bereiter and Scardamalia's findings and our own results? Although the emphasis on creativity in these students' school may account for some of the discrepancy between Bereiter and Scardamalia's observations and our own, another likely explanation for our 2nd and 3rd graders' elaborate planning is that children in our investigation worked in *collaboration* to develop a plan for their project. With only one exception, Bereiter and Scardamalia's research focuses on individual as opposed to collaborative processes. In the one instance when Bereiter and Scardamalia observed a group of four 6th grade children collaborating on a written project they noted that the group engaged in sophisticated planning comparable to adult planning and consistent with our own findings. They infer that this single observation might be attributed to some features of collaboration. Similarly, Flower, Higgins and Petraglia (1990) suggest that: 'The presence of a partner forces writers to explain, elaborate, or in some cases try to articulate thoughts, doubts, fragments, assumptions and ambiguities that are often left unsaid in thinking to one's self' (p. 6). In the next section we discuss the collaborative methods that the group employed during the playcrafting sessions and examine how collaboration is integral to the planning process.

Social organization of creative planning

In our use of the playcrafting event as the unit of analysis, we consider the roles of individuals involved as they constitute and are constituted by the coherence of the overall event. It is relevant to ask how the individuals co-ordinated their efforts and their relative responsibilities for the management of planning, and the extent to which their thinking was shared.

Although the six girls differed in writing skill and leadership strength, and they varied in friendship histories, they consistently worked together throughout the sessions. Even when they attempted to work independently, each writing her own lines or developing her own characters, they consulted each other constantly on fitting their contributions together, assisting each other in spelling and reminding each other of decisions that had already been made or of the basic story model in which they were working.

Working together was not easy – early sessions were full of conflict and mismatches of assumptions and ideas. At times subgroups worked together simultaneously or several girls worked actively while others observed. There were four girls who played a more dominant role in decision making, but the other two were always attentive and all six contributed ideas and management at one point or another. (Of the two girls who were less dominant, one was the only 2nd grader in the group and the other was quieter than the other four 3rd graders. After the teacher had put this group together, she noticed that it was composed of a number of strong personalities and expressed concern about the potential for explosion in the group.)

In any case, the girls were all engaged, with shifting leadership from day to day. There were *very* few moments spent off-task, by any of the six girls. On a few occasions the group fooled about around play development, but this seemed often to serve a function of reducing tension or getting past an impasse in planning. The only occasion when the group really spent time off-task was a three to four minute period when the student teacher interrupted the group in an attempt to organize it in his own fashion.

Initial anchors for planning

To begin the process of planning, the girls faced the problem of anchoring their imaginations so that they could work from a common ground. Without such anchors, there would be little hope of co-ordinating their individual efforts. Some of the anchors drew upon constraints and resources of the cultural institution in which the children worked – school. Before the first session, the teacher provided anchors for the planning process in her management of the classroom to choose four plays as a basis of the projects and to determine with the children who was to work on which play, after lessons on the structure of fairy-tales. Her requirement to produce a written script also channelled the process.

Another means of anchoring the process, and of encouraging planning at higher levels, was the teacher's provision of the planning sheet requesting the children to determine the characters, the setting and the main events. The use of this sheet was managed in the first session by Stacy, who repeatedly directed the group back to determining characters or main events when they strayed into too much detail on planning props or dialogue, as in the following example:

> When the girls got involved in discussing how to make a talking mirror, Stacy tried to get them back to general planning. She interrupted, tapped the girl who was leading the mirror discussion with her pencil, and said 'Main Events'.
> But the discussion remained on the mirror topic.
> Stacy tried again, exasperated: 'We are going to do the Main Events.'
> When the others continued discussing the mirror, Stacy asked: 'What are the Main Events?'
> Finally the girls turned to reconstructing their memories of the main events of the tale. But after some progress, the girls began to worry about how they would produce the setting.
> Stacy tried to move away from this level of planning, insisting: 'We aren't doing this right now. We are on the Main Events right now.' And the girls returned to listing the main events.

At the end of the first session, the main events for *Snow White* were written as:

> the queen wats snow white
> kiled. Snow wite eats a pousand
> banana snow white gets strageld
> snow white gets bered and the
> price comes and they get meryd.

The girls also used the traditional story line of the play as an anchor for their planning during the first day, relying on cultural knowledge outside the structure provided by the teacher. However, since the girls did not share a common story line (due to having seen two different video versions of the tale), their common ground here was not solid. Intersubjectivity was repeatedly disrupted, until the girls understood the basis of the misunderstanding. Eventually they checked understandings with each other.

> In Session 2, when Heather and Robin disagreed on how the dwarves should carry their shovels, Heather checked, 'Have you seen the Walt Disney one?' before going on with a proposal; 'OK, well you know how they swing back? [*she demonstrated*] They go like that.'

Many of the girls' disputes could be traced to *apparent* consensus but with different underlying assumptions that later surfaced as problems. The problem of differing assumptions was resolved when the teacher suggested that they make up a modern version of the play, and the girls eagerly accepted this solution to their interpersonal trouble.

Hence the decision to create rather than reproduce a play resulted from interpersonal difficulties in establishing a common ground. The idea of modifying the traditional tale had been suggested before the beginning of the sessions by the teacher, and during the session by several girls. But it was not until it appeared as a solution for the difficulties in co-ordinating ideas across people that it was adopted:

> The teacher suggested: Why don't you guys think up a totally new version? A modern-day version?'
>
> The group made favourable comments, and Robin supported the idea: 'I think that it would be neat to come up with a modern-day version. Like Snow White eats a poison lemon or something.'
>
> After further discussion, Robin gave more support to the idea of a new version as a way of achieving consensus: 'We could have a whole new thing and then everybody would be figuring it out all together and then nobody would have seen it [i.e. quarrel about the "real" story].'
>
> The group began immediately to brainstorm.

For the second session, the anchor for planning was elaborated by Robin's production, at home, of a modified story line in which many events were made to be opposite to the original tale. She reported to the group that she was following their group decision: 'I just totally changed it. Remember how we were going to make a new one? So I just did that.' When she read the story to the group they were largely enthusiastic.

Although this version did not persist intact, Robin's play served as a new anchor point, both for those who accepted it and for those who argued against it. The argument derived from a girl who had been absent at the previous session and was not pleased with changes occurring in her absence: 'Well, she shouldn't have done it until all of us like it . . . It's supposed to be *Snow White*, not *Black Night*.' With the teacher's support, the group pulled together to reach a new agreement, and this resulted in a change of the name of the play, from the revised name offered by Robin:

> The teacher probed: 'What could you do to solve the problem?'
>
> Leslie suggested: 'We could change it? . . . Could we just change the name instead of *Black Night*? Would that help?'
>
> The girls discussed alternative names. After much more discussion, and attempts by the group to have each girl write individual ideas to be mixed together, Leslie offered an efficient compromise: 'If we have a little of Robin's *Black Night*, if you want to, we could have *Snow White Black Night*.' In discussion, the idea of *Blue Sky* came up, and Leslie suggested: 'How about *Blue Night*? Cuz, some of your [Robin's] idea and some of their idea?'

At this suggestion, all agreed and planning moved along collaboratively. The group's solution was to combine parts of each idea, to get a new one. This is a recipe for creative planning, and it is essential to note that interpersonal processes were central in necessitating the mixing of ideas and guiding the resulting creative elaboration.

Means of co-ordinating efforts

Over the course of the playcrafting sessions the group was able to develop effective ways to manage both the play-planning task and the social relationships.

Division of tasks

One collaborative method the group attempted involved the division of various tasks. Here, a task is divided into subtasks and individuals are assigned to perform one or more of the subtasks. Once the subtasks have been performed, individual products are integrated to form a whole. Sometimes, tasks were divided with parallel contributions from all, by distributing character roles and having each participant create her own actions, dialogue and motivations, as in the following proposal in the second session: 'Everybody get a piece of scratch paper . . . *write down their parts*, and what they want to say. Then we'll discuss them . . . and see if everybody likes it.' On some occasions, subgroups divided tasks and worked simultaneously within subgroups. For example, the three dwarves worked on their dialogue and actions, speaking across the table through the conversation of the king and queen who were developing their piece of the script.

At other times, the division involved specialization, with distribution of individual jobs (e.g. playwright, director, set designer), and later integration of the products according to a master plan. This social organizational model is common in professional theatre (see Schechner, 1985, for an anthropological discussion of theatre). One advantage of this model is that it takes into consideration variation in individual skills. For example, a child who has difficulty writing can create props. However, the group must decide who will divide the task and who will integrate individual products once they have been created. Without a clear distinction in resources or status, it is difficult to determine who should take what role. In fact, during the planning of *Snow White* a great deal of the conflict revolved around one or another of the four dominant girls protesting about too much leadership by another.

A cultural tool – writing – was often used by the girls to take control of the planning process. As in ancient times, the scribe and the literate had power over those who did not write or read. In the first session, Stacy took the job of writing down decisions on the teacher's planning sheet. She also kept the group on task by reminding them of the need to make decisions at the level of the planning sheet (e.g., main events). However, this gave her a dominant role about which other girls later protested. Leslie scolded: 'You are supposed to be writing down what we *all* want!' and later Heather asked Stacy if she could write the next part, since Stacy had written everything so far (but Stacy did not yield the pencil and paper).

In other sessions, other girls also used writing as a means of influence – Robin writing the play at home, Carol gaining authority in decision-making as the only girl who could find her script from the session before, and Leslie later being nominated to be the writer of the script (with admonitions to write the group consensus) on the basis of her more complete manner of writing. When there were difficulties in establishing group consensus, the written word was often used as an anchor point and as a way of exerting leadership. Perhaps because the group members were basically similar in resources and skills and involved four girls who vied for the leadership role, asymmetry in roles was often rejected, in favour of discussion, negotiation and compromise.

Shared decision-making

This collaborative method was used throughout the creation of *Snow White* with ideas developed through a process of brainstorming and evaluated and adapted for use. Each child has a say in the decision-making process even though individual children do not make equivalent contributions to proposals or to carrying them out. During one dispute, the girls complained that Leslie was being bossy in protesting about the inclusion of a part that was not her character's; she replied, 'it's my play, too', disputing the idea that decisions could be made unilaterally by people playing specific parts.

The process was often chaotic, filled with interruptions, topic and task changes. Likewise, the play under construction was sometimes disjointed, since the individual parts often did not comprise a coherent whole. This was complicated by the likelihood that individuals were working from differing models of the goal or differing background information.

To progress, the group must be able to work together on a shared task, with shared attention, shared communication, and the ability to adjust individual activities to facilitate the group. At times the girls proposed ways of co-ordinating their individual or subgroup ideas:

TEACHER: Can you think of how you would like it [the play]?
STACY: I'd like to change the form. Like make [the ideas] exactly opposite . . .
ROBIN: Why don't we mix them up? . . . Like we can get everybody to make the ideas so everybody will have their own idea and then we can mix them up together . . . We can figure out a way to mix them all up on somebody's piece of paper.

The social–cognitive collaborative methods of division of tasks and shared decision making that the group used to create their play served as both a planning *process* that propelled the group to its goal and as a *tool* that facilitated the creation of the play, with indivisible social and cognitive processes. During the initial four playcrafting sessions sociocognitive vehicles for the co-ordination and generation of ideas were built by the group, and as they were built, the group was able to use them to create its play. On the fourth day the group was able to achieve a coherence between cognitive activities and social organization. After the fourth day it spent most of its time planning specific dialogue and action, and rehearsing.

The *Snow White* group's methods and product contrasted with many of the other groups' playcrafting sessions, which did not employ a method of shared decision making. For example, in one of the other fairy-tale groups an adult needed to remain with the group for all ten sessions in order to dictate the method of collaboration and to structure the task. The adult became responsible for generating ideas, negotiating conflict, and attempting to motivate the group's efforts. Another group elected not to collaborate on a joint project, but rather to work on individual products that were later performed separately. In these instances the groups did not develop a means of collaborative management of ideas, and their interactions and plays were of a much different nature from those of *Snow White*, in which the group developed successful interaction patterns and used them to develop a play together, working almost independently of adult direction. We argue that collaborative methods of social organization were essential to the group's handling of a variety of cognitive tasks.

Summary

In this paper we have argued that creative planning can best be understood as a sociocultural process involving both advance and improvisational planning. Whereas many traditional perspectives view creativity and planning as cognitive products, mental possessions or individual traits, our purpose has been to explicate sociocultural processes in children's collaborative creative planning. We emphasize both the process and the sociocultural nature of planning by arguing that in order to plan collaboratively children need to develop ways of managing both social relations and the cognitive problems inherent in the project. Social interaction patterns constitute the cognitive course of the creative process and, in mutual fashion, cognitive processes constitute social organizational patterns.

We stress the dynamic, sociocultural nature of the processes of creative planning. Sociocultural contexts provide fertile ground for the development of new ideas and structure creative planning as ideas emerge and evolve in new ways. Regardless of whether we investigate artistic, scientific or everyday creative planning, all take place within sociocultural communities. The individual contribution to creative planning is only a part of a broader dynamic sociocultural process, in which the whole is greater than the sum of the parts.

Note

1. This research was funded by a grant from the Spencer Foundation. We would like to express our gratitude to Cindy Berg, Batya Elbaum, Denise Goldsmith, Artin Goncu, Wendy Haight, Pilar Lacasa, Shellie Manning, Christine Mosier, Carol Randell and Cindy White for their assistance and insights during various stages of this project. In addition, many thanks to the students, teachers and parents at Washington Elementary School for allowing us to observe and tape the playcrafting process. The names of the children in this chapter are pseudonyms.

References

Azmitia, M. (1988), 'Peer interaction and problem solving: when are two heads better than one?', *Child Development*, 59, pp. 87–96.

Bereiter, C. and Scardamalia, M. (1987), *The Psychology of Written Composition* (Hillsdale, NJ: Erlbaum).

Bouchard, T.J. (1971), 'Whatever happened to brainstorming?', *Journal of Creative Behavior*, 5, pp. 182–9.

Brown, A. and DeLoache, J. (1978), 'Skills, plans, and self-regulation', in R. Siegler (ed.), *Children's Thinking: What develops?* (Hillsdale, NJ: Erlbaum), pp. 3–35.

Csikszentmihalyi, M. (1988), 'Society, culture, and person: a systems view of creativity', in R.J. Sternberg (ed.), *The Nature of Creativity* (Cambridge: Cambridge University Press).

Dean, R.T. (1989), *Creative Improvisation: Jazz, contemporary music and beyond* (Philadelphia: Open University Press).

Flower, L. and Hayes, J.J. (1980), 'The dynamics of composing: making plans and juggling constraints', in L.W. Gregg and E.R. Steinberg (eds), *Cognitive Processes in Writing* (Hillsdale, NJ: Erlbaum), pp. 31–50.

Flower, L., Higgins, L. and Petraglia, J. (1990), 'Collaboration and the construction of meaning', unpublished manuscript, Center for the Study of Writing, Carnegie Mellon University.

Gardner, W. and Rogoff, B. (1990), 'Children's deliberateness of planning according to task circumstances', *Developmental Psychology*, 26, pp. 480–7.

Gearhart, M. (1979), 'Social planning: role play in a novel situation', paper presented at the meetings of the Society for Research in Child Development, San Francisco.

Göncü, A. and Kessel, F. (1988), 'Preschoolers' collaborative construction in planning and maintaining imaginative play', *International Journal of Behavioral Development*, 11, pp. 327–44.

Hayes, J.R. and Flower, L.S. (1980), 'Identifying the organization of writing processes', in L.W. Gregg and E. R. Steinberg (eds), *Cognitive Processes in Writing* (Hillsdale, NJ: Erlbaum), pp. 3–30.

Hayes-Roth, B. (1985), 'A blackboard architecture for control', *Artificial Intelligence*, 26, pp. 251–322.

Hayes-Roth, B. and Hayes-Roth, F. (1979), 'A cognitive model of planning', *Cognitive Science*, 3, pp. 275–310.

John-Steiner, V. (1985), *Notebooks of the Mind: Explorations of thinking* (New York: Harper & Row).

Leont'ev, A.N. (1981), 'The problem of activity in psychology', in J.V. Wertsch (ed.), *The Concept of Activity in Soviet Psychology* (Armonk, NY: Sharpe).

McCrohan, D. (1987), *The Second City: A backstage history of comedy's hottest troupe* (New York: Putnam).

Pea, R. and Hawkins, J. (1987), 'Planning in a chore scheduling task', in S. Friedman, E. Scholnick and R. Cocking (eds), *Blueprints for Thinking: The role of planning in psychological development* (New York: Cambridge University Press), pp. 273–302.

Perkins, D.N. (1981), *The Mind's Best Work* (Cambridge, MA: Harvard University Press).

Radziszewska, B. and Rogoff, B. (1988), 'Influence of adult and peer collaborators on children's planning skills', *Developmental Psychology*, 24, pp. 840–8.

Radziszewska, B. and Rogoff, B. (1991), 'Children's guided participation in planning errands with skilled adult or peer partners', *Developmental Psychology*, 27, pp. 381–9.

Rogoff, B. (1982), 'Integrating context and cognitive development', in M.E. Lamb and A.L. Brown (eds), *Advances in Developmental Psychology*, vol. 2 (Hillsdale, NJ: Erlbaum).

Rogoff, B. (1990), *Apprenticeship in Thinking: Cognitive development in social context*, (New York: Oxford University Press).

Rogoff, B. and Gauvain, M. (1986), 'A method for the analysis of patterns, illustrated with data on mother–child instructional interaction', in J. Valsiner (ed.), *The Individual Subject and Scientific Psychology* (New York: Plenum), pp. 261–90.

Rogoff, B., Gauvain, M. and Gardner, W. (1987), 'The development of children's skills in adjusting plans to circumstances', in S. Friedman, E. Scholnick and R. Cocking (eds), *Blueprints for Thinking: The role of planning in psychological development* (New York: Cambridge University Press), pp. 303–20.

Rogoff, B., Lacasa, P., Baker-Sennett, J. and Goldsmith, D. (in preparation), *The Sociocultural Context of Children's Errand Planning: Girl Scout cookie sales and delivery*.

Schechner, R. (1985), *Between Theater and Anthopology* (Philadelphia PA: University of Pennsylvania Press).

Vygotsky, L.S. (1978), *Mind in Society* (Cambridge, MA: Harvard University Press).

Weisberg, R.W. (1986), *Creativity: Genius and other myths* (New York: Freeman).

Wellman, H., Fabricius, W. and Sophian, C. (1985), 'The early development of planning', in H. Wellman (ed.), *Children's Searching: The development of search skill and spatial representation* (Hillsdale, NJ: Erlbaum), pp. 123–49.

Winokur, Jon (1990), *Writers on Writing* (Philadelphia: Running Press).

Chapter 7

Desituating cognition through the construction of conceptual knowledge

Giyoo Hatano, *Dokkyo University*
Kayoko Inagaki, *Chiba University*

In this chapter, we will draw on our research findings to try to answer the following two questions:

1. How do people construct knowledge applicable to a variety of situations as they gain expertise?
2. What conditions enable them to do so?

We will be concerned particularly with the question of the situated nature of cognition, in other words, the context-boundness of our knowledge and competence, and its possible change in the course of acquiring expertise.

This chapter consists of three principal parts. First, after a short introductory section suggesting that the acquisition of mental models makes cognition less situated, we report two contrasting cases of children accumulating experiences of raising animals, one of which resulted in mere procedural sophistication, while the other led to the construction of mental models of the target animals. Second, we specify how a person can construct mental models of the target object through repeated experiences in dealing with it. Third, we discuss why a person acquires less situated knowledge in some conditions but not in others – that is, we consider the motivational conditions enhancing the construction of mental models.

Gaining expertise and desituating cognition

When we are novices, our everyday problem solving is heavily dependent on devices and materials, and also other people's knowledge or knowledge given in an externalized symbolic form. For example, when we cook, we may refer to a printed recipe or ask the advice of an experienced cook. In addition, what we do is constrained by available devices and materials. In fact, it is often much easier actually to perform a step in cooking (e.g. making grated white radish) than to state or comprehend that step verbally, because what we can comfortably do is highly restricted by these external constraints. Thus a large amount of specific knowledge is not needed to perform the task successfully; what is minimally required is to be able to comprehend instructions, use devices, and process materials properly. However, our competence is highly situated or context-bound, because it is entirely dependent on such external support. We may no longer be competent when any minor portion of the support is taken away. For example, when we find a few lines of the printed recipe missing, we are at a loss, wondering what we should do next. In other words, these external aids have a large *effect with* (i.e. making the task performance easier when they are used), but not necessarily a large *effect of* (i.e. being facilitative even after they are no longer used) (Salomon, Perkins and Globerson, 1991), probably because successful problem solving is the first concern of people who are in charge of providing the aids.

After some experience, our task performance becomes dependent on our acquired knowledge and mental representations. We can make dishes relying on recipes stored in long-term memory. We can anticipate what will come later, and thus perform the preceding steps so that their products can easily be used in later steps. Although the physical environment, such as a frying pan filled with oil, may serve as a reminder, we can tell what we should do next even when our eyes are closed. Further experience makes us more and more skilful in performing the task. At this stage, however, what we know of the 'domain' primarily consists of procedures which are rigid in the dual sense – the order of actions or steps within a procedure is fixed, and none of them can be replaced by comparable ones. Thus our knowledge is still situated in the sense that it does not have general applicability across situations. Such knowledge often fails to transfer; even a minor situational change often makes an attempt to solve problems unsuccessful. For example, we cannot make a designated dish if some materials are missing or some devices are not available.

Qualitatively different progress is made when we acquire conceptual knowledge, which means more or less comprehensive knowledge about the nature of the objects of the procedures (i.e. what they are like). Forms of conceptual knowledge that change in response to mentally exerted actions, and thus can be used to run mental simulation (Collins and Gentner, 1982), are often called mental models (Gentner and Stevens, 1983). When we possess a mental model of the target object we can understand the meaning of each step of a given procedure in terms of the change it produces in the object. By running the mental model we can also predict what will occur in unexperienced situations.

Those who have acquired conceptual knowledge of the major objects of the domain, in addition to procedures for solving problems, are called 'adaptive experts' (Hatano and Inagaki, 1986), and contrasted to 'routine experts', who are experts by virtue of their efficiency in applying acquired procedures. Problem-solving competence of adaptive experts is not context-bound in the same sense as that of novices or routine experts. Adaptive experts are able to achieve the goal in spite of the lack of some external support, and to solve various novel problems of the domain. Their knowledge is still situated in the sense that it reflects the history of its acquisition and its use, but is desituated in the sense that it is no longer associated tightly with the situation in which it was originally acquired.

Therefore, for desituating cognition, the acquisition of conceptual knowledge in the form of mental models seems critical, though a few other routes to 'high road transfer' (Perkins and Salomon, 1989) may be available. Adaptive experts in cooking can differentiate those interchangeable steps from those to be performed in the prescribed order, add different materials from the standard recipe, use different devices when needed, and still make essentially the same and equally delicious dish. They may invent new dishes by mentally combining a variety of materials and modes of cooking. According to Hatano and Oura (1991), college students who were subjectively good at and liked cooking, though not grand experts, possessed their own individual recipe for curry sauce, and could cope with imaginary situations where they had to make curry sauce without some standard ingredients.

We will present below two contrasting cases of children accumulating experiences of raising animals, one of which resulted in the mere procedural sophistication and the other in the construction of conceptual knowledge of the target animal. The latter case deals with children who were not yet real experts in raising goldfish, but whose mental models of goldfish enabled them to transfer their experience to unfamiliar situations.

Knowledge acquired through experiences of raising animals

Young children often engage in an activity of raising animals in their infant facility or at home. Many pre-schools and kindergartens have small animals, such as rabbits, hamsters, chickens, etc. in order to allow children to take care of them as an activity for science education. At home, parents ask their child to help them take care of such animals as dogs, cats, goldfish or Java sparrows. In either case children initially perform procedures for raising an animal (e.g. feeding a pet animal, cleaning up its 'residence', and so on) under an adult's guidance by taking partial charge of it, then gradually take on larger responsibility, and finally become able to do the whole by themselves. In the process of raising animals, therefore, young children apply the prescribed procedures to a target animals hundreds, or often, thousands of times.

Children become procedurally proficient

Namiki and Inagaki (1984) examined characteristics of knowledge that 6 year olds have acquired through raising rabbits as a duty over a year at their kindergarten. These children were, in rotation, in charge of taking care of rabbits and four kinds of birds (i.e. bantams, ducks, wild ducks and parakeets) since they had moved up to senior classes. They were firmly expected to follow the prescribed procedures for looking after animals, which were taken over from the preceding seniors, by their teachers (who were concerned about the possibility of animals dying, primarily for financial reasons).

After one year of experience of raising animals, these children could apply the procedures to the raised animals efficiently (i.e. in a much shorter time than before). In addition, when asked about what things were important in raising rabbits, they listed both feeding and cleaning up the rabbits' residence equally reliably. This was in sharp contrast to a corresponding group of 6 year olds, used as 'control' subjects, from another kindergarten where teachers, instead of children, were in charge of taking care of rabbits, and thus children had no direct experience of raising rabbits. These latter children did not recognize the importance of cleaning up the residence, though a majority of them realized the importance of feeding.

Those children who had direct rabbit-raising experience also correctly predicted more often than the control children who had no direct experience that rabbits would die if we continued to give only food that the rabbits liked or if we did not clean up their residence. However, these children could seldom give any reasonable reasons concerning why such treatments would lead rabbits to die; they understood the meaning of each step of the raising procedures no better than the children without direct raising experience.

Namiki (1985) reported that another group of children from the above kindergarten who were required to take care of animals in rotation over a year possessed more correct factual knowledge about the raised animals than their counterparts, but their knowledge was not so integrated. For example, although the children correctly answered that ducks were egg-laying while rabbits were not, they could not consistently give correct answers to questions asking whether ducks or rabbits grew bigger by drinking milk.

The findings described above suggest that, although children are likely to acquire factual and procedural knowledge through raising animals as a duty over an extended period in their kindergarten, they do not go further to acquire the conceptual knowledge, that serves as the basis for explaining the necessity of the procedure. It is likely in the above case that the children were not always motivated to engage in an activity of raising animals in the kindergarten, because the activity was not initiated by children's strong volition. The animals had already been raised in the kindergarten before the children entered it, and all the children, irrespective of their interest, were required to engage in the activity in rotation for the purpose of science education.

Imagine a case where children raise an animal at home. In this case children usually begin to raise it of their own volition. If they lose their interest in its care, other members of their family will take it over. To the extent that children are interested in the raised animal, they are likely to be involved in the raising activity, and thus the cognitive consequences of this activity may be different. We shall examine such a case in the next subsection.

Children acquire conceptual knowledge of the raised animal

Inagaki (1990) investigated what kind of knowledge is acquired, using as subjects those children who had raised goldfish at home. (An ideal comparison would be with children raising rabbits at home, but such cases were very hard to find.) Of thirty kindergarteners who reported they had raised goldfish, eighteen children were selected as those who actively engaged in raising goldfish for an extended period. That is, they were taking care of their goldfish (including feeding them) by themselves either almost every day or every two days. Sometimes, they helped their parent(s) to change the water in the fishbowl. They had been raising goldfish for a long time: one-third of them had raised goldfish for the last three months, and two-thirds for about one year or more. By individual matching to the above goldfish-raising children in terms of chronological age, another group of eighteen children who had never raised any animal at home were selected as control or 'not-raising' subjects. It was confirmed that these two groups of children did not differ in factual knowledge about other animals than goldfish, through their answers to questions on mammals, such as 'Does a monkey lay eggs?' or 'Does a panda have nails?'

Both goldfish-raising and not-raising children were individually given factual or procedural knowledge questions concerning goldfish, and prediction questions about reactions not only of a goldfish but also of a frog, a novel aquatic animal, to situations which they had never experienced. The knowledge questions for goldfish consisted of items on routine raising procedures (e.g. 'How many times is a goldfish fed a day?'), observable properties of the goldfish (e.g. 'Does a goldfish sleep at night?') and its unobservable properties (e.g. 'Does a goldfish have a heart?').

The prediction questions concerned four biological phenomena (i.e. too

much eating, inevitable growth, spontaneous recovery and excretory function). Example questions, each of which was followed by the question, 'How
come?', were as follows: 'What will happen with X if we feed it ten times a
day?' 'Does X excrete?' (when a child's answer was 'Yes') 'Does X excrete if
it is not fed for a number of days?' The situations used were supposed to be
novel even for the goldfish-raising children, because, generally speaking,
children have few opportunities to observe the phenomena used in this study
when taking care of their goldfish in everyday life. For example, children
seldom have a chance to learn through everyday experience that a goldfish
does not excrete if it is not fed for a number of days, because nobody will
intentionally try a procedure that may lead to the death of their pet goldfish.
Thus answering such questions is supposed to require some inference based
on conceptual knowledge for most children.

Results were as follows: the goldfish-raising children acquired a greater
amount of factual or procedural knowledge about goldfish than the children
who had never raised any animal; they possessed not only more procedural-
observable-factual knowledge but also more knowledge about unobservable
attributes, such as having a heart or blood.

The goldfish-raising children were also superior to the non-raising
children in terms of giving explanations for goldfish-raising procedures.
When asked why they fed their goldfish X times a day, about half the
goldfish-raising children answered that too much feeding would lead to the
death of the goldfish, and one of them said, 'too much feeding will hurt the
stomach', whereas such a response (referring to the relation between too
much feeding and illness or death) was found in only one among the non-
raisers; more than half of the non-raising children gave tautological reasons
or no reasons. When asked why the water in a fishbowl was sometimes
changed, eleven of the eighteen goldfish-raising children answered that the
dirty water would lead to the goldfish's death or ill health, and three of them
explicitly referred to the relationship between the dirty water and goldfish's
excretion, saying, 'Because the water is made dirty by the goldfish's excretion, they will die [if we leave the water unchanged]'. Only four non-
raising children gave similar reasons, and only one of them referred to the
relation between dirty water and excretion.

The goldfish-raising children made reasonable predictions for the
prediction questions about a goldfish more often than the children who had
never raised any animal. When generating predictions for goldfish's reactions
to novel situations, both goldfish-raisers and non-raisers used the person
analogies (e.g. 'Goldfish will grow bigger by eating food, as a human does'),
but the former children did so more often than the latter; a great majority
(94 per cent) of the goldfish-raising children used at least one person analogy
for the four situations, while 60 per cent of the non-raising children did so.

It is noteworthy that the goldfish-raising children tended to generalize the
knowledge acquired through goldfish-raising experience in predicting

reactions of an unfamiliar aquatic animal (i.e. the frog) in novel situations, though they had never raised it. That is, they used their knowledge about goldfish as the source in making analogies about the frog, and produced reasonable predictions with some explanations for it more often than their counterparts. For example, one of the goldfish-raising children answered, when asked whether we could keep the baby frog the same size for ever: 'No, we can't, because the frog will grow bigger as the goldfish grew bigger. My goldfish were small before, but now they are big.' It might be added that the goldfish raisers tended to use person analogies as well as goldfish analogies for a frog. In other words, the goldfish raisers could use two sources for making analogical predictions.

Kondo and Inagaki (1991) found, in another study with goldfish-raising children, that having two highly familiar domains of animals (i.e. a human and a raised animal) helped young children to enlarge their narrow conception of animals. Previous studies have reported that young children tend to underattribute unobservable animal properties (shared by all animals, e.g. breathing) to animals that are phylogenetically far from and dissimilar to people, dependi.ig upon how dissimilar the targets are (Carey, 1985; Inagaki and Sugiyama, 1988). Contrary to the previous findings, young children who had raised goldfish attributed those properties of having a heart, having blood, breathing and excreting, which are shared by humans, to goldfish at a high rate. In addition, when asked to attribute those properties to a variety of animals, the goldfish raisers were superior in attributing them to a majority of animals phylogenetically in between humans and goldfish. Having the two familiar domains of object changed children's patterns of attribution (see Figure 7.1 overleaf for example). This suggests that the goldfish raisers have come to recognize that not only goldfish but also other animals apparently dissimilar to a human share properties with a human.

In summary, it is suggested that active, spontaneous engagement in raising animals may lead children to acquire a sort of conceptual knowledge or a mental model of them, based on which they can produce reasonable predictions for their reactions to novel situations and give explanations about the prescribed procedures. Furthermore, mental models that children acquire can be applied to another animal of which they have no direct experience.

Processes through which mental models are constructed

How did the goldfish-raising children acquire conceptual knowledge, or more specifically, mental models, of what goldfish are like? Before trying to answer this specific question, let us examine the general issue of how people construct mental models spontaneously. Although previous studies have suggested that it is very hard to construct mental models of the target object

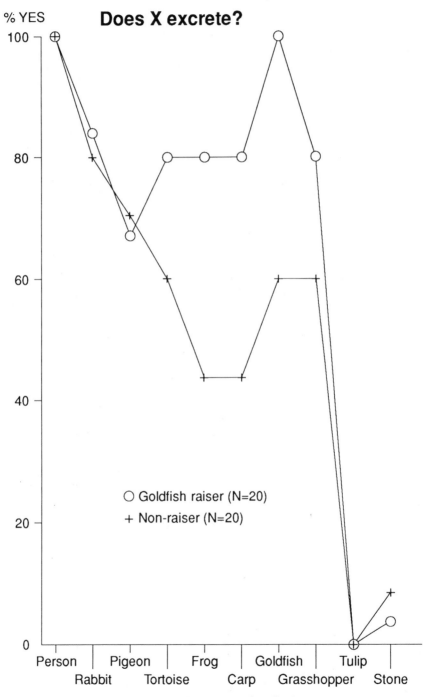

Figure 7.1 An example of children's patterns of attribution.

(especially of a complex artifact) without being taught them explicitly, we assume that it is possible, or even likely, if people engage in performing procedures for the object actively and repeatedly. Spontaneously constructed mental models may be fragmentary, inconsistent, or even somewhat erroneous, but possessing them does have a few advantages over having only a set of procedures in terms of problem-solving competence, as pointed out in the introductory section, and also of understanding and perceived control of realities.

There are two prerequisites for the construction of mental models. First, some observational data about the target object, that is, its reactions to various external actions, must be available. Second, unless the models can be built by directly perceiving the inside of the object, some 'source' models that can be transferred to the target object must also be available. It is usually impossible to construct mental models just by direct perception, because of the limited number of observations, the opacity of the object, the invisible nature of mechanisms, etc., and therefore, models must usually be borrowed from elsewhere and tailored to the target. We may generalize some old mental models to represent the new target. We may generate a new model from old ones relying on analogies. Even when the new object is only partially similar to what we know, and thus the generalization or full analogy cannot be applied, we can still selectively use parts of our old models to construct a new one.

How do people pick out and impose a good candidate model, which is to be checked later with the entire data set about the target object? We assume that abduction is a principal (if not *the* principal) mechanism through which a candidate model is applied. 'Abduction' means constructing a hypothesis to explain a set of puzzling facts. People often attribute a cause for observed events to characteristics of the object, and this will lead them to hypothesize what the object is like. For example, a conspicuous similarity in behaviour suggests that the target object is similar to a familiar object in related dimensions as well as the one directly relevant to the behaviour; in other words, the familiar object's mental model can be transferred to the target object with some adjustments.

The construction of mental models by abduction is nearly impossible when one does not possess a usable old model. People tend to be at a loss when they cannot think of any model that can explain the observed unexpected events. Even when we observe behaviour of a complex machine a number of times, and recognize some unexpected events, we are seldom able to construct its model even at a global level, unless we possess a familiar prototype of such a machine. In fact Miyake (1986) found that her highly intelligent subjects could not imagine mechanisms by which a sewing machine makes stitches before they were allowed to look inside.

Abduction seems to have played a significant role in the case of raising goldfish described above. More specifically, the goldfish-raising children may have recognized similarities between humans and goldfish as biological entities through this process, and so constructed mental models of goldfish by transferring their knowledge about humans through analogy, with some modifications based on the observations they had made of goldfish. When children encountered some unexpected reactions of goldfish (e.g. becoming ill) and adults' remarks (such as 'Don't feed too much'), they may have interpreted these as implying goldfish had human-like bodily structures. In other words, in order to make these reactions and remarks understandable, they may have borrowed knowledge about a human, though they could not see the internal bodily structure of goldfish. They may have recognized goldfish's characteristics that are shared with humans (e.g. having hostility to a newcomer, preference for novelty) and thus comfortably applied the person analogy to goldfish.

Since human beings have an intrinsic motivation for understanding (Hatano and Inagaki, 1987), as we describe later in detail, it is likely that the goldfish-raising children tried to understand the meaning of the procedures they were applying and also the 'why' of their observations. They may also have been motivated to understand the nature of the pet goldfish which they were taking care of. The process of abduction should be taken as a manifestation of human intrinsic motivation for understanding.

Interestingly, the studies reported in the previous section offer some evidence that even young children can build models selectively, or with parts from what they already know. Careful examination of protocols suggests that the goldfish-raising children revealed good insight into the characteristics of a frog, not by reasoning that a frog and a goldfish were very similar, but by selecting and extending the goldfish-like nature to build a new model for a frog. Inagaki and Hatano (1991) also showed that personifying (or animistic) responses of young children occur selectively to some human-like aspects of the target object. Kindergarten children (6 year olds) knew very well that a tulip does not speak, and thus did not say that it would shout for attention even when its owner was about to leave it behind, while those same children often inferred that the tulip would feel sad when its owner, who had taken care of it every day, died. One of the children said, 'The tulip will surely be sad. It cannot say "sad", but it will feel so inside.' (This child predicted that the tulip would go bad when we watered it ten times a day, by justifying as follows: 'The tulip cannot drink the water so much, so it will wither.') Human-like properties were not transferred indiscriminately.

It should be noted that children do not always select appropriate properties from the old model in constructing a new model; as shown in the above example of a tulip, they sometimes overtransfer some properties from the old model to a new one. In the study mentioned above (Kondo and Inagaki, 1991), the goldfish-raising children attributed a property of feeling pain, which biologists would attribute only to higher animals, not only to goldfish but also to a carp, frog and grasshopper, more often than the children who had never raised any animal. It is suggested that the goldfish-raising children had constructed overly humanized models of goldfish, projecting knowledge about humans to them. Because young children lack knowledge about the relation between a brain and sensation or feeling (Johnson and Wellman, 1982), they overattribute sensation and feeling to the target animal when they construct its human-like models.

Motivational conditions enhancing construction of conceptual knowledge

As we have seen, repeated experience of raising animals ended in the acquisition of procedural knowledge alone in one case, and in another it led children to acquire conceptual knowledge as well. In everyday life, we often see that repeated experiences of cooking meals lead some people to cook quickly within the conventional recipes and others to go beyond them to invent new dishes. Why do people in some conditions but not in others construct mental models of the objects of the procedures they often use? We will discuss this issue in this section, focusing our attention on motivational aspects of the contexts.

Although human beings are intrinsically motivated to understand the world (Hatano and Inagaki, 1987), they do not always try to do so. People may not be motivated to understand the target deeply, because to do so requires much time and mental effort, and procedural knowledge is often quite sufficient to deal with problems that are frequently encountered. In this section we discuss (a) conditions under which motivation for comprehension is likely to be elicited, and (b) how these characterizations can explain why conceptual knowledge was constructed by the goldfish-raising children, but not by the children who took care of rabbits as a duty.

We have proposed a theory of motivation for comprehension elsewhere (Hatano and Inagaki, 1987). This theory assumes that cognitive incongruity – that is, a state where people feel that their comprehension is inadequate – motivates them to pursue subjectively adequate comprehension or satisfactory explanations. Cognitive incongruity induces enduring comprehension activity, including offering a possible interpretation, deriving a prediction from the interpretation, testing the prediction, proposing another interpretation and so forth. More specifically, when people encounter an event or information that disconfirms a prediction based on prior knowledge, they will be motivated to understand why the prediction has failed and how to repair the prior knowledge by incorporating the new information. When people are aware of equally plausible but competing ideas related to the target object or procedure, they will seek further information in order not only to choose one of the alternatives with confidence but also to find justifications for the choice. Or, when people recognize that available pieces of knowledge involved are not well connected, or that other pieces of related information cannot be generated by transforming the existing ones, they will engage in comprehension activity.

Moreover, only when people experience cognitive incongruity about a target that they value in their lives are they likely to engage in comprehension activity. When they love the target object, they may also engage in active and enduring attempts to understand it better. Otherwise, they will be reluctant to engage in comprehension activity, and they may suppress the motivation to comprehend.

Since the construction of mental models is based on motivation to understand a given set of observations better, conditions arousing cognitive incongruity and inducing comprehension activity will also enhance the construction of mental models. We propose four such conditions below, the first two of which are concerned with the arousal of cognitive incongruity, and the last two with the elicitation of committed and persistent comprehension activity in response to induced incongruity. Some varieties of the conditions may specifically enhance abduction, and thus will be most effective in encouraging people to construct conceptual knowledge.

The first condition is to encounter fairly often a phenomenon that disconfirms a prediction based on prior knowledge. Such an encounter induces cognitive incongruity in general, and motivates abduction in particular. This condition tends to be met when procedures are applied to a natural object, because of the inherently occurring variations in its critical parameters (e.g. we may find that the original version of the procedure no longer works). On the other hand, such an encounter is very rare when the object dealt with is highly standardized.

Let us take an example from cooking. Cooking with an automatic device (e.g. an electronic oven) and a detailed recipe involving precise quantification will ensure a standard dish, so will provide less opportunity to observe an unexpected event and thus acquire mental models of dishes. On the contrary, a less specified recipe and less controlled procedures of cooking may produce unexpected variations in taste, and so motivate the construction of the mental models.

Raised animals are typical natural objects. An exactly identical procedure may induce different reactions of the target animals, depending on their physical and other conditions. Even an attempt to please a pet animal may bring about a totally different reaction, and this may well motivate comprehension activity of the owner. Motoyoshi (1979) reported the following episode collected in her daycare centre. Boys who loved to take care of raised rabbits were curious about what kinds of food the rabbits liked best. After carefully observing the rabbits' reactions to different kinds of food given over a month, they discovered that the animals liked carrot best, lettuce second, and Chinese cabbage least, but they ate, quite unexpectedly, lettuce ahead of carrot after being given only carrot for ten consecutive days. One of the boys said: 'When we continue to eat only food we like, we are tired of it. The rabbits are the same as we are.' This utterance can be taken as an expression of his interpretation by abduction of the unexpected event – that is, assigning human-like properties to the rabbits in terms of delicate food preference (and probably also of internal bodily states).

Therefore, it is conceivable that children acquire mental models of raised animals through their experience of taking care of them. The reason why the children raising rabbits as a duty failed to do so may be that they just followed the prescribed procedures blindly without paying much attention to the rabbits' reactions. In addition, many of them did not love the rabbits much, and were not interested in taking care of them. In other words, recognition of an unexpected event often requires prior commitment, which is strengthened by the deep concern with the target object, as well as the freedom to vary and adjust procedures.

The second condition is that frequent dialogical interaction, such as discussion, controversy and reciprocal teaching, are involved in the activity of the domain. Four reasons are proposed for this to be motivating comprehension activity.

1. Dialogical interaction invites a person to 'commit' to some ideas by requiring the person to state the ideas to others, thereby placing the issue in question in the domains of interest. This helps one recognize the inadequacy of his or her comprehension (which otherwise is likely to be ignored) and thus to induce comprehension activity.
2. One has to make explicit what has been known only implicitly in the process of trying to convince or teach others. This will lead one to examine one's own comprehension in detail and thus to become aware of any, thus far unnoticed, inadequacies in understanding.
3. Because persuasion or teaching requires the orderly presentation of ideas, one has to organize better intra-individually what has been known. This will make one realize one's inadequacies of comprehension.
4. For effective argumentation or teaching, one must incorporate opposing ideas – that is, co-ordinate different points of view inter-individually between proponents and opponents or between tutors and learners. This will also induce comprehension activity.

Miyake (1986) presents a good example of how dialogical interaction motivates persons to engage in enduring comprehension activity that would not be induced without a partner, and to produce jointly a detailed mental model of an artifact, a sewing machine. When asked to find why a sewing machine can make stitches, pairs of intelligent adult subjects spent as long as sixty to ninety minutes trying to integrate different perspectives and knowledge bases through discussion in order to construct an elaborated mental model. One member of a pair claimed before long that he had achieved understanding, but criticism by the partner created once again the state of non-understanding (cognitive incongruity) that motivated further comprehension activity.

As mentioned above, the children in Motoyoshi's daycare centre continued to examine rabbits' preference for food over a month. This was originally initiated by discussion between two children who loved the rabbits: one child insisted that the rabbits liked lettuce better because they ate lettuce ahead of carrot, but the other disagreed with him for the reason that when he fed the rabbits the other day, they ate carrot first. When a child of the study group reported the 'discovery' of that day (i.e. the rabbits' reactions) during the period of investigation, other children listened to him with interest. These social interactions seemed to lead these children to engage in the comprehension activity over a month. The present authors would speculate that if the goldfish-raising children had talked to one another about their observations, they could have been motivated more strongly and developed more elaborated mental models of goldfish.

The third condition for people to be involved in comprehension activity is that people are free from urgent external need (e.g. material rewards, positive evaluations or correct answers). People can pursue comprehension only when the pressure to obtain rewards is not so strong, because engaging in comprehension activity is seldom the surest and shortest way to rewards. If people perform a procedure to obtain rewards, they will refrain from being involved in comprehension activity even when incongruity is induced. They will certainly be reluctant to risk varying the procedure, because they usually believe that safety lies in relying on the conventional version. Thus, obtaining rich data by continuous experimentation is often made impossible by external rewards.

These predictions have been supported, though indirectly, by studies showing that the expectation of rewards reduces the quality of performance and intrinsic motivation (Lepper and Greene, 1978). As suggested by Inagaki (1980), and partially confirmed by Inagaki and Hatano (1984), expectation of external rewards may prevent learners from understanding things or events deeply by changing their orientation from towards comprehension to towards success or efficiency.

In the case of raising rabbits as a duty described in the previous section, we can easily imagine that trying to avoid teacher's punishment for the animals' deaths made children hesitate to do anything with the animals beyond the conventional procedures, which inhibited the data collection and thus the construction of mental models. In fact, it was observed in the process of the care that one of the children hesitated to give a piece of (unusual) vegetable, though he was interested, saying that 'I don't know what I shall do if the rabbit dies by being given this'.

In the case of raising goldfish at home, on the other hand, parents' anxiety about goldfish's death that would inhibit children's comprehension activity was not so strong, because goldfish were cheap and were considered as short-life animals in nature. Thus children may sometimes have tried to give them new food. Although most children reported they usually gave them the prescribed food for goldfish at home, they correctly answered, when asked, that goldfish would also eat a small piece of bread (Inagaki, 1990).

The fourth condition is that understanding is valued by reference group members. The encouragement of comprehension by reference group members will lead an individual to form metacognitive beliefs which emphasize the significance and capability of comprehension (at least in the domain in which expertise is acquired). This will make comprehension activity likely to occur when cognitive incongruity is induced. In a reference group which values comprehension, people are often required to explain the appropriateness of the procedure, largely in relation to others, but sometimes to themselves. As mentioned above, individuals may try to construct mental models of the target as the basis for explanation.

In contrast, a reference group which highly values the prompt performance of a procedure and its outcome discourages individuals to seek explanations or to examine new variations of the procedure. Such a reference group may regard asking why or forming corresponding conceptual knowledge through experimentation as extraneous or even detrimental to the efficiency of performance.

As aptly pointed out by Goodnow (1990), the society or culture may impose selected values on its members, especially its less mature members. Metacognitive beliefs about knowing, for example, what kind of knowledge and skills are important, are included in these values. Thus the beliefs about the importance of understanding shared by the developed people in a reference group would be internalized by its developing members, because the latter's metacognitive goals of knowing would often be acquired through joint activities with developed members (Wertsch, 1979). This imposition of internalization usually does not take a form of direct teaching of values. The learning of values is often inseparable from the learning of knowledge and skills. In other words, as pointed out by Lave and Wenger (1990), becoming competent in a domain is almost synonymous with becoming an acceptable member of the community which comprises experts in the domain.

In an unpublished study by Namiki and Inagaki we could see an inhibitory effect of comprehension-disfavouring metacognition on comprehension activity in the kindergarten where children's experience of raising animals resulted in mere procedural sophistication. In this kindergarten, children, in a group of five, were supposed to engage in the care about half an hour immediately after their arrival at the kindergarten. Efficiency was valued by teachers who were afraid that spending a longer time in the animal care might hinder the subsequent main activity they planned for that day. Thus a child's curiosity or question was often suppressed by this efficiency-orientation that the children also seemed to share. Three months after they had begun to engage in the raising activity, the investigators suggested that one of the teachers should prepare an unusual food box for the raised animals, one which was much smaller than the one usually employed, to examine the children's understanding of the meaning of the activity. Finding only a much smaller food box, one of the children said, 'Something is strange with the box'. However, his question ended without being pursued further, because another, influential, child directed him to carry the food box with vegetables promptly to the raised rabbits, and also because other children who were busy in performing their own part of the job ignored his question. Hence, those children did not recognize that they could not feed the animals enough with the small food box they used.

The goldfish-raising children were apparently not much affected by values of the reference group, because they were in a sense isolated. However, we can see in another case a facilitative effect of the comprehension-favouring metacognition on comprehension activity. A teacher in Motoyoshi's daycare centre described earlier put high value on children's interaction with the animal they were raising, so she encouraged the children to run an active 'experimentation' whenever they had some questions or wanted to test their own ideas. This must have led them to continue to examine the rabbits' food preference over a month.

Children in this daycare centre did another experiment on growing plants (Motoyoshi, 1979). That is, they sowed flower seeds at places they liked and compared the results; half the children sowed them in the flower bed, but the other half sowed at very different places, such as in the sandpit, next to a hen house, under a hedge, and so on. They found that some seedlings did not come up, and that whereas some seedlings grew well, others did not. These children learned a lot about growing of plants. After accumulating observations, one of the children said: 'Flowers are like people. If flowers eat nothing, they will fall down from hunger. If they eat too much, they will be taken ill.' The shared belief that it is fun to discover something new by engaging in active experimentation, even when it resulted in a failure, supported these children's comprehension activity and helped them construct mental models of plants.

Conclusion: active mind in context

As Kuhn (1989) aptly pointed out, young children as well as lay adults often possess mental models of the objects they encounter repeatedly that capture some of the objects' essential characteristics, though they are not very good at modifying the models based on newly offered evidence. This suggests that they can build mental models spontaneously and intuitively, without systematic teaching, probably helped by innate and early cognitive constraints in each of the domains (Gelman, 1990).

As long as our competence in problem solving is based on knowledge consisting only of procedures, it must be highly situated or context-bound, and we will be at the mercy of even a minor change in the environment. We cannot be very flexible, and have to cope with novel situations by local adjustment or pure trial and error. It is only by acquiring conceptual knowledge, in the form of mental models of the target objects, that we can be adaptive and inventive. The competence of adaptive experts, who possess such models of the major target objects in the domain, is no longer restricted to familiar situations. Certainly their knowledge is still situated in the sense that it reflects its history (how it was acquired and has been used); however, the knowledge is desituated in the sense of being useful even outside of these experienced situations.

Thus our answer to the first of the two questions posed at the beginning of this chapter is as follows. People may construct mental models of the objects in the domain as they gain expertise in it. The mental models serve as the basis for flexibly modifying familiar procedures and inventing new promising procedures. In other words, knowledge involving mental models can be applied to a variety of situations.

Our answer to the second question is: since human beings have intrinsic motivation to understand, and are equipped with capacities to generate new knowledge from old knowledge or observations, they tend to construct mental models primarily through abduction and analogy in the course of seeking a subjectively satisfactory explanation for the set of observations, providing that the conditions encourage them to engage in enduring comprehension activity and allow them to find usable prior knowledge.

Our findings revealing that even young children can spontaneously construct mental models, if they have engaged in practice repeatedly, exemplifies the power of the active mind of human beings. Its situated nature is one side of our cognition, but we should not miss the other side, namely, that cognition is often pushed forward by the active mind to go beyond the situations which engendered it.

References

Carey, S. (1985), *Conceptual Change in Childhood* (Cambridge, MA: MIT Press).

Collins, A. and Gentner, D. (1982), 'Constructing runnbale mental models', *Proceedings of the Fourth Annual Conference of the Cognitive Science Society*, Ann Arbor, MI, August.

Gelman, R. (1990), 'Structural constraints on cognitive development: introduction to a special issue of cognitive science', *Cognitive Science*, **14**, pp. 3–9.

Gentner, D. and Stevens, A.L. (eds) (1983), *Mental Models* (Hillsdale, NJ: Erlbaum).

Goodnow, J.J. (1990), 'The socialization of cognition: what's involved?', in J.W. Stigler, R.A. Shweder and G. Herdt (eds), *Cultural Psychology: Essays on comparative human development* (Cambridge: Cambridge University Press).

Hatano, G. and Inagaki, K. (1986), 'Two courses of expertise', in H. Stevenson, H. Azuma and K. Hakuta (eds), *Child Development and Education in Japan* (New York: Freeman), pp. 262–72.

Hatano, G. and Inagaki, K. (1987), 'A theory of motivation for comprehension and its application to mathematics instruction', in T.A. Romberg and D.M. Stewart (eds), *The Monitoring of School Mathematics: Background papers. Vol. 2: Implications from psychology; outcomes of instruction* (Madison WI: Wisconsin Center for Education Research), program report 87–2, pp. 27–46.

Hatano, G. and Oura, Y. (1991), *Expertise and Generation of Knowledge*, paper presented at the 33rd Meeting of Japanese Educational Psychology Association, Joetsu [in Japanese].

Inagaki, K. (1980), 'Effects of external reinforcement on intrinsic motivation', *Japanese Psychological Review*, **23**, pp. 121–32 [in Japanese with English summary].

Inagaki, K. (1990), 'The effects of raising animals on children's biological knowledge', *British Journal of Developmental Psychology*, **8**, pp. 119–29.

Inagaki, K. and Hatano, G. (1984), *Effects of External Evaluation on Reading Comprehension and Intrinsic Interest*, paper presented at the American Educational Research Association Annual Meeting, New Orleans.

Inagaki, K. and Hatano, G. (1991), 'Constrained person analogy in young children's biological inference', *Cognitive Development*, **6**, pp. 219–31.

Inagaki, K. and Sugiyama, K. (1988), 'Attributing human characteristics: developmental changes in over- and underattribution', *Cognitive Development*, **3**, pp. 55–70.

Johnson, C.N. and Wellman, H.M. (1982), 'Children's developing conceptions of the mind and brain', *Child Development*, **53**, pp. 222–34.

Kondo, H. and Inagaki, K. (1991), *Effects of Raising Goldfish on the Grasp of Common Characteristics of Animals*, paper presented at the 44th Annual Meeting of Japanese Early Childhood Education and Care Association, Kobe [in Japanese].

Kuhn, D. (1989), 'Children and adults as intuitive scientists', *Psychological Review*, **96**, pp. 674–89.

Lave, J. and Wenger, E. (1990), *Situated Learning: Legitimate peripheral participation*, report no. IRL90–0013, Institute for Research on Learning, Palo Alto, California.

Lepper, M.R. and Greene, D. (eds) (1978), *The Hidden Cost of Reward* (Hillsdale, NJ: Erlbaum).

Miyake, N. (1986), 'Constructive interaction and the iterative process of understanding', *Cognitive Science*, **10**, pp. 151–77.

Motoyoshi, M. (1979), *Essays on Education for Day Care Children: Emphasizing daily life activities* (Tokyo: Froebel-kan) [in Japanese].

Namiki, M. (1985), 'Young children's activity of raising animals and their biological concepts', *Psychological Science*, **8**, pp. 19–29 [in Japanese].

Namiki, M. and Inagaki, K. (1984), *Cognitive Consequences of Raising Animals at a Kindergarten*, paper presented at an Annual Meeting of Japanese Educational Psychology Association, Kyoto [in Japanese].

Perkins, D. and Salomon, G. (1989), 'Are cognitive skills context-bound?', *Educational Researcher*, **18**, pp. 16–25.

Salomon, G., Perkins, D.N. and Globerson, T. (1991), 'Partners in cognition: extending human intelligence with intelligent technologies', *Educational Researcher*, **20**, pp. 2–9.

Wertsch, J.V. (1979), 'From social interaction to higher psychological processes', *Human Development*, **22**, pp. 1–22.

Chapter 8

The pragmatic bases of children's reasoning

Vittorio Girotto, *Istituto di Psicologia, CNR, Rome*
Paul Light, *University of Southampton*

Introduction

If cognitive development is characterized by a high degree of domain-specificity, so too is the *study* of cognitive development. Research is frequently conducted in microworlds which are relatively insulated from one another. These research microworlds are, in turn, often focused around a single experimental 'paradigm task'. This is certainly true of the research to be discussed in this chapter. At the broadest level we are concerned with the nature and development of human reasoning. More specifically, we are concerned with hypothetico-deductive reasoning, and more specifically again, with the use of deductive (and metadeductive) inferences to evaluate the truth status of conditional rules. One experimental task has dominated work in this field for the last quarter of a century: the Wason (1966) selection task.

Against a backcloth provided by Piagetian ideas concerning reasoning and its development, we shall introduce the selection task and the general pattern of adult responses to it. The context sensitivity of such responses was established early on, as we shall see. Our focus in this chapter will be upon the explanation of such context sensitivity.

Drawing upon recent research with adults, and our own studies with children, we shall argue that the concept of 'pragmatic schemas' has much to offer. However, more is involved than simply the evocation of an appropriate reasoning schema. Our analysis highlights the need for psychological bridge-building between research on human reasoning and research on early sociocognitive development.

Limitations of the Piagetian view of reasoning

Until the 1970s the predominant view on the development of reasoning was that founded on Piaget's theory. Central to this approach was the claim that during adolescence children acquire an ensemble of rules of inference which permit the drawing of valid inferences from premises independently of the specific *contents* of these premises and of the *contexts* in which they are presented. These rules of inference constitute the formal operational competence characteristic of adolescents and adults, and are considered as equivalent to the schemas of inference of standard logic. Inhelder and Piaget captured the essence of this view when they claimed that 'reasoning is nothing more than the propositional calculus itself' (1955/1958, p. 305).

While Piaget's theoretical account emphasized logical or logico-mathematical development (e.g. Piaget, 1953), his experimental work tended to concentrate on scientific rather than strictly logical reasoning. Thus the development of reasoning was typically assessed using tasks which involve obtaining and interpreting empirical evidence. The most famous example is probably the pendulum task (Inhelder and Piaget, 1955/1958). Subjects had to determine which of a number of factors (e.g. weight attached, length of string, force of push) affected the period of oscillation of the pendulum. The analysis of children's responses focused upon the systematic control of variables, and interpreted the emergence of this control strategy in terms of a group of inferential operations forming a schema of hypothetico-deductive reasoning.

The emergence of deductive reasoning, then, is seen as one aspect of a much wider transition to a formal or scientific mode of reasoning, a transition which typically occurs in early adolescence. Beth and Piaget (1961/1966) explicitly include the inferential processes necessary to solve deductive reasoning problems in their characterization of 'formal operational' thinking. Consider, for example, problems which involve assessing conditional statements of the type *if p then q* against evidence. Formally, this requires the ability to use simple rules of inference such as *modus tollens* (which permits the derivation of the conclusion *not p* from the conditional statement *if p then q* together with the premise *not q*). But also crucial to this kind of problem is the ability to see how certain kinds of evidence (e.g. the co-occurrence of *p* and *not-q*) are relevant for establishing the truth or falsity of the conditional statement. In other words these problems, although different in form from, for example, the pendulum task, also require the ability to reason in a meta-inferential or hypothetico-deductive manner. This ability to search for the potential counter-examples which could falsify a proposition is seen by Piaget as a hallmark of formal operational thought.

Over the last two decades, this Piagetian approach has been seriously challenged by the results of two lines of research, both of which have

employed hypothetico-deductive reasoning problems. Tasks used have
included problems requiring the postulation of hypotheses and the combina-
torial analysis of their consequences (e.g. Wason, 1978; Griggs, 1983;
Girotto and Legrenzi, 1989), problems requiring rule discovery strategies
(e.g. Wason, 1960) and problems involving assessing the truth status of a
conditional rule (e.g. Wason, 1966).

One of the challenges to the Piagetian position hinges on the issue of
whether adults really do show competence in hypothetico-deductive reasoning. It transpires that the performance of even highly educated adults is often
dramatically poor on such tasks. Moreover, the results suggest that the
content of the premises can often affect the responses which adults give to
these problems. Evans (1989) offers a good recent review of this body of
research into adult reasoning.

The second challenge to the Piagetian position concerns the abilities of
children at ages below that associated with the achievement of formal
operational thinking. As we shall see in the section which follows, under
suitable circumstances even quite young children seem to be able to solve
meta-inferential problems. Moreover, the same contexts and contents which
facilitate adults' reasoning serve to facilitate the performance of young
children.

Research findings in these two fields will be discussed in relation to an
emerging alternative to the Piagetian position, namely, a *pragmatic view* which
ascribes a crucial role to the context of reasoning tasks and to the goals of
subjects engaged in them.

The 'pragmatic schemas' view of reasoning

Since so much of the research to be discussed in this section involves variants
on Wason's (1966) selection task, it will be necessary to provide a brief
outline of the task here. In its basic version, the selection task consists of four
cards, set out as shown in Figure 8.1. Each card is known to have a letter on
one side and a number on the other, and they are set out so that the visible
faces of the four cards show one vowel, one consonant, one even number and
one odd number. Subjects are given the conditional rule: 'If there is a vowel
on one side of the card then there is an even number on the other' (i.e. *if p
then q*). The subjects' task is to indicate which of the cards must be turned
over to establish whether the rule is true or false.

The correct solution is to select only those cards which could conceivably
represent disconfirming counter-examples to the rule – that is, which could
combine a vowel (*p*) and an odd number (*not-q*). The only relevant cards are
thus the one which shows a vowel and the one which shows an odd number.

Despite the simple structure of this task most adult subjects, including

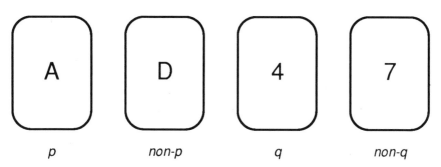

p   non-p   q   non-q

Figure 8.1 An array of cards for the selection task, together with their logical values.

undergraduates with a formal training in logic (Cheng, Holyoak, Nisbett and Oliver, 1986), perform very poorly on it. Only about 10 per cent usually choose the correct cases of vowel and odd number (i.e. p and *not-q*). The commonest pattern of response is to choose the vowel and the even number (i.e. p and q).

The difficulty that adults have with this type of task may be taken to reinforce the view that the ability to assess conditional rules depends on a sophisticated stage of formal reasoning, so that demonstrations that *children* have great difficulty with such tasks (e.g. Kuhn, 1977; Moshman, 1979; O'Brien and Overton, 1980, 1982) seem hardly necessary. Alternatively, the poor performance of adults on such tasks might be taken as an indication that adult reasoning does not in fact conform to the formal operations prescribed by Piagetian theory. Brain and Rumain (1983), for example, suggest that a *general confirmation bias* lies at the heart of adults' problems with the selection task. Most subjects perform poorly, so this argument goes, because they have a strong bias to evaluate propositions by trying to verify them rather than trying to falsify them.

The picture is complicated by the existence of a considerable body of evidence indicating that in suitable circumstances adults are actually able to solve 'selection task' problems rather easily. For example, Johnson-Laird, Legrenzi and Sonino-Legrenzi (1972) asked their adult subjects to imagine that they were postal workers examining sealed and unsealed letters with stamps of different value (40 and 50 lire). Presented with four envelopes, one with a 50 lire stamp, one with a 40 lire stamp, one sealed and one not sealed, they had to decide which would have to be turned over in order to determine whether the rule 'If a letter is sealed then it has a 50 lire stamp on it' was violated. Despite the obvious similarity between this and the original letters/ numbers version of the task, subjects' performance turned out to be very different. Almost all subjects (c. 90 per cent) solved the postal version, turning over the sealed envelope (p) and the envelope with the 40 lire stamp (*not-q*) – that is, just those cases which could potentially show a violation of the rule.

These very marked effects of context and content pose problems for any explanation of reasoning purely in terms of formal rules of inference such as *modus tollens*, since such rules are essentially content independent. In order to retain such an explanatory approach, Piagetian researchers have had to assume that context and content variables act as moderating variables, affecting the accessing of the underlying logical competences once these competences have been acquired (e.g. Overton, 1990). This builds on Piaget's own concession (Piaget, 1972) that formal operations may be applied only to familiar contents. Such an approach, of course, involves retaining the assumption that the relevant competences are not available prior to adolescence.

The literature on context effects on selection task performance is now a considerable one (e.g. Griggs, 1983). It is apparent that in fact familiarity *per se* is neither necessary nor sufficient for facilitation of performance, and nor indeed is concreteness. The conditions for facilitation have in fact proved quite elusive, but in recent years a distinctive interpretive stance has emerged which has taken the debate forward somewhat. Cheng and Holyoak (1985, 1989; Cheng *et al.*, 1986) have suggested that what is crucial about the postal version of the selection task, for example, is not that the rule is familiar, nor that the contents are concrete, but rather than it taps into deontic rules about permission and obligation.

Cheng and Holyoak suggest that people typically reason using not formal rules of inference but *pragmatic reasoning schemas*. These schemas are defined as clusters of context-sensitive rules which, while potentially applicable to different content domains, are none the less constrained by particular classes of 'pragmatically important goals and relationships to these goals'. Some of the schemas lead to correct performance of the selection task in a way which appears consistent with standard logic, but this is essentially little more than a coincidence.

Among deontic schemas, conditional permission ('If one wants to take action A then one must satisfy precondition C') and obligation ('If condition A occurs, then action B must be taken') activate rules which broadly correspond with those of the logic of implication. For example, the permission schema can be defined in terms of four production rules which, although not coinciding (given that they include modal verbs such as 'must' and 'can'), correspond with those of logical implication. Consider the permission rule given above. From this it is possible to derive the contrapositive rule: 'If precondition C is not satisfied, then action A cannot be taken', which implies that one cannot have 'action A' (*p*) with 'precondition C not satisfied' (*not-q*). Moreover, one can derive the conclusion that: 'If action A is not to be taken, then it is irrelevant whether or not precondition C is satisfied'; and that: 'If precondition C is met, it doesn't matter whether action A is taken or not'. From the initial and the contrapositive rules it is possible to infer the relevance of p and *not-q* cases. From the other two rules it is possible to infer the irrelevance of the other two cases.

This analysis was supported by Cheng and Holyoak's own studies using American college students. They showed that subjects without experience on a particular permission or obligation rule (but with a rationale enabling them to understand it as such) could produce the same performance as subjects with direct experience of using the rule. For example, in the case of the postal rule described earlier, American students unfamiliar with such a rule could do as well as students in Hong Kong who had experience of such a rule 'in real life' (Cheng and Holyoak, 1985). In the same paper they report a study in which even an abstractly stated version of a permission rule (i.e. literally, 'If one is to take action A then one must satisfy precondition C') produced significant facilitation when compared to a version similar to Wason's original one. This finding was replicated in a later study, where 62 per cent of subjects succeeded on a version of the problem concerning an abstract precautionary rule: 'If one is engaged in hazardous activity H, then one must have protection P' (Cheng and Holyoak, 1989).

Taken together, these and other results in the adult literature lend considerable support to the view that people can reason by using semi-abstract clusters of rules relating to such things as permission and obligation. While the use of such rules may produce apparently logical responses, the generation of these responses may not in fact depend in any way upon formal logical competences of the kind envisaged in Piagetian theory.

Interpretation of reasoning in terms of such pragmatic schemas offers a quite different perspective on what might be expected by way of responses to selection tasks from young children. Work on sociocognitive development suggests that children have considerable expertise in such matters as permission and obligation from an early age (e.g. Turiel, 1983). To the extent that such expertise underlies performance on the selection task, one should hypothesize that children's performance might be very much like that of adults, and that the same conditions which facilitate adults' reasoning should facilitate that of children on such tasks. This is the hypothesis which has guided our own experiments in this area, some of which we shall outline in the next section.

Children's performance on the 'reduced array' selection task (RAST)

Several of our studies have employed a 'reduced array' version of the selection task (cf. Johnson-Laird and Wason, 1970). In this version, subjects have to draw inferences only about the q and *not-q* cases. This reduction of cognitive load does not eliminate the crux of the problem, since in the full selection tasks subjects typically have little or no difficulty in seeing the relevance of the *p* card and the irrelevance of the *not-p* card. It is the choice of the *q* and/or *not-q* cards which causes difficulty. Where the RAST has been used with adults (Johnson-Laird and Wason, 1970; Mazzocco, 1972; Wason and Green, 1984) most subjects still do not solve it unless the context and content of the rule refer to deontic matters.

As well as reducing the choice to just the *q* and *not-q* sets, the RAST procedure typically involves actually allowing the subject to test elements (i.e. to turn over cards or whatever) in order to determine the status of the rule. This feature allows the RAST procedure to be built into a more game-like scenario, which was one of the features which attracted us to it for our studies of children's reasoning. In our first experiment (Girotto, Light and Colbourn, 1988) we actually adapted an existing children's game involving a battery-operated device. However, in subsequent studies (e.g. Girotto, Blaye and Farioli, 1989) we used a computer-based simulation of the original game, and this is the version we shall describe here.

Children were presented with a computer screen displaying some schematic bees. It was explained to the children that some of the bees were 'buzzers' and some were 'non-buzzers'. When touched on the screen with a light pen the buzzers emitted a tone while the non-buzzers were silent. After an initial familiarization phase, the screen changed to show where the bees lived – it showed a central area which was 'inside' (i.e. the hive) and a peripheral area which was 'outside' (i.e. a field 'outside'). Some bees were shown inside and some others outside (see Figure 8.2).

It was explained to the children that the Queen Bee had made a rule that 'If a bee buzzes, then it must stay outside'. It was explained that the Queen had made the rule so that she would be able to rest and not be disturbed by the buzzing. The children had to imagine that they were officers of the Queen Bee, and they had to check that her rule was being obeyed. They were first asked which of the bees – those inside, those outside, or both – they would need to check on. Then they were allowed to test all those that they wished to with the light pen. Finally, they were asked for a judgement as to whether they thought the rule was being obeyed (in fact it always was). Thus the correct solution required:

1. Correct anticipation of the need to test all and only the *not-q* set (i.e. the bees inside the hive).
2. The systematic testing of all and only these bees.
3. A final judgement that the rule was being obeyed.

The performance of children even as young as seven was very good on this task. For example, Girotto, Blaye and Farioli (1989, Experiment 3) found that 70 per cent of 7 year olds succeeded with the permission rule. A

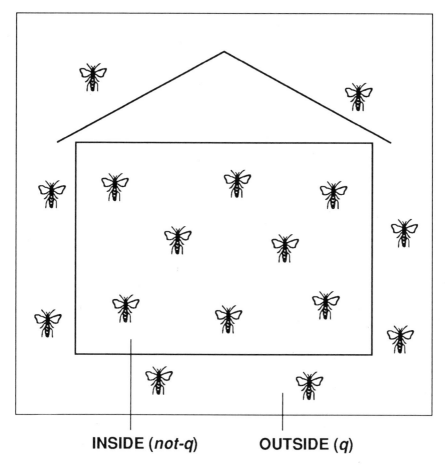

Figure 8.2 Screen presentation for the 'buzzing bees' task.

similarly high rate of success was found in a condition in which the tested rule had the form of an obligation (e.g. 'If a bee is sick then it must stay outside'; the sick bees in this case produced a coughing sound when tested!). A control condition was used in which the rule 'If a bee buzzes, then it is outside' was offered without supporting context. The rule in the case was simply 'If a bee buzzes, then it is outside'. This condition produced a mere 5 per cent success rate from the 7 year olds.

Success on the task in any of its conditions involves searching for potential counter-examples to conditional rules, which as we have noted has been seen as an achievement peculiar to the formal operational stage of reasoning. The high rates of success activated by young children on the 'permission' and 'obligation' versions of the task thus present some problems to a Piagetian account. These problems would not be resolved by positing the earlier appearance of the relevant formal competences, since these would be expected to support successful performance on the control condition too.

Nor can results of these experiments be readily explained in terms of familiarity with the content of the rule or the specific context of the task (cf. Griggs, 1983). However, while the children had no direct or specific familiarity with the rule or the context of testing it, the *general situation* posited in the permission and obligation versions was certainly familiar and recognizable to them. The pragmatic view of reasoning highlights the significance of such 'general situations' as bases for interpretation. The demonstration that even 7 year olds are able to solve reasoning problems which defeat adults provided that they are framed as permissions or obligations seems to lend considerable support to such a view.

In fact, age differences are not at all conspicuous on these tasks. In particular, for an arbitrary ('control') version of the RAST, Girotto, Blaye and Farioli (1989, Experiment 1) found there were no significant differences between the performances of 9/10 year olds, 14/15 year olds, and adults. All three groups showed about a 10 per cent success rate. By contrast, one of our studies involving a RAST test of an obligation rule showed 70 per cent success even from children in their first year of schooling (Light, Blaye, Gilly and Girotto, 1989).

Children's performance on the full selection task

The results we have reported using the RAST are at variance with those of a series of American studies using the full selection task (Overton, Ward, Noveck, Black and O'Brien, 1987; Ward and Overton, 1990). These authors have been concerned to retain the Piagetian concept of formal operations, explaining the role of content and context variables as *moderators* of the deployment of an underlying competence once that competence has been acquired. In the case of the selection task, the necessary competence is not considered to be present before adolescence, so that the facilitatory effects of context should be apparent only *after* that age.

In support of this position, Overton and colleagues offer evidence that pre-adolescent children perform poorly on the full selection task even with relevant (i.e. non-arbitrary) content. For example, Ward and Overton (1990) obtained about 20 per cent correct solutions from a group of 11 year olds, both with 'relevant' and with 'irrelevant' content. However, their procedures involved children being given a number of selection tasks, which varied in character, including some which might be interpreted as threats or warnings (e.g. 'If a student is caught running in the school halls then the student must be punished') and some which might most readily be interpreted in descriptive terms (as a co-variation) rather than in deontic terms (e.g. 'If a student is in a school, then the student is not playing the radio'). The carry-over or interference effects arising from the use of several quite different kinds of rule on a within-subject basis are difficult to estimate.

Another difference between these studies and our own, reported in the previous section, is that Overton and colleagues used the full selection task involving all four options (*p*, *not-p*, *q* and *not-q*) whereas we had used the reduced array version of the task involving only two options (*q* and *not-q*). To assess the significance of this we carried out a number of experiments using the full selection task (Girotto, Gilly, Blaye and Light, 1989). In these, we sought to examine only one type of rule ('permission'), and carried out all comparisons on a 'between subjects' basis. Contrary to those of Overton and colleagues, these studies show that 10 year olds as well as 14 year olds can do well in situations where the rule was contextualized as a permission, even if the rule itself is novel and unfamiliar.

For example, the (clearly unfamiliar) rule: 'If you drive over 100 km/hr, then you must have a fluorescent car', was presented to 10 and 14 year olds as one of the road safety rules of an imaginary country. They were asked to think of themselves as policemen, having responsibility for checking that the rule was obeyed. In one condition an explicit rationale for the rule was given, namely, that at high speed, cars need to be visible at a distance, so the fluorescent bodywork is a safety measure. In another condition no rationale for the rule was given. For comparison, a third condition used a *familiar* road safety rule: 'If you sit in the front of a car then you must wear a seat belt'. Finally, a control group of subjects were given the original vowel/even number version of the selection task. In all cases, they were presented with four cards showing the various cases and they had to decide which cards they would need to turn over, just as in the original task.

Predictably, performance in the control condition was poor (about 8 per cent success). Performance with an unfamiliar rule *without* rationale was better (about 55 per cent success), while that on the unfamiliar rule *with* rationale was as good as that on the specifically familiar rule (about 80 per cent success). There were no significant differences between the results for the two age groups.

These results confirm and extend those obtained with the reduced array version of the task. They show that direct experience with a permission rule is not a necessary condition for searching for potential violations. Even 10 year olds are able to test an unfamiliar rule appropriately if a rationale explaining the motives of the authority that introduced it is available. The fact that significant facilitation is evident even without such a rationale being explicitly available may mean that the fact of presentation as a permission (i.e. it contains the modal verb 'must', it has been produced by an authority, and the subjects have to check whether it is being obeyed) is sufficient in itself to support solution. However, an alternative interpretation is that the facilitation occurring in the case of a non-rationalized permission may depend in some measure on the children inventing a plausible rationale for themselves. If so, it should depend on the intrinsic plausibility of the rule.

To investigate this, we sought to compare the facilitatory effects of more and less plausible versions of a rule (Girotto, Gilly, Blaye and Light, 1989, Experiment 2). One group of 10 year olds were given a selection task with the 'fluorescent car' rule as given above, without a rationale. Another group of 10 year olds were given an intrinsically less plausible rule: 'If you want to drive a fluorescent car, then you must drive at over 100 km/hr'. For the first group the results of the previous experiment were replicated, with about 55 per cent of subjects succeeding. For the second group results were poorer, with only about 20 per cent succeeding.

The children in both conditions were asked for a possible reason why the government of this imaginary country might have introduced this rule. Sixty five per cent of children given the first rule were able to provide some intelligible reason, only 10 per cent of children given the second rule were able to provide any kind of reason for it. Furthermore, the ability to think of a reason was significantly correlated with the ability to solve the selection task.

It is apparent from the studies discussed in this section that the contextualization of a selection task rule as a permission *can* evoke responses which coincide with the formal solution even from pre-adolescent children. However, it is equally apparent that more is involved than simply an automatic triggering of the appropriate schema – for example, the plausibility of the rule and the accessibility of a rationale for it have significant effects upon subjects' responses. In the next section we shall take a closer look at some of these issues, at the same time shifting our focus from rules relating to permissions to rules relating to promises.

Schema activation, perspective taking and the representation of potential violations

Deontic rules can be broadly divided into two categories in terms of the possibilities for violation (Gigerenzer and Hug, 1991). The first category, which includes the permission and obligation rules discussed in previous sections, is characterized by a 'unilateral violation option'. Here the subject is typically aligned with the authority (or the group/institution) which has promulgated the rule, and is required to check on potential violations by the party to whom the rule is applied. The second category includes rules characterized by a 'bilateral violation option' – that is, rules which can very plausibly be violated by either of the parties involved. This is the case, for instance, with a conditional contractual promise,[1] having the general form 'If you fulfil condition C then I will give you reward R'.

Such a promise can be violated by the promisor deciding not to give the promised reward to a deserving promisee. Alternatively it can be violated by the promisee gaining the proposed reward without performing the requested action. If such a rule has to be checked in the context of a selection task, then, we should expect that the pattern of results will depend upon the *specific perspective* which subjects are cued to adopt. The appropriate pragmatic representation of the rule depends upon this perspective (cf. Politzer and Nguyen-Xuan, in press).

Where the subject takes the promisee's perspective an obligation schema will be activated, and the pragmatic representation of the rule from this point of view becomes: 'If condition C is met then reward R must be given'. The potential violation by the promisor is therefore 'Condition C met, reward R not given'. When the subject takes the promisor's perspective a permission schema is activated and the pragmatic representation of the rule from this point of view becomes: 'If reward R is to be given condition C must be met'. The potential violation by the promisee is thus 'Reward R given, condition C not met'.

If the original rule is represented formally as: 'If p [i.e. condition C] then q [i.e. reward R]', then from the promisee's perspective the subject could be expected to select the options corresponding to p and *not-q*, whereas from the promisor's perspective the predicted selections would be those corresponding to *not-p* and q.

Several recent studies, though not always framed in terms of pragmatic schemas, have borne out these predictions. For example, Manktelow and Over (in press) explored a situation in which a shop manager made a conditional contractual promise to his customers, namely: 'If you spend more than £100, then you may take a free gift'. The majority (62 per cent) of their adult subjects who had to test this rule from the customer's point of view selected the pragmatically correct cards p (i.e. more than £100 spent) and *not-q* (i.e. no gift). When the same rule had to be tested from the point of view of the shop manager, the majority (85 per cent) of subjects chose the complementary cards *not-p* (i.e. less than £100 spent) and q (i.e. gift taken). The fact that the results were more clear cut in this latter case may suggest that violations by the customer are intrinsically more plausible than violations by the shopkeeper.

Similar results have been reported by Gigerenzer and Hug (1991) using the rule: 'If an employee works on the weekend then that person gets a day off during the week', again with adult subjects. We have ourselves recently reported a study using conditional contractual promises with children. Light, Girotto and Legrenzi (1990) asked their subjects (11/12 year olds) to check on a promise made by a headteacher to his pupils. The school was one in which 'housepoints' were awarded by the teachers for good work or behaviour. The headteacher's promise was: 'If you get more than ten housepoints this week then you can have a sweet'. In one condition the

subjects were asked to check the rule from the headteacher's perspective –
that is, they had to check whether any of the children had cheated (the
children were left to help themselves to sweets if they met the condition).
The most frequent single pattern of response (50 per cent) was choice of
cards showing a child with less than ten housepoints (*not-p*) and a child with
a sweet (*q*).

In this situation cheating by the promisor is not a plausible option, so we
devised a more complex variant of the scenario in which the headteacher
implemented his promise by giving the sweets to the house captains (i.e.
selected senior pupils) to distribute to those children who met the condition.
This allowed us to suggest, for example, that the headteacher subsequently
decided to check on whether the house captains had cheated by keeping too
many sweets for themselves.

Here the predicted pattern of choice was 'child with ten or more
housepoints' (*p*) and 'child without sweet' (*not-q*). However, only 22 per cent
of children chose just these two cards. The most frequent pattern of choice
(39 per cent) involved these two cards plus that showing 'child with sweet'
(*q*). After the selection task (which was, of course, undertaken individually by
the children) we discussed the task with them in groups of four to six. In this
context they frequently mentioned the possibility that the house captains
might not simply retain sweets for themselves but give them to their
undeserving friends. So even where this possibility of nepotistic violation of
the rule was not suggested, it was clearly available to many of the children –
presumably on the basis of their experience with house captains!

Politzer and Nguyen-Xuan (in press) conducted a study with 15 to 18 year
olds using a conditional contractual promise very similar to the Manktelow
and Over's 'shop' role described earlier. The rule, supposedly made by a
famous Paris jeweller, was: 'If the purchase exceeds 10,000 Francs, then the
salesman must stick on the back of the receipt a gift voucher for a gold
bracelet'. When asked to test the rule from the customer's point of view (in
the role of consumers' association representative) only 35 per cent of subjects
chose solely the predicted cards corresponding to 'more than 10,000F' (*p*)
and 'no gift voucher' (*not-q*). When testing from the manager's point of view
only 17 per cent chose solely the predicted cards, corresponding in this case
to 'less than 10,000F' (*not-p*) and 'gift voucher' (*q*). These percentages
compare to the 62 per cent and 85 per cent obtained by Manktelow and Over
(in press) with an apparently virtually identical rule.

How can these differences in response be explained? We suggest that the
difference may lie in the motives and opportunities for violation suggested by
the two scenarios. In Politzer and Nguyen-Xuan's scenario, the promisor or
his agent (the famous jeweller's salesman) had no apparent motive for
violating the promise, while the promisee (the customer) had no apparent
opportunity to do so. By contrast, in Manktelow and Over's scenario both the
promisor (a shop manager in an industrial town during the depression who

was suspected of cheating his customers) and the promisee (a customer suspected of) taking more than he/she was entitled to) had motive and opportunity.

Another of Manktelow and Over's (in press) studies offers support for such an interpretation. Their (adult) subjects were presented with a promise made by a mother to her son: 'If you tidy up your room then you may go out to play'. When cued to the mother's perspective 68 per cent chose cards corresponding to 'room not tidied' (*not-p*) and 'went out to play' (*q*). However, when cued to the son's perspective only 23 per cent chose the cases 'room tidied' (*p*) and 'not allowed out to play' (*not-q*). But when the scenario was modified to include the suggestion that the mother has a history of being unfair to her children the percentage of 'correct' selections from this point of view rose to 63 per cent.

The rather chequered results of these studies using conditional contractual promises as selection task rules seem, then, to indicate just how sensitive deontic reasoning can be to contextual constraints upon the representation of potential violators. Even when the rule clearly has the form of a promise, and is set in an intelligible context, and even when the perspective from which the rule has to be tested is specified, the responses of both adults and children are highly variable. Systematic searching premissed upon violations of the rule from particular perspectives depends upon the intrinsic plausibility of such violations, given what is known about the situations and agents involved. Such contextual factors clearly need to be taken into account in some way if we are to have a satisfactory account of the pragmatics of reasoning.

Thus far, apart from showing that children as young as primary school age respond rather similarly to adults in these kinds of task, we have had little to say about the origins of such reasoning. In the next section we shall look briefly at one recent approach to this issue.

The evolution of conditional reasoning

The notion of pragmatic reasoning schemas rests on the idea that certain patterns in the flow of human experience, and especially perhaps social experience (i.e. patterns related to permissions, obligations, etc.) become the basis for fairly general reasoning schemas. Grounded initially perhaps in specific experiences, with development they come to offer available interpretative frames for dealing with a range of situations. Little has been written concerning the development processes involved, but one suggestion is that the relevant development may be better conceived in phylogenetic than in ontogenetic terms (Cosmides, 1989; Cosmides and Tooby, 1989).

Cosmides argues that human reasoning may be underpinned by species-specific mechanisms very akin to the pragmatic schemas we have been discussing. What she terms 'Darwinian algorithms' are envisaged as specialized mechanisms which organize experience into adaptively meaningful schemas or frames: 'When activated by appropriate problem content, these innately specified frame builders ... call up specialised procedural knowledge that will lead to domain-appropriate inferences, judgements and choices' (Cosmides, 1989, p. 195).

In particular, Cosmides argues that responses to the selection task are interpretable in terms of adaptations based on the social development of the species over long periods of evolutionary time. For the vast majority of their evolutionary ancestry humans have lived in pre-agricultural hunter-gatherer groups. Thus, she argues, the exigencies of life under these conditions must be seen as the source of the adaptive pressures which have shaped the evolution of our thinking. Various types of interpersonal 'deals' involving paying some kind of cost to secure some kind of benefit can plausibly be thought to have played an important part in the life of such groups. Avoidance of getting cheated in such 'social contracts' would thus be highly adaptive. Cosmides suggests that it is an evolved facility for operating with such social contracts which underpins successful responses to schematized versions of the selection task.

This argument should perhaps be seen in the context of a wider one concerning the roots of human intelligence. It has long been argued that the distinctive success of the human species may owe more to its social organization than to any more specific adaptations at the individual level (e.g. Bruner, 1972). One corollary of this argument is that adaptive success for the individual will always have depended more upon successful integration into (and manipulation of) social relationships than on almost any other attribute. Intellectual propensities or strategies which are effective in the context of such social negotiations will therefore have been subject to heavy selection pressure (e.g. Byrne and Whiten, 1988).

The difficulty with this kind of argument, of course, is not so much any lack of plausibility as a lack of pertinent evidence. Cosmides (1989) attempts to adduce at least some circumstantial evidence using the selection task. Her argument is that if facilitation depends on the elicitation of a 'social contract' schema, then it should occur *only* in situations which involve the parties in paying some kind of cost in order to secure some kind of benefit.

In practice, Cosmides's attempts to demonstrate this have not been entirely convincing (Cheng and Holyoak, 1989; Pollard, 1990; Girotto, 1991). Indeed, some of the rules which are best established as facilitative of selection task performance do not readily lend themselves to analysis in cost-benefit terms. For example, rules such as 'If someone is drinking beer then they must be over 18' have been established as facilitative of selection task performance (e.g. Griggs and Cox, 1982). However, being over 18 cannot sensibly be construed as a *cost* incurred in order to drink beer. To take another example from one of our own studies mentioned earlier, in the case of the facilitatory rule 'If a bee is sick then it must stay outside', being outside cannot be construed as a cost incurred in order to be sick! Rather these rules involve authority, and the imposition of collective rules upon the individual.

Thus facilitatory effects appear to extend beyond the kind of social contract which Cosmides emphasizes. Cosmides herself argues that permission from institutional authority cannot plausibly be envisaged as central to the life of our hunter-gatherer ancestors (Cosmides, 1989, p. 255; see also Pollard, 1990).

Although on present evidence her evolutionary argument seems unsubstantiated, Cosmides has done a valuable service to the field by highlighting the essentially social grounding of facilitatory schemas and the unresolved issue of their origins. We have seen from the previous section that taking perspectives and analysing situations in terms of motives has a part to play in this type of reasoning. Cosmides's work adds to this an emphasis on the importance of being alert to the possibilities for cheating or deception. As Gigerenzer and Hug (1991) note, these are areas which have recently begun to attract the attention of developmental psychologists interested in 'the child's theory of mind'. In the section which follows we shall briefly dip into this literature from the point of view of what it might offer for our understanding of the development of pragmatically grounded reasoning.

Pragmatic schemas and children's theory of mind

Much of the recent work on children's theory of mind has employed tasks which involve assessing the young child's ability to attribute false beliefs (i.e. beliefs which are at variance with the child's own knowledge) to others (e.g. Perner, Leekham and Wimmer, 1987). It appears that 3 year olds have a great deal of difficulty with this, whereas 4 year olds do not. The 'false belief' issue is clearly related to that of cheating or deception. The emergence of deceptive strategies in the context of games has been studied over a considerable period (e.g. De Vries, 1970; Light, 1979; Sodian, 1991). Here again it is clear that by 4 or 5 years of age children can engage in deliberate deception, whereas the weight of evidence suggests that children of 3 years and younger cannot.

More generally, between 3 and 5 years of age there seems to be a marked development in children's ability to predict or appreciate the beliefs, actions, intentions and goals of others (see Astington and Gopnik, 1991, for a recent review). Moreover, individual differences on tasks across this range tend to co-vary – that is, children who are good at one such task tend to be good across the range of such tasks (Light, 1979; Astington and Gopnik, 1991).

Though these observations give some indication of the developmental timetable, they do not in themselves offer much insight into the developmental processes involved. Some researchers in this field share with Cosmides the belief that specific innate abilities are involved. For example Leslie (e.g. 1988; Leslie and Thaiss, in press) argues for the existence of an innate, domain-specific cognitive mechanism which underlies the ability to understand others' behaviour in terms of mental states. The deficits shown by autistic children are held to arise from an impairment (i.e. a failure of maturation) of this mechanism.

Other researchers interested in the conditions for development of such understanding have looked to the social experiences of children during their early years. Dunn (1988), for example, offers detailed observationally based accounts of the contexts within which young pre-schoolers come to understand and utilize deceit. She also devotes close attention to the issue of how children develop their appreciation of social rules (of permission, prohibition and so on) within the context of the family.

Dunn emphasizes the mother's role: rules and discussions relating to such rules make up a significant fraction of the mother–child talk which Dunn has analysed:

> Our conversational analyses show that the social rules of the world in which the children were growing up were continually discussed by their mothers: discourse on what was acceptable, what unacceptable, surrounded them . . . The moral order of their parents' world was conveyed to the children again and again in the repeated events of their daily lives. (Dunn, 1988, p. 73)

Other evidence is available to suggest that the way in which mothers speak to, and about, their pre-school children is a significant correlate of their children's facility on a range of tasks involving the recognition of others' points of view (Light, 1979). However, it is hard to establish cause and effect in this area, and as Dunn points out, the available evidence does not exclude the possibility of rather specific innately given contributions to such development.

What, then, has this brief excursion into the psychology of early socio-cognitive development offered? Our earlier analysis suggests that the kinds of later reasoning performance in which we are interested depends upon a familiarity and facility with certain forms of social rules and an ability to reason in terms of the motives and perspectives of others. It is thus of some interest to see current developmental research suggesting that critical developments in this regard probably occur between 3 and 4 years of age. However, beyond this there seems to be little agreement either about how to characterize what develops or about the developmental processes involved (Astington and Gopnik, 1991). We can hope that the high level of current interest in researching the development of 'children's theory of mind' will help to change this situation, and allow firmer bridges to be built between this research area and that concerned with the pragmatic bases of later reasoning performance.

Conclusion

In this chapter we have discussed the pragmatic basis of children's hypothetico-deductive reasoning, with particular reference to deontic matters, in relation to recent developments in the study of adult reasoning. We have reviewed research showing that even quite young children can, under suitable circumstances, solve problems demanding the ability to search for possible violations of conditional rules.

Such problems are difficult even for intelligent adults when presented in arbitrary contexts. The fact that children as young as 6 or 7 years can reach very high levels of success in certain contexts raises difficulties for the traditional Piagetian view of reasoning development. It seems that children at what ought to be different stages of intellectual development (i.e. concrete and formal operations) respond very similarly using deontic rules. Taken together with the fact that even at supposedly 'formal operational' ages subjects typically fail with abstract or arbitrary rules, this seems to militate against the idea that reasoning development is characterized by the emergence of formal, general-purpose rules of inference during adolescence.

Recent versions of the Piagetian position assume that expression of the formal competence is moderated by contextual factors (e.g. Overton, 1990). This does not explain the evident facility of pre-adolescent children with deontic rules. Moreover, if the moderating contexts are *always* required for the expression of the formal competence, the explanatory value of the latter concept seems questionable.

Some other recent attempts at explaining reasoning have also retained the concept of formalistic rules or schemas of inference. The 'natural logic' position (e.g. Politzer, 1986; Braine, 1978) assumes that reasoning is determined in some cases by simple schemas such as *modus ponens*. However, these are considered to be early acquisitions. Their operation is seen as constrained by a class of pragmatic factors which we have not touched on in this chapter (though we might with advantage have done so), namely, those related to the rules of conversation.

In discussing the origins of the early competence which children appear to show in the deontic domain, we considered Cosmides's (1989) suggestion that such reasoning is grounded upon an evolved facility for operating with 'social contracts'. Our own demonstrations of children's early ability to deal with tasks requiring the testing of deontic conditional rules could be said to be at least consistent with her claim for the existence of specific innate procedures for 'looking for cheaters'. However, as we have seen, there are weaknesses in her argument that facilitatory rules can always be understood in narrowly 'cost-benefit' terms.

The nature versus nurture issue could potentially be addressed in terms of the cultural variability of responses to reasoning tasks. There appears to be very little research on this using the selection task (our own studies have been conducted in the UK, Italy and France, but that hardly counts!). The wider cross-cultural literature (e.g. Scribner, 1977) indicates that culture, literacy and schooling can have significant effects on responses to cognitive tests including tests of syllogistic reasoning.

The issue of the effects of training has received more attention. Cheng and Holyoak (1989) compared the effects of formal training (i.e. training in the elementary rules of logic) with those of pragmatic training (based on general characteristics of permissions and obligations). Pragmatic training bearing on the nature of obligations was found to improve college students' performance on problems amenable to interpretation in terms of obligation. However, neither the comparable formal training nor indeed a six-month course in propositional logic had any substantial effect on students' ability to solve either arbitrary or deontic versions of the problem. Only one of our own studies (Light *et al.*, 1989) has involved any form of training, but that indicated that pragmatic training can be effective even with 7 year olds.

A number of more naturalistic studies have indicated that courses in, for example, mathematics can have significant effects on conditional reasoning (Jackson and Griggs, 1988; Lehman and Nisbett, 1990). Overall, then, it appears that the type of reasoning called for by the selection task can be improved through both extended/naturalistic and short-term/experimental training, and that there is a specific positive effect of training on deontic matters.

At its simplest, the concept of pragmatic schemas might be seen in terms of the automatic triggering of a particular schema, given a particular syntactic framing of the conditional rule. However, even from Cheng and Holyoak's initial (1985) research it was clear that this is not the case, at least to the extent that some *rationale* is necessary in the case of unfamiliar rules. The complex pattern of results emerging from the more recent studies we have reviewed suggests that the responses of both children and adults are influenced not only by the plausibility of the rule as a deontic regulation, but also by the role subjects take up in searching for potential violations and the representation of what counts as a violation.

To the extent that these factors involve perspective-taking and the representation of motives for violation, there is a potentially rich connection with research on the development of the young child's 'theory of mind'. One possible direction for future research would involve investigation of the relationship between the capacity for attributing mental states to others, behaving deceptively, etc., on the one hand, and the ability to evaluate deontic rules on the other.

Representation of what counts as a violation in the case of a deontic rule could be considered as a special case of representing counter-examples to any type of conditional rule. The importance of such representation of counter-examples has been stressed by proponents of the 'mental models' theory of reasoning (Johnson-Laird, 1983). The mental models theory is perhaps the most radical alternative to any conception of reasoning in terms of inferential rules. Reasoning is conceived as a matter of representing the contents of the premises and searching for possible examples which are at variance with this representation, in order to draw a valid conclusion. Searching for a counter-example depends on the ease of representing it – that is, on the load such representation imposes on working memory (Oakhill and Johnson-Laird, 1985).

This theory assumes that there is only one crucial step in the acquisition of deductive competence, and this involves the ability to search for counter–examples (Johnson-Laird, 1990). This ability is constrained by the processing capacity of working memory, which develops with age. Some support for this in the field of syllogistic reasoning comes from the finding that children's performance depends on the number of models or representations required by the premises (Johnson-Laird, Oakhill and Bull, 1986). However, no significant correlation was found between syllogistic reasoning performance and a measure of working memory.

More generally, it is not clear how the mental models theory could accommodate the very different performances produced by children of the same age when seaching for counter-examples in syllogistic as opposed to deontic selection tasks. Moreover, as we have seen in this chapter, despite presumed increases in working memory, responses to any given selection task are often very similar for subjects of very different ages (e.g. Girotto, Blaye and Farioli, 1989).

The pragmatic schemas approach which we have drawn upon in this chapter does offer a way of understanding the evident domain-specificity of reasoning. It allows us to understand how responses are shaped by the specific domain of knowledge activated by the content of the reasoning problem and the scenario within which it is presented. Having said that, we have seen that our conception of the operation of such schemas needs to be considerably enriched to take account of the full range of contextual influences which shape subjects' responses to reasoning tasks. We have concentrated here on a rather narrow range of deontic contents; it remains for future research to establish whether there are other equally well-demarcated domains of pragmatic reasoning to be found.

Note

1. We use the term 'conditional contractual promise' to refer to a social rule in which a promisor specifies a certain condition that the promisee has to satisfy in order to obtain a given reward or undertake a desired action (e.g. 'If you meet condition C then I'll give you reward R'). In an unconditional promise the promisor states only the action which he or she is committed to carry out (e.g. 'I promise you that I

shall be back in a week'). In a conditional *non*-contractual promise the promisor promises something to the promisee on the basis of the occurrence of a certain event which may not depend on his/her will (e.g. 'If I win the lottery, I'll buy you dinner').

References

Astington, J. and Gopnick, A. (1991), 'Theoretical explanations of children's understanding of the mind', *British Journal of Developmental Psychology*, 9, pp. 7–31.

Braine, M.D.S. (1978), 'On the relation between the natural logic of reasoning and the standard logic', *Psychological Review*, 85, pp. 1–21.

Braine, M.D.S. and Rumain, B. (1983), 'Logical reasoning', in Flavell, J. H. and Markman, E.M. (eds), *Handbook of Child Psychology: Vol. 3, Cognitive Development*, fourth edition (New York: Wiley).

Bruner, J. (1972), 'Nature and uses of immaturity', *American Psychologist*, 27, pp. 687–708.

Byrne and Whiten, A. (1988), *Machiavellian Intelligence: Social expertise and the evolution of intellect in monkeys, apes, and humans* (Oxford: Oxford University Press).

Cheng, P. and Holyoak, K. (1985), 'Pragmatic reasoning schemas', *Cognitive Psychology*, 17, pp. 391–416.

Cheng, P.W. and Holyoak, K.J. (1989), 'On the natural selection of reasoning theories', *Cognition*, 33, pp. 285–313.

Cheng, P.W., Holyoak, K.J., Nisbett, R.E. and Oliver, L.M. (1986), 'Pragmatic versus syntactic approaches to training deductive reasoning', *Cognitive Psychology*, 18, pp. 293–328.

Cosmides, L. (1989), 'The logic of social exchange: has natural selection shaped how humans reason? Studies with Wason selection task', *Cognition*, 31, pp. 187–276.

Cosmides, L. and Tooby, J. (1989), 'Evolutionary psychology and the generation of culture, Part II case study: a computational theory of social exchange', *Ethology and Sociobiology*, 10, pp. 51–97.

De Vries, R. (1970), 'The development of role-taking as reflected by behaviour of bright, average and retarded children in a social guessing game', *Child Development*, 41, pp. 759–70.

Dunn, J. (1988), *The Beginnings of Social Understanding* (Oxford: Blackwell).

Evans, J. St B.T. (1989), *Bias in Human Reasoning. Causes and consequences* (Hillsdale, NJ: Erlbaum).

Gigerenzer, G. and Hug, K. (1991), *Reasoning about Social Contracts: Cheating and perspective change*, manuscript submitted for publication.

Girotto, V. (1991), 'Deontic reasoning: the pragmatic schemas approach', *Intellectica*, special issue, and in Politzer, G. (ed.), *Reasoning and Pragmatics* (in press).

Girotto, V., Blaye, A. and Farioli, F. (1989), 'A reason to reason: pragmatic basis of children's search for counterexamples', *European Bulletin of Cognitive Psychology*, 9, pp. 227–321.

Girotto, V., Gilly, M., Blaye, A. and Light, P.H. (1989), 'Children's performance in the selection task: plausibility and familiarity', *British Journal of Psychology*, 80, pp. 79–95.

Girotto, V. and Legrenzi, P. (1989), 'Mental representation and hypothetico-deductive reasoning: the case of the THOG problem', *Psychological Research*, **51**, pp. 129–35.

Girotto, V., Light, P.H. and Colbourn, C.J. (1988), 'Pragmatic schemas and conditional reasoning in children', *Quarterly Journal of Experimental Psychology*, **40**, pp. 469–82.

Griggs, R.A. (1983), 'The role of problem content in the selection task and THOG problem', in Evans, J. St B.T. (ed.), *Thinking and Reasoning: Psychological approaches* (London: Routledge & Kegan Paul).

Griggs, R. A. and Cox, J. R. (1982), 'The elusive thematic materials effect in Wason's selection task', *British Journal of Psychology*, **73**, pp. 407–20.

Inhelder, B. and Piaget, J. (1958), *The Growth of Logical Thinking from Childhood to Adolescence* (London: Routledge & Kegan Paul) (original work published 1955).

Jackson, S.L. and Griggs, R.A. (1988), 'Education and the selection task', *Bulletin of the Psychonomic Society*, **26**, pp. 327–30.

Johnson-Laird, P.N. (1983), *Mental Models* (Cambridge: Cambridge University Press).

Johnson-Laird, P.N. (1990), 'The development of reasoning ability', in Butterworth, G. and Bryant, P. (eds), *Causes of Development: Interdisciplinary perspectives* (London: Harvester Press).

Johnson-Laird, P. N., Legrenzi, P. and Sonino-Legrenzi, M. (1972), 'Reasoning and sense of reality', *British Journal of Psychology*, **63**, pp. 395–400.

Johnson-Laird, P.N., Oakhill, J. and Bull, D. (1986), 'Children's syllogistic reasoning', *Quarterly Journal of Experimental Psychology*, **38A**, pp. 35–58.

Johnson-Laird, P.N. and Wason, P.C. (1970), 'Insight into a logical relation', *Quarterly Journal of Experimental Psychology*, **22**, pp. 49–61.

Kuhn, D. (1977), 'Conditional reasoning in children', *Developmental Psychology*, **13**, pp. 342–53.

Lehman, D.R. and Nisbett, R.E. (1990), 'A longitudinal study of the effects of undergraduates' training on reasoning', *Developmental Psychology*, **26**, pp. 952–60.

Leslie, A. (1988), 'Some implications of pretence for mechanisms underlying the child's theory of mind', in Astington, J., Harris, P. and Olson, D. (eds), *Developing Theories of Mind* (New York: Cambridge University Press).

Leslie, A. and Thaiss, L. (in press), 'Domain specificity in conceptual development: evidence from autism', *Cognition*.

Light, P.H. (1979), *The Development of Social Sensitivity* (Cambridge: Cambridge University Press).

Light, P.H., Blaye, A., Gilly, M. and Girotto, V. (1989), 'Pragmatic schemas and logical reasoning in six to eight year olds', *Cognitive Development*, **4**, pp. 49–64.

Light, P.H., Girotto, V. and Legrenzi, P. (1990), 'Children's reasoning on conditional promises and permissions', *Cognitive Development*, **5**, pp. 369–83.

Manktelow, K.I. and Over, D.E. (in press), 'Social roles and utilities in reasoning with deontic conditionals', *Cognition*.

Mazzocco, A. (1972), 'Due esperimenti sul ragionamento deduttivo: il probleme della conversa', *Rivista di Psicologia*, **56**, pp. 47–65.

Moshman, D. (1979), 'Development of formal hypothesis-testing ability', *Developmental Psychology*, **15**, pp. 104–12.

Oakhill, J.V. and Johnson-Laird, P.N. (1985), 'Rationality, memory and the search for counterexamples', *Cognition*, **20**, pp. 79–84.

O'Brien, D.P. and Overton, W.F. (1980), 'Conditional reasoning following contradictory evidence: a developmental analysis', *Journal of Experimental Child Psychology*, **30**, pp. 44–60.

O'Brien, D.P. and Overton, W.F. (1982), 'Conditional reasoning and the competence-performance issue: a developmental analysis of a training task', *Journal of Experimental Child Psychology*, **34**, pp. 274–90.

Overton, W.F. (1990), 'Competence and procedures: constraints on the development of logical reasoning', in Overton, W. F. (ed.), *Reasoning, Necessity and Logic: Developmental perspectives* (Hillsdale, NJ: Erlbaum).

Overton, W.F., Ward, S.L., Noveck, I.A., Black, J. and O'Brien, D.P. (1987), 'Form and content in the development of deductive reasoning', *Developmental Psychology*, **23**, pp. 22–30.

Perner, J., Leekham, S. and Wimmer, H. (1987), 'Three year olds' difficulty with false belief: the case for a conceptual deficit', *British Journal of Developmental Psychology*, **5**, pp. 125–37.

Piaget, J. (1953), *Logic and Psychology* (Manchester: Manchester University Press).

Piaget, J. (1972), 'Intellectual development from adolescence to adulthood', *Human Development*, **15**, pp. 1–12.

Politzer, G. (1986), 'Laws of language use and formal logic', *Journal of Psycholinguistic Research*, **15**, pp. 47–92.

Politzer, G. and Nguyen-Xuan, A. (in press), 'Reasoning about promises and warnings: Darwinian algorithms, mental models, relevance judgements or pragmatic schemas?', *Quarterly Journal of Experimental Psychology*.

Pollard, P. (1990), 'Natural selection for the selection task: limits to social exchange theory', *Cognition*, **36**, pp. 195–204.

Scribner, S. (1977), 'Modes of thinking and ways of speaking: culture and logic reconsidered', in Freedle, R. (ed.), *Discourse Production and Comprehension* (Hillsdale, NJ: Erlbaum).

Sodian, B. (1991), 'The development of deception in young children', *British Journal of Developmental Psychology*, **9**, pp. 173–88.

Turiel, E. (1983), *The Development of Social Knowledge* (Cambridge: Cambridge University Press).

Ward, S.L. and Overton, W.F. (1990), 'Semantic familiarity, relevance and the development of deductive reasoning', *Developmental Psychology*, **26**, pp. 488–93.

Wason, P.C. (1960), 'On the failure to eliminate hypotheses in a conceptual task', *Quarterly Journal of Experimental Psychology*, **12**, pp. 129–40.

Wason, P.C. (1966), 'Reasoning', in Foss, B. (ed.), *New Horizons in Psychology* (Harmondsworth: Penguin).

Wason, P.C. (1978), 'Hypothesis testing and reasoning', Unit 25, Block 4, *Cognitive Psychology* (Milton Keynes: The Open University).

Wason, P.C. and Green, D.W. (1984), 'Reasoning and mental representation', *Quarterly Journal of Experimental Psychology*, **36A**, pp. 597–610.

Chapter 9

Contexts and cognitions: taking a pluralist view

Jacqueline J. Goodnow
Pamela M. Warton, *Macquarie University*[1]

Our starting point is a concern with the limitations of some conventional accounts of context and cognition. These accounts often proceed as if the individual encounters *a* culture or *a* context, as if cultures or contexts provide a single message, a single explanation of events, or unequivocal pieces of information. They also often proceed as if the outcome of cognitive development were the acquisition of a single understanding of events, a single way of defining a task or of looking at the world.

A singular view, we propose, may fit some particular problems, some particular domains of knowledge. More often, it seems that a singular view does not have a good fit with the nature of contexts or the nature of development. Many contexts, for instance, may best be described as containing a collection of messages, with some of these at odds with others. The advice may be given, for example, both to look before you leap and to remember that he who hesitates is lost – that is, to treat all problems in scientific, rational fashion and, at the same time, to regard at least some problems as not amenable to such analysis. In similar fashion, achievement may be presented as a matter sometimes of talent and sometimes of effort. Personality may be described as indefinitely improvable and as limited by temperament, by genes, or by one's astrological sign. The way in which the body works may be described as closely linked to states of mind or as independent of one's mood. Overall, the presence of a single position on a topic or of a single correct solution to a problem might indicate the exceptional context rather than the norm.

This chapter expands upon these general proposals, developing what we shall call a 'pluralist' view. We use this term to refer to context and to cognition. In the references to context, it indicates that the situations within

157

which ideas are absorbed or constructed often contain more than one view of an event, with the views sometimes in conflict or competition with one another. In the references to cognition, it indicates that an individual may take on board more than one point of view, sometimes resolving them to generate a new blend and sometimes simply flipping from one to the other without a sense of conflict.

The first section of the chapter outlines an area of research built around a singular view of contexts and of development. The research deals with the acquisition of an understanding of conservation: for instance, acquiring the principle that the weight of an object does not change when its surface appearance does. The section describes briefly the way in which, within this area, questions of context and cognition have been approached. It also points to several reasons for regarding tasks of this kind as providing a limited understanding of contextual effects and of cognition. Few areas of knowledge, we shall argue, are of the type represented by tasks such as conservation.

The second section considers several examples of pluralist views, drawn from accounts of cultural models (e.g. Quinn and Holland, 1987) and of social representations (e.g. Duveen and Lloyd, 1990). In the main, these accounts have emphasized the pluralist nature of contexts. They point, for instance, to the presence of expert and lay theories in many areas of knowledge, together with variations within formal and informal views. They underline also the need to ask how these several points of view co-exist and influence one another, and suggest that contexts may be described in terms of the range of theories and the nature of their co-existence (e.g. scorn or respect for each other, mutual borrowing or strict distance).

A pluralist view does more than provoke a second look at the nature of contexts. It alters as well our understanding of the way context and cognition are intertwined. Accordingly, we shall include in this section several suggestions dealing with cognitive development in the form of a tolerance for ambiguity and contradiction, and with processes such as the selective appropriation of culturally available ideas, adopting some as one's own and rejecting others.

The third section concentrates on some research applications of a pluralist view, bringing together some material in earlier sections but asking more explicitly: what kind of research does a pluralist view lead to? The applications considered are to the analysis of context and to the analysis of cognition, with the larger space given to the latter type of application. The section mentions briefly material on concepts of intelligence (Mugny and Carugati, 1985; Carugati, 1990) and concepts of children (Emiliani, Zani and Carugati, 1981; Molinari and Emiliani, 1990). It then considers in more detail an application to parents' ideas about the place of money in the family system (more specifically, the use of money rewards for children's household jobs), based on data gathered at Macquarie (Warton and Goodnow, 1990).

All three sections take a broader view of cognition than is contained in research that concentrates upon performance on school tasks or psychometric tasks. Under the heading of cognition we include ideas about such topics as the nature of a 'task', the bases of success or failure, divisions of responsibility between teacher and learner or among family members, and the nature of intelligence, childhood or development. Ideas of this kind have sometimes attracted attention because they appear to underlie performance on the cognitive or academic tasks that psychologists present. They have also attracted attention as forms of social cognition: the understanding of people, emotions, intentions or relationships, often set in arbitrary opposition to the understanding of objects, time or space. Both bases for interest will emerge in the following sections.

An example of research based on a singular view

We shall start from analysis of the way in which children acquire an understanding of physical conservation: that is, of the principle maintaining that changes in the surface appearance of an object do not change such intrinsic properties as its amount, weight or volume. It has long been argued that an understanding of this principle is a hallmark of change in a child's cognitive level. In particular, it marks a shift from thinking that is driven by appearances to thinking based on a logical understanding of transformations, and on the ability to distinguish transformations which matter from those which do not.

On a variety of conservation tasks, children have been shown to proceed through three positions. In the first, they firmly believe that the intrinsic properties (e.g. amount or weight) change when the surface appearance changes. In the second, children may entertain two possibilities (change and no change), vacillating between the two. In the third, they come down firmly on the side of no change. At this point, to use the Piagetian phrase, they have 'a sense of logical necessity'. They see no other view as possible, are surprised that any other view could be held, and resist attempts at persuasion in the form of statements that other children, or the experimenter, take a different view. Overall, the transition is from the one incorrect view to one scientifically correct view. The former is abandoned when the latter is achieved. The latter is endorsed by adults as not only correct but also as a mark of competence. Failure to achieve it is then considered to be a mark of delayed development.

How is this form of cognitive development linked to the analysis of contextual effects? By and large, researchers interested in conservation tasks have not regarded social contexts as the main source of change in the level of thinking. They have, instead, placed a great deal of emphasis on such processes as biological unfolding, discovery, and the individual's abstraction or construction of logical order from the events encountered in the course of exploratory activity.

This is not to say that questions about contextual effects and the processes underlying them have been lacking. Such questions have been asked, most often in the form of attention to whether the social setting provides the conditions seen as needed for children to abstract or generate a correct understanding of the problem. These conditions may be thought of in terms of schooling, in terms of the opportunity for exploratory activity, or – more subtly – in terms of the presence of encounters with views other than one's own: encounters which may lead to reflection, a resolution of differences, and a move from one level of thought to another (e.g. Doise and Mugny, 1984).

The main departure from this type of approach comes in research documenting the extent to which an adult's questions and actions are open to several interpretations by the child. Children may, for instance, not understand the specific connotation of 'same' that an adult has in mind when asking, say, whether two objects are the same amount or will displace the same amount of water. Children may also be inclined, when adults ask questions to which they must surely know the answer, or when adults ask the same question twice, to consider that some unusual answer is called for or that their first answer may be wrong. A 'wrong' answer, then, may not show a lack of intellectual competence but a social misunderstanding of the question. In addition, development may now be regarded not only as the acquisition of a logical understanding of transformations but also as the acquisition of shared meanings between adult and child: for example, the acquisition of an understanding of the kind of answer an interrogator has in mind (e.g. Hundeide, 1988; Light and Perret-Clermont, 1989).

Documenting the ambiguity of an adult's questions in most con- servation tasks is one step towards asking about the special features of conservation tasks. Besides the ambiguity of questions, however, two further features have been noted. Both lead towards the suggestion that the situations that conservation tasks represent, and the answers they suggest for the interplay of cognition and context, or for the description of cognitive development, may be limited.

One of these features has to do with aspects of proof. Proof in laboratory tasks is usually easy to obtain. As Glick (1985) has noted, the child working on the Piagetian task of understanding how a pendulum operates usually has easy access to pendula which yield accurate results. In real life, pendula may be owned by others, inaccessible, or rigged to give the results that the owner has in mind. Regardless of these material circumstances, conservation tasks also present problems which people regard as open to proof. As Lloyd and Duveen (1990) have pointed out, the very expectation that scientific proof will provide an unequivocal answer means that conservation problems are of a particular kind. If one adopted Habermas's (1979) classification of problems in terms of the kind of validation people regard as appropriate (e.g. turning to evidence, to faith, to custom or to morality), conservation problems would fall into the group of questions generally regarded as referable to a world of scientific evidence. A different view of proof or validation may well apply, however, to the nature of social categories or social invariants, or to the understanding of emotions, of personality, of social events. The development of thinking with regard to these phenomena may then follow a quite different course.

The second feature noted for conservation tasks is a lack of social pressure towards understanding. This may sometimes occur because adults expect that children will inevitably acquire some forms of understanding. Conservation of amount or of weight might fall into this category. A lack of social pressure may also arise because the issue is not seen as important. Conservation of volume provides an example. For most people, this form of understanding is relevant to few tasks and is of no great social or interpersonal importance (Goodnow, Knight and Cashmore, 1985). Under either of these circumstances, there may be no social pressure applied to move towards a particular understanding of events. A child's error may be left uncorrected. The views of others may not be seen as relevant to one's own or as calling for any great degree of thought. It may well take, for instance, an experimenter's or a teacher's insistence that people emerge with a single, agreed answer to generate much interest in resolving any awareness of people taking more than one view of most problems involving volume. If only by default, then, the major processes will have to do with individual curiosity and discovery.

In effect, one might well argue that problems of the kind typified by conservation problems are likely to encourage a singular view of contexts and cognitions: one correct answer, demonstrable by some form of scientific proof; one direction of development (towards the unshaded acceptance of the correct answer as logical and inevitable); and one major process (namely, individual discovery).

For strong alternatives, often based upon the analysis of different areas of knowledge or understanding, we shall turn to the notions of plurality contained in some accounts of social representations and cultural models.

Examples of pluralist views

We shall draw from two approaches to questions of culture and cognition, one emphasizing cultural models, the other social representations. As Goodnow and Collins (1991) point out, these two approaches are seldom brought together, although both make a number of the same points. An emphasis on plurality is one of these.

Cultural models

The analysis of cultural models covers both what a culture may provide and the way an individual may think about events. The term comes from the discipline known as cognitive anthropology (e.g. Reid and Valsiner, 1986; Super and Harkness, 1986; D'Andrade, 1987; Quinn and Holland, 1987). That discipline has come 'to stand for a new view of culture as shared knowledge – not a people's customs and artifacts and oral traditions, but what they must know in order to see as they do, make the things they make, and interpret their experience in the distinctive way they do' (Quinn and Holland, 1987, p. 4). It is this shared knowledge that is at the heart of cultural models. They are 'presupposed, taken-for-granted models of the world that are widely shared (though not to the exclusion of other alternative models) by the members of a society' (*ibid.*).

As an example of co-existing alternatives, researchers interested in cultural models have pointed to the presence in most cultures of both formal models (the models advocated by the accepted experts) and of informal models or 'everyday knowledge'. Along with a formal model of education or medicine, for example, there co-exists a theory of alternative education or alternative medicine. Within each there may also be alternatives. Formal models of education, for instance, may contain both the view that intelligence has to do with the capacity to manipulate symbols and solve abstract problems (a view that Mugny and Carugati, 1985, term a cybernetic definition of intelligence), and some acceptance of a definition of intelligence as having to do with the capacity to deal with everyday life, to interact effectively with other people, or to adapt to new circumstances. The same plurality may well be found also within the informal models held by parents (Mugny and Carugati, 1985). In a sense, the polyglot nature of society may be reflected in the individual's state of mind.

To say that alternative models may co-exist, however, does not mean that they have equal status. In Salzman's (1981) terms, a culture at any one time contains both 'dominant' and 'recessive' views on most topics. Formal medicine, to take an example from Foucault (1980), generally enjoys a higher status in most sections of the population than does alternative medicine. Alternative medicine may be turned to, however, and used as a way of criticizing the formal model, when disappointment with the formal model reaches a certain level, or when there is a sense of the formal model being too entrenched or too unresponsive to the needs of its clients.

What consequences of plurality are considered within accounts of cultural models? They have mainly to do with the nature of cognition. To start with, cognition is expected to be marked by a tolerance for ambiguity and contradiction. This emerges both from the plurality of views and from the tendency of people to adopt a scientific mode of thinking only with certain kinds of problems or under certain kinds of pressure. This combination of events means that 'a folk theory does not present a totally consistent whole the way a conscious, expert theory does' (Kay, 1987, p. 76).

A second consequence has to do with the extent to which an individual's ideas are responsive to new information. The tendency to see folk models as not primarily issues of 'hard evidence' may mean a slow response. Ideas are firmly held to in the face of what others may see as overwhelming evidence. Alternately, ideas may display an easy flip from one view of events to another, in a fashion which is again not in keeping with the pace of evidence (Gergen, 1982). The easy change, it has been suggested, arises because 'folk theories are not "believed" in the way conscious theories are but are used or presupposed as the occasion of thought or communication demands' (Kay, 1987, p. 76). As a result, 'individuals find it relatively easy ... to invoke conflicting proverbial advice for the solution of different problems and to adopt one or another contradictory folk theory of language depending on which one better fits the linguistic case at hand' (Quinn and Holland, 1987, p. 10).

Within this account of cultural models, it is not clear when people will lag behind or outstrip the pace of information. To use a Quinn and Holland (1987, p. 10) example, we may well change easily from one theory of how a thermostat works to another theory. We may also cling to particular views of 'marital commitment, career choice, gender relations, and kinship obligations' (*ibid.*) in the face of clear disagreement with the views of experts or even the evidence of one's own life. For the latter cases, one suspects psychologists might well turn towards Abelson's (1986) view that some beliefs are 'like possessions'. They have become part of one's sense of self and sense of place, cherished and held dear in spite of changes in the world's fashions and, if ever abandoned, set aside only with reluctance and a sense of lost comfort.

This type of suggestion (a link to issues of identity) is one we shall return to in later sections. The adoption and retention of particular views or schemas, it suggests, is not simply a matter of information encountered, accepted or ignored. It is as well a matter of one's sense of identity and group membership. Some areas of knowledge, some views of the world, some ways of approaching problems, some styles of thought: these become part of one's sense of self as a person who is 'scientific', 'perceptive', 'intuitive', or 'sound'. The adoption of some and the rejection of others are influenced, then, by the extent to which they are in keeping with the image one wishes to hold of oneself or to have others hold (Goodnow, 1990).

Social representations

Where anthropologists speak of cultural models or folk theories, social psychologists are likely to speak of 'social representations'. A definition from

Moscovici and Hewstone (1983, p. 15) brings out several points of overlap. Social representations are 'cognitive matrices coordinating ideas, words, images and perceptions that are all interlinked; they are commonsense theories about aspects of the world'.

Some of the questions considered in analyses of social representations have to do with their content. Like cultural models, social representations may cover more than one idea about an event, with relatively little concern for the way the several ideas hang together. The primary role of social representations is to make possible both easy communication and social interaction (a function made possible by their being shared views). As long as this function is met, everyday beliefs 'may include inconsistent and actually contradictory elements' (Duveen and Lloyd, in press, pp. 3–4).

Analyses of social representations also contain questions about their source. One approach has taken the form of asking about the interplay of formal and informal knowledge, of 'science' and 'commonsense'. It is this interest, for instance, which prompts Moscovici (1961) to analyse the way in which terms from psychoanalytic theory have become part of everyday speech (e.g. terms such as neurosis, repression, superego, the unconscious, oral personality) and Chombart de Lauwe (1984) to consider the way in which formal theories about children are taken up in informal theory.

In a more novel approach to content, it has also been proposed that social representations may contain an iconic aspect. Our views of children, for instance, are often attached to particular visual images (D'Alessio, 1977; Chombart de Lauwe, 1984; Molinari and Emiliani, 1990). These iconic typifications may then account for the lack of change in the face of new information (we become attached, for instance, to an image of children as 'babies' or an image of homes as 'havens'). They may also account for the presence of change when some new icon is made available. The picture of a battered child, for example, weakens the standard icon of a child surrounded by loving parents.

A different kind of approach to sources is illustrated by Sarchielli's (1984) analysis of becoming a member of an occupational group. Any work setting, Sarchielli argues, contains a number of social groups. Some are co-workers, some are subordinates, some are one's managers. This variety of groups means first that the individual is exposed not to a single message but to a variety. It also means that the individual, rather than accepting some inexorable process of occupational socialization, may adopt a 'questioning and critically active stance to the organization setting and ... to the influencing pressures exerted within the working environment' (Sarchielli, 1984, p. 283). In effect, the variety of views encountered offers the individual some opportunity to resist some of the views offered and to choose among them. 'Transmission' then needs to be thought of in terms of processes such as selective appropriation or resistance (Goodnow, 1990), and one needs to ask how these aspects of process come into play, rather than concentrating only on the absorption of a prevailing view or the construction of an inevitably correct solution.

The last feature of social representations approaches to which we shall draw attention again has to do with the factors which give rise to the selection of a particular viewpoint or to the holding of several. The representations one develops, it is argued, are strongly influenced by one's social position, by the nature of one's participation in the social life of the group. The ideas held by children about the nature of authority, for instance, or about the extent to which resources should be distributed on the basis of equality or equity, are likely to reflect not only their age and cognitive capacity (the variables usually considered) but also their social class and the forms of participation in social life that this influences (Emler, Ohana and Dickinson, 1990).

This particular way of defining context, as we shall see again in the third section, opens a number of interesting research possibilities. In effect, context becomes specified in terms not of reality external to the individual and imposing itself upon him or her, but in terms of the place of the individual within the social group. The individual may, for instance, be mainstream or minority, at the centre or marginal, a member of an ingroup or an outgroup. In a particularly interesting application of this concept, attention may be especially directed towards the ideas of people who hold a double social position. Few parents, for instance, occupy only the social role of parents. Even mothers, often thought of as occupying only one social role, may be both mothers and, in their paid work, teachers. The two social positions do not promote identical views of children, giving rise to research asking whether the two sets of views come to be blended or whether they lead to some particular sources of frustration and unease (e.g. Mugny and Carugati, 1985; Molinari and Emiliani, 1990).

Research uses of a pluralist perspective

In this third and final section, we ask: how can we put a pluralist perspective to research use? Some research possibilities have already been indicated. We now wish to draw these together and extend them.

Two broad lines of research application may be noted. In one, the starting point is an interest in analysing the nature of contexts. In the other, the starting point is an interest in analysing the nature of cognition, with particular attention given to the concepts and categories people use when considering topics such as the nature of children, of intelligence, or of family.

We do not wish to imply that the analysis of context and the analysis of cognition are neatly separate from one another. When cognition is defined, for instance, in terms of the informal models that individuals come to hold, then context may be described in terms of the range of alternate views that are likely to be encountered. In some contexts, one meets only like-minded people. In others, one encounters a range, and may even be engaged in a constant defence of one's ideas.

For all the interconnections, however, we shall for the moment keep separate research starting from a primary interest in context and research starting from a primary interest in cognition. We shall also give the larger space to the second line of research. That imbalance stems in part from cognition being the starting point more often preferred by psychologists. It stems also from the analysis of cognition being the point of origin for some research in which we have been directly engaged: research that has suggested a novel way of interweaving context and cognition, a way which may be of value to other researchers looking at the same issue.

Analyses of context

One way of approaching context is to ask about the nature of the models held by the people who surround one and are in some position to argue for their views as warranting attention or acceptance. This approach leads readily to a concern with the nature of formal theories or expert advice: the nature of formal theories of intelligence, for example, or of advice to parents from educators or pediatricians. Clarke-Stewart's (1978) analysis of 'primers for parents' is one example. Zelizer's (1985) analysis of changing legislation (e.g. legislation related to paid child labour) and changing advice in parents' magazines, is another.

For these aspects of context (the nature of the formal models) there is the advantage of a written record. For informal or everyday models, one needs to turn to survey material: to the analysis, for instance, of parents' views about the use of punishment in public and in private, asking which ideas about punishment display some fair degree of consensus and which are held by smaller pockets of people (Reid and Valsiner, 1986).

Documenting the presence of variety, however, stops short of describing the nature of people's encounters with the views of others. This type of description opens a further way of differentiating among contexts. One might ask, for instance, about the way in which the holders of formal and informal models regard each other's. Are everyday models looked upon with scorn, treated as 'naive' theories? Or are they regarded with some degree of respect? In turn, are expert models treated with respect or regarded with suspicion, regarded as the products of people who 'wouldn't know' what the real situation is like? One might also ask about the degree of distance, or the nature of the blend, between formal and informal models. That is, for example, the kind of step taken by Moscovici (1961) in his analysis of the extent to which concepts from psychoanalytic theory have become part of everyday language.

Less easy to document are aspects of context related to the nature of the encounters people have with ideas other than their own. The nature of 'lay' encounters with formal or expert models have yet to be detailed, and may be difficult to determine. One may know, for instance, how many copies of *Dr Spock* have been bought but not how many are then read or used. Perhaps the easier possibility is the documentation of encounters with the informal views of other individuals. On an Israeli kibbutz, for instance, differences in opinion about child rearing cannot be glossed over to the extent that they can be among parents living in town. On the kibbutz, the differences are not only difficult to hide; it is also expected that differences will be aired and worked through (Orr, personal communication). From a pluralist perspective, the critical feature differentiating these contexts would then be the likelihood of encounters with discrepant views, accompanied by some demand for discussion and perhaps resolution.

The analysis of cognition

As a first example, we shall note a particular approach to concepts of intelligence (Mugny and Carugati, 1985; Carugati, 1990). In brief, the argument proposed is that people hold several definitions of intelligence. They may endorse, for instance, the view that intelligence refers to the ability to solve abstract problems and manipulate symbols (a 'cybernetic' definition of intelligence). They may also endorse a definition of intelligence as 'adaptive' (the ability to change as circumstances change) or as 'social' (the ability to learn the rules and expectations of one's social group). The degree of endorsement for each of the three may then vary from one parent to another, with one source of variation being the extent to which a parent has been exposed to champions of one view or another. Once their children enter the school system, for instance, with emphasis on cybernetic definitions and its rewards for this kind of intelligence, most parents move towards a stronger endorsement of the cybernetic definition than they had previously made.

As a second example, consider some research on parents' concepts of children. Like the research by Mugny and Carugati (1985), this research stems from an interest in social representations. It also contains an interest in the idea that the endorsement of one model rather than another reflects not only exposure but also one's social position. To be more concrete, one study by Molinari and Emiliani (1990) asks about the extent to which parents emphasize the importance of independence, both in theory and in action. Of particular interest is the presence of difference between mothers who are full-time homemakers and mothers who are also teachers in schools. (The latter are viewed as occupying a double social position, with a potential conflict between the view that adults should accept a child's dependence and the view that they should foster independence.) Mothers who are also formal teachers turn out to place the stronger value on independence, to find more frustrating a child's dependent actions, and to take a more didactic approach to a task such as reading with a child. The 'teacher' view of children apparently swamps the more accepting view that is part of the 'motherly' model.

The degree to which one's formal role may take over is even more strongly exemplified in a study of nursery-school teachers in centres with contrasting routines (Emiliani *et al.*, 1981). One centre emphasized strict routines. The other emphasized the importance of flexibility and the need to consider the child's preferences. Caregivers in the two centres endorsed quite different views of the child and of what children need in order to develop well or to feel secure. The views held of children were consistent with the practices. That might be because people choose to work in centres where the practices endorse what the caregivers believe from the start. It seems equally likely, however, that caregivers can hold both concepts of what a child needs. They move towards one or the other when one particular point of view is publicly praised or when it is more or less called for as part of one's position. To the extent that a particular point of view is linked to aspects of identity (a school teacher who questions the value of schooling, for instance, would be regarded as suspect), then the push towards endorsement of one model, with a possible derogation or downgrading of alternative views, seems likely to become even stronger. One view becomes part of the definition of the 'in-group'. The other belongs to people different from oneself.

The last example comes from parents' ideas about the place of money in the family system. More specifically, what ideas do parents hold about money rewards for children's household jobs? At this point, we shall begin to draw upon some direct experience, gained in the course of some recent research on children's household jobs and the possible links between parental practices and parental ideologies (Warton and Goodnow, 1990; Goodnow and Warton, 1991).

The research began with an awareness of Zelizer's (1985) historical account of public debate in the USA about pocket money and jobs. This left no doubt that 'Anglo' cultures have contained a diversity of expert views. Some experts have favoured a close linking of jobs and money. The majority of experts, however, have favoured a separation of money from jobs, a distinction between the concept of 'allowance' and the concept of 'wage'. They have then felt it was reasonable to chide parents for their tendency to use allowances as an instrument of discipline, rewarding children for jobs done or fining them for jobs not done.

This historical account, combined with some data from a study with English parents of 7 year olds (Newson and Newson, 1976), led us to expect that we might find two major views on the subject of pocket money in relation to household jobs. One may be labelled, 'Keep them Separate'; the other, 'Link the Two'. We also hoped that we might be able to identify groups of parents in terms of the degree to which they endorsed these two positions.

Parents, we thought, might not be completely dedicated to one position or the other, but they might well be expected to lean strongly towards one rather than the other.

With these expectations in mind, we put together a set of thirteen statements produced by a group of Australian mothers in the course of open-ended questions about their views on pocket money in relation to jobs. Some of these statements argued, in strong or weak forms, for separation: for example, 'Arrangements in the family and arrangements in the paid work force are quite separate issues'; 'Payment shouldn't be necessary: doing a job well should be its own reward'; 'Children should want to help without necessarily being paid'. Others argued for a link, again in either a strong or soft form: for example, 'It's the same as hiring someone else; if I had to bring someone in to do that work, I'd expect to pay for it', or 'If they're getting pocket money anyway, they should do something in return'.

We then proceeded to ask a new sample of 118 parents (mothers and fathers) to rate each statement for the degree to which they agreed with each statement. The options were: (1) agree completely; (2) agree somewhat; (3) disagree somewhat; and (4) disagree completely. The next step – factor analysis – reflected the hope that we could, as Mugny and Carugati (1985) had done for concepts of intelligence, locate clusters of statements and then identify groups of parents in terms of their scores on the several factors.

To cut a long statistical story short, we found not two factors, but three. The first loaded on statements supporting the position, 'Keep them Separate'. The second factor supported the position, 'Link the Two'. The third factor loaded on statements suggesting a completely pragmatic view of the problem. Here the positive loadings were for statements such as the following: 'It's OK to pay them if that's the only way to save a lot of argument'.

The three factors made conceptual and intuitive sense. Unfortunately, between them they accounted for only 35 to 40 per cent of the variance. Moreover, several attempts to locate parents in terms of their scores on the three factors were unsuccessful. When we divided parents, for instance, in terms of whether they displayed high, middle or low scores on the three factors, the largest subgroup (a clear 25 per cent of the sample) occupied a middle position on all three factors.

That type of outcome, we came to recognize, is not out of line with the view that people may incorporate several cultural models into their own understanding and may then not be aware of, or bothered by, the presence of contradictions within their ideas. The level of co-existence, however, seemed high to us. In addition, to leave the matter as a happy co-existence of opposites seemed an insufficient account of the way parents thought and felt about the issue. From the interviews, we had the sense that co-existence was more complex than a *laissez-faire* tolerance of several positions would imply. We had the sense, for instance, that a sizeable group of parents went along with many positions but at some point found their 'bottom line': a position they absolutely could not endorse.

At this point, we decided to turn the problem of agreement on its head and to ask about disagreement. We then came up with a different view of how people may select from, or live with, a variety of culturally available viewpoints.

We turned especially to the rating (4) 'disagree completely' and asked: how many statements do parents disagree with? Can we perhaps describe subgroups in terms of how many statements (and what kinds of statement) they find intolerable? Perhaps, we thought, parents might be far more clear cut about what they do not like or cannot stand than about what they positively endorse.

This attempt at analysing co-existence was far more rewarding than had been our concentration on the statements with which parents agreed. We began by noting that parents did differ widely in the number of statements with which they disagreed. The range was from 0 to 11 of the 13 statements.

We then asked about groups of parents, starting with those who did not disagree completely with any statement. In the sample of 118, there were 12 of these (6 mothers, 6 fathers). They are not simply people who avoid the ends of the range (they make ample use of the rating [1] 'agree completely'). Nor are they people who agree to some extent with everything. They did use the rating (3) 'disagree somewhat'. There was simply no statement with which the parents in this subgroup completely disagreed.

In contrast was a sizeable group (N = 24: 12 mothers, 12 fathers) who disagreed completely with only one statement. These are the parents whom we see as having one 'bottom line'. Most positions seem somewhat reasonable to them until they encounter one which they are totally unwilling to endorse. The item disagreed with by 7 of these 24 is one which argues for a close similarity between 'home' and 'shop', between an 'allowance' and a 'wage': 'It's the same as hiring someone else; if I had to bring in someone else to do that job, I'd expect to pay for it'. Attracting disagreement from another 6 of the 24 was the instrumental view: 'Paying them is OK if it's the only way to get the job done without a lot of argument'. That statement seems to be rejected because it has the air of a loss of parental authority. For the remaining parents, the items with which they disagreed were diverse, with no single item attracting more than two votes.

At the other end of the scale were 10 parents (5 mothers, 5 fathers) who disagreed with more than half of the statements offered for rating. One of the striking features of this group was their avoidance of the rating (3) 'disagree somewhat'. They might agree 'completely' or 'somewhat' (they used both of these ratings), but they were crystal clear about what they did not like.

It is among this group that we find the purists, the people who have selected one ideological message and hold firmly to it. Some of these parents are strongly of the view that money and jobs need to be kept completely separate from one another. As they explain, 'children need to learn to take responsibility for their place in the family and share the jobs that need to be done' (a mother's statement).

A few others hold, again without reservations, the view that jobs and money go together. To use the words of another mother:

> Children have to learn that they will get money only if they work for it when they enter the work force. They must learn it won't come from sitting down and doing nothing. They must budget their earnings so as to alleviate the debt problems people put themselves into because they haven't saved for one reason or another.

In effect, each of these mothers has chosen one of the several positions available in the culture, and then discarded the rest as unacceptable.

How, one might ask, do the great majority live with their endorsement of a variety of positions? (The purists above have no such problem.) They do so in part by placing their several positions in some sort of hierarchy, with a preferred position set aside when it turns out not to work. For example, one mother starts off by arguing for separateness:

> I have always felt that children and women are entitled to a share of the family income. Personally, I hate having to ask for money – being dependent on the whim of another person is awful. I think children should have the wherewithal to buy something without having to ask for and to justify why they want the money. But this backfires when the regular job is not done without considerable nagging, at which point the threat that money will be withheld usually works.

Managing several positions may also be made possible by regarding them as differentially appropriate for children of different ages or experience. 'Pocket money for jobs,' says the father of a 14 year old, 'is most useful when they're younger – say, under the age of 10, when you want to encourage some specific behaviours.' As they get older, a mother comments, the link to money should become weaker:

> Pocket money was introduced when the child began school as an incentive to contribute to family chores by making his bed and receiving 20 cents each morning. As he has grown (the child is now 10), pocket money has been paid less for specific chores and more for the child's initiative and attitudes towards helping. I believe children should not be paid for each task they perform. But special thoughtful actions occasionally deserve praise plus a financial reward.

The final form of management, and a very prevalent one, is to think in terms of two categories of jobs. For many parents, some jobs are 'never paid for'. Others may be. An example is the following statement from the mother of a 14 year old:

> The children are expected to look after their own rooms, their school clothes, to make breakfast and to be self-reliant, and this is not part of pocket money because they are learning to be responsible for their lives. We don't want the children to think that every time they do something extra they should be paid for it, as they are part of a family, not a company. However, if a child wants something which we are

not prepared to buy, we will allow him to do extra jobs (e.g. gardening) and negotiate a price first.

It is in relation to these extra jobs that the ethos of value for effort, of a contractual set of norms, is most likely to be brought into play. In the words of one father:

> Apart from a regular allowance, there are discretionary jobs which allow extra money to be earned. Certain jobs have a pre-set value: e.g. washing the car, vacuuming the car. Non-regular jobs have either a total value struck or an hourly rate struck before the job is started. The child should have the opportunity to earn additional money on a value for effort basis.

This same father, however, also pointed out that 'chores are not paid for, as it is a duty'. In effect, some jobs should indeed be kept separate from issues of money, while others may be linked. The double category for jobs, especially if combined with the view that one basically uses what 'works' with a particular child, allows the acceptance of several messages within the cultural collection, rather than the single selections displayed by those more purist in their style.

Even here, however, distinctions are not always black-and-white. In a fashion reminiscent of the bottom-line position that appeared earlier, most parents again have a clear sense of the jobs they would 'never pay for'. Once out of this category, however, there is a great deal of movement and flexibility. One might, for instance, never pay children for making their beds or brushing their teeth. Washing the car, however, might be sometimes paid for, sometimes not, depending upon circumstances or mood, and with no great sense on the part of parents that the status of the job, and their stand, need tidying or clarification. It might be possible to reduce the apparent ambiguity by writing out an array of variables, the various weights of which in particular circumstances lead to a parent's adopting a particular position or taking a particular action. It is equally possible, we are suggesting, that neither parents nor children are bothered by the presence of ambiguity or apparent contradiction in a number of context areas. The interesting questions then become: when is a consistent single message, preferably explicitly stated, sought by either generation? When are ambiguity and an acceptance of two views of a problem, delaying or not bothering with a resolution, preferred states of mind? And what functions do these alternatives serve, not only within the mental life of each, but also in their social interactions with one another?

Extensions to children

The research applications we have outlined have been mainly in terms of the ideas that adults come to hold and the ways in which these ideas may come to change. We now wish to ask whether we can describe children's contexts and children's cognitive development in similar terms.

On the first score – describing children's contexts – there certainly appears to be ample opportunity to describe the contexts children encounter in terms of the range of opinions they meet, the extent of demands that differences be resolved, and the degree of respect accorded to a child's opinion and ability. To take one example, there is currently a great deal of debate over the credibility of young children as witnesses, especially in situations of abuse. A child is likely to encounter either the view that he or she is competent unless proved otherwise or, more likely, the view that young children remember poorly and are prone to fantasy. The adult, in this latter view, has a monopoly of cognitive competence.

The second issue – extensions to the analysis of children's cognitive development – has been the particular concern of Duveen and Lloyd (1990). To take an example that is the particular focus of their own research, the acquisition of gender schemas may be regarded in terms of the child's coming to understand the several ways in which its social group defines 'male' and 'female'. That understanding, they argue, is first demonstrated at the level of action and then more abstractly. Children display, for instance, sex-role stereotyping first in the toys they play with and then in the way they use gender as a dimension for categorizing photographs of males and females (Lloyd and Duveen, 1990). In both cases 'the development of a social representation can be traced through an analysis of the child's capacity to use signs in accordance with the conventions of the community' (*ibid.*).

Gender schemas will serve also as a bridge to a further possibility. Boys, it has been argued, learn not only how to think and act like boys. They also learn how *not* to think or act like girls. Girls, in contrast, have some greater leeway but they must still learn what is regarded as out-of-bounds as well as what is permitted or encouraged. This kind of pattern suggests that children, in the course of coming to understand the social world, are learning where the boundary lines are, where their actions or ideas come close to what they must not do or must not know about. This sense of what is prohibited may even be acquired before any clear idea of what is permitted (Goodnow, in press).

One last possibility to be considered is that the schemas children acquire, especially in their understanding of parents, often have to do with gradations in acceptability of their actions and ideas to parents. It is the knowledge of gradations of acceptability that allows children to move in steps towards a parent's limits, without producing an open war. That knowledge, combined with the knowledge of what parents have least tolerance for, may also be what allows some adolescents to select an especially challenging area of difference – a parent's 'bottom line' – when they decide to declare themselves as different from their parents.

A final comment

We have outlined two general perspectives on the issue of the way context and cognition are interrelated: one labelled 'singular', the other 'pluralist'. Each perspective raises interesting research questions. Each also forces one to ask: what is the nature of any particular area of knowledge or understanding? To what extent does it seem to fit best with a singular or a pluralist view of acquisition?

In these last comments, we shall argue for the need to avoid any sense of dividing areas of knowledge into physical cognition and social cognition, regarding these as respectively the areas where a singular and pluralist view fit best. There can be, it might be said, only one correct answer to questions about the conservation of properties such as amount, weight or volume, and all development must be directed towards the acquisition of this single truth. This rather simplistic view, however, ignores the presence of diverse views about some events which, in expert ideas, should allow for only one correct answer (conservation of volume is the example we used earlier). It ignores also the evidence that the understanding of physical events can be improved by encountering and resolving different points of view (e.g. Doise and Mugny, 1984). Finally, it ignores the way in which even problems involving objects may call for gradations of acceptability within a variety of answers. To say that 2 plus 2 equals 4, for instance, may be the only completely correct answer. The answer '5' may none the less be regarded as less incorrect than the answer '100'. In effect, even for problems where the issue seems to be one of fact, there may well be a hierarchy of acceptable answers, with part of cognitive development having to do with understanding when approximations will serve.

In similar fashion, we would argue against any simple alignment of a singular view with accounts of cognitive development based upon Piaget, and a pluralist view with accounts based upon theories which place a stronger emphasis upon social context and upon forms of cognitive development other than the emergence of logical structures. We have, for instance, made considerable use of a way of describing social context that has emerged from the analysis of logical structures: namely, description in terms of the likelihood of encountering people who hold a viewpoint different from one's own and argue for some resolution of the difference rather than simply for the imposition of their own view of the world. That form of description is the kind used by Piaget (1965) in his comments on the importance of peers for the development of moral reasoning and by a later Genevan group for the development of both physical and social cognition (e.g. Doise and Mugny, 1984).

The optimal research position, in our view, is one where we set aside the easy dichotomies. We have accordingly argued in this chapter for a pluralist view of cognition and context, not with the intent of forcing a choice but with the aim of asking what would follow for a pluralist perspective, both in the form of research questions and in the form of recognizing new possibilities, breaking up the old habits of thought that we may bring to the interweaving of context and cognition.

Note

1. We happily acknowledge financial support from the Australian Research Grants Committee and the Macquarie University Research Committee. Intellectually, we wish to express our appreciation of discussions at various times with several colleagues: in particular and in alphabetical order, Jennifer Bowes, Judy Cashmore, Andy Collins and Joan Grusec. Authors' address: Macquarie University, Sydney, NSW, Australia 2109 (School of Behavioural Sciences for Goodnow, School of Education for Warton).

References

Abelson, R.P. (1986), 'Beliefs are like possessions', *Journal for the Theory of Social Behavior*, **16**, pp. 223–50.

Carugati, F. (1990), 'From social cognition to social representation in the study of intelligence', in G. Duveen and B. Lloyd (eds), *Social Representations and the Development of Knowledge* (Cambridge: Cambridge University Press), pp. 27–46.

Chombart de Lauwe, M.J. (1984), 'Changes in the representation of the child in the course of social transmission', in R.M. Farr and S. Moscovici (eds), *Social Representations* (Cambridge: Cambridge University Press), pp. 185–210.

Clarke-Stewart, K.A. (1978), 'Popular primers for parents', *American Psychologist*, **33**, pp. 359–69.

D'Alessio, M. (1977), 'Bambino generalizzato e bambino individualizzato nella steroetipia d'eta', in E. Ponzo (ed.), *Il bambino semplificato o inesistente* (Rome: Bulzoni), pp. 231–42.

D'Andrade, R.G. (1987), 'A folk model of the mind', in D. Holland and N. Quinn (eds), *Cultural Models in Language and Thought* (Cambridge: Cambridge University Press), pp. 112–50.

Doise, W. and Mugny, G. (1984), *The Social Development of the Intellect* (Oxford: Pergamon Press).

Duveen, G and Lloyd, B. (1990) (eds), *Social Representations and the Development of Knowledge* (Cambridge: Cambridge University Press).

Duveen, G. and Lloyd, B. (in press), 'An ethnographic approach to social representations' in G. Breakwell and D. Cantor (eds), *Empirical Approaches to the Study of Social Representations* (Oxford: Oxford University Press).

Emiliani, F., Zani, B. and Carugati, F. (1981), 'From staff interaction strategies to the social representations of adults in a day nursery', in W.P. Robinson (ed.), *Communication in Development* (London: Academic Press), pp. 89–107.

Emler, N., Ohana, J. and Dickinson, J. (1990), 'Children's representations of social relations', in G. Duveen and B. Lloyd (eds), *Social Representations and the Development of Knowledge* (Cambridge: Cambridge University Press), pp. 47–69.

Foucault, M. (1980), *Power-knowledge: Selected interviews and other writings* (London: Harvester Press).

Gergen, K.J. (1982), *Toward Transformation in Social Knowledge* (New York: Springer).

Glick, J. (1985), 'Culture and cognition revisited', in E. Neimark, R. DeLisi and J.L. Newman (eds), *Moderators of Competence* (Hillsdale, NJ: Erlbaum), pp. 99–115.

Goodnow, J.J. (1990), 'The socialization of cognition: what is involved?', in J.W. Stigler, R.A. Shweder and G. Herdt (eds), *Cultural Psychology* (Cambridge: Cambridge University Press), pp. 259–86.

Goodnow, J.J. (in press), 'Parents' ideas, children's ideas: the bases of congruence and divergence', in I. Sigel, A. McGillicuddy-DeLisi and J.J. Goodnow (eds), *Parental Belief Systems*, second edition (Hillsdale, NJ: Erlbaum).

Goodnow, J.J. and Collins, W.A. (1990), *Development According to Parents* (London: Erlbaum).

Goodnow, J.J., Knight, R. and Cashmore, J. (1985), 'Adult social cognition: implications of parents' ideas for approaches to social development', in M. Perlmutter (ed.), *Social Cognition: Minnesota symposia on child development* (Hillsdale, NJ: Erlbaum), vol. 8, pp. 287–324.

Goodnow, J.J. and Warton, P.M. (1991), 'The social bases of social cognition: interactions about work and their implications', *Merrill-Palmer Quarterly*, **37**, pp. 27–58.

Habermas, J. (1979), *Communications and the Evolution of Society* (London: Heinemann).

Hundeide, K. (1988), 'Metacontracts for situational definitions and for presentation of cognitive skills', *The Quarterly Newsletter of the Laboratory of Comparative Human Cognition*, **10**, pp. 85–91.

Kay, P. (1987), 'Linguistic competence and folk theories of language', in D. Holland and N. Quinn (eds), *Cultural Models in Language and Thought* (Cambridge: Cambridge University Press), pp. 67–77.

Light, P. and Perret-Clermont, A-N. (1989), 'Social context effects in learning and testing', in A. Gellatly, D. Rogers and J. A. Sloboda (eds), *Cognition and Social Worlds* (Oxford: Oxford University Press), pp. 99–112.

Lloyd, B. and Duveen, G. (1990), 'A semiotic analysis of the development of social representations of gender', in G. Duveen and B. Lloyd (1990), *Social Representations and the Development of Knowledge* (Cambridge: Cambridge University Press). pp. 27–46.

Molinari, L. and Emiliani, F. (1990), 'What is an image: the structure of others' images of the child and their influence on conversational styles', in G. Duveen and B. Lloyd (eds), *Social Representations and the Development of Knowledge* (Cambridge: Cambridge University Press), pp. 91–106.

Moscovici, S. (1961), *La psychoanalyse, son image et son public* (Paris: Presses Universitaires de France).

Moscovici, S. and Hewstone, M. (1983), 'Social representations and social explanations: from the "naive" to the "amateur" scientist', in M. Hewstone (ed.), *Attribution Theory* (Oxford: Blackwell), pp. 89–125.

Mugny, G. and Carugati, F. (1985), *L'intelligence au pluriel: les représentations sociales de l'intelligence et de son développement* (Cousset: Editions Delval).

Newson, J. and Newson, E. (1976), *Seven Years Old in the Home Environment* (London: Allen & Unwin).

Piaget, J. (1965), *The Moral Judgment of the Child*, transl. by M. Gabain (New York: The Free Press; first publ. 1932).

Quinn, N. and Holland, D. (1987), 'Culture and cognition', in D. Holland and N. Quinn (eds), *Cultural Models in Language and Thought* (Cambridge: Cambridge University Press), pp. 3–42.

Reid, B. V. and Valsiner, J. (1986), 'Consistency, praise, and love: folk theories of American parents', *Ethos*, **14**, pp. 1–25.

Salzman, P. C. (1981), 'Culture as enhabilmentis', in L. Holy and M. Stuchlik (eds), *The Structure of Folk Models* (London: Academic Press), pp. 233–56.

Sarchielli, G. (1984), 'Work entry: a critical moment in the occupational socialization process', in W. Doise and A. Palmonari (eds), *Social Interaction in Individual Development* (Cambridge: Cambridge University Press), pp. 261–78.

Super, C.M. and Harkness, S. (1986), 'The developmental niche: a conceptualization of the interface of child and culture', *International Journal of Behavioral Development*, **9**, pp. 546–69.

Warton, P.M. and Goodnow, J.J. (1990), 'For love or money: parents' practices and ideologies related to children's household tasks', paper presented at 6th National Developmental Conference, Perth, WA.

Zelizer, V. (1985), *Pricing the Priceless Child* (New York: Basic Books).

Index

Index